Science the "Write" Way

Science the "Write" Way

Edited by Jodi Wheeler-Toppen

NSTA press
National Science Teachers Association

Arlington, Virginia

National Science Teachers Association

Claire Reinburg, Director
Jennifer Horak, Managing Editor
Andrew Cooke, Senior Editor
Wendy Rubin, Associate Editor
Agnes Bannigan, Associate Editor
Amy America, Book Acquisitions Coordinator

Science and Children
Linda Froschauer, Editor
Valynda Mayes, Managing Editor
Stephanie Andersen, Associate Editor

Science Scope
Inez Luftig, Editor
Kenneth L. Roberts, Managing Editor

Art and Design
Will Thomas Jr., Director, Interior Design
Linda Olliver, Cover

Printing and Production
Catherine Lorrain, Director
Nguyet Tran, Assistant Production Manager

National Science Teachers Association
Francis Q. Eberle, PhD, Executive Director
David Beacom, Publisher
1840 Wilson Blvd., Arlington, VA 22201
www.nsta.org/store
For customer service inquiries, please call 800-277-5300.

Library of Congress Cataloging-in-Publication Data
Science the "write" way / edited by Jodi Wheeler-Toppen.
     p. cm.
  Includes bibliographical references and index.
   ISBN 978-1-936137-40-4 (print) -- ISBN 978-1-936959-97-6 (e-book) 1. Science--Study and teaching (Elementary)
2. Science--Study and teaching (Middle school) 3. Technical writing--Study and teaching (Elementary) 4.
Technical writing--Study and teaching (Middle school) 5. Diaries--Authorship--Study and teaching (Elementary)
6. Diaries--Authorship--Study and teaching (Middle school) 7. Language arts--Correlation with content subjects.
I. Wheeler-Toppen, Jodi.
 LB1585.S395 2011
   507.1'2--dc23
                                        2011030758

Contents

Introduction ix

Part 1: Writing and Learning in Science

Why Writing?

Chapter 1   *On Writing in Science* 1
       By Sandra K. Abell

Chapter 2   *Science the "Write" Way: Nonfiction Writing Activities Help Students Learn Science* 5
       By Valarie L. Akerson and Terrell A. Young

Chapter 3   *Unlocking Reading Comprehension With Key Science Inquiry Skills* 11
       By Roxanne Greitz Miller

Chapter 4   *14 Writing Strategies* 17
       By Thomas Turner and Amy Broemmel

Chapter 5   *This Isn't English Class! Using Writing as an Assessment Tool in Science* 25
       By Michael Rockow

Building Basic Skills

Chapter 6   *Making Thinking Visible: A Method to Encourage Science Writing in Upper Elementary Grades* 31
       By Roxanne Greitz Miller and Robert C. Calfee

Chapter 7   *Writing to Learn* 41
       By Brian Hand, Vaughan Prain, and Keith Vance

Chapter 8   *Helping Students Write About Science Without Plagiarizing* 45
       By Jodi Wheeler-Toppen

Chapter 9   *Learning to Write and Writing to Learn in Science: Refutational Texts and Analytical Rubrics* 49
       By Amy Singletary and Victor Sampson

Chapter 10   *Peanut Butter and Jelly Science* 57
       By Donna Farland

Chapter 11   *Write It, Do It* 59
       By Erin Peters

Chapter 12   *Comments on Students' Writing* 63
       By Inez Fugate Liftig

Writing With English Language Learners

Chapter 13   *From Speaking to Writing in the Structured English Immersion Science Classroom* 69
       By Conrado Laborin Gómez and Margarita Jimenez-Silva

Chapter 14   *Integrated Assessments for ELL: Students—and Teachers—Benefit From Incorporating Writing and Drawing in Science* 75
       By Joan Armon and Linda J. Morris

Contents

Chapter 15   *What Writing Represents What Scientists Actually Do?* 81
By William C. Robertson

Chapter 16   *Writing Through Inquiry* 85
By Paul Jablon

Chapter 17   *Getting Students to Become Successful, Independent Investigators* 91
By Jeffrey D. Thomas

Chapter 18   *Kinesthetic Writing, of Sorts* 101
By Kirstin Bittel and Darrek Hernandez

Chapter 19   *Multigenre Lab Reports: Connecting Literacy and Science* 105
By Leonora Rochwerger, Shelley Stagg Peterson, and Theresa Calovini

Chapter 20   *Lab Report Blues* 111
By Andrew Diaz

Part 2: Classroom-Tested Lessons
Writing Across the Genres

Chapter 21   *The Nature of Haiku: Students Use Haiku to Learn About the Natural World
and Improve Their Observational Skills* 115
By Peter Rillero, JoAnn V. Cleland, and Karen A. Conzelman

Chapter 22   *Keeping Science Current* 123
By Barbara Timmerman

Chapter 23   *Extra! Extra! Learn All About It* 127
By Kristen Curry, Jerilou Moore, and William J. Sumrall

Chapter 24   *Science Newsletters* 135
By Melissa Nail

Chapter 25   *Scientific Journals: A Creative Assessment Tool* 139
By Larissa Beckstead

Chapter 26   *A Natural Integration: Student-Created Field Guides Seamlessly Combine
Science and Writing* 145
By Tracy Coskie, Michelle Hornof, and Heidi Trudel

Chapter 27   *Nature Detectives: First Graders Study Yearlong Changes in Nature and
Create a School Yard Field Guide* 153
By Natalie Harr and Richard E. Lee Jr.

Chapter 28   *Students as Authors: Illustrated Science Information Books Created
During Integrated Units Are Windows Into Student Understanding* 161
By Maria Varelas, Christine C. Pappas, Sofia Kokkino, and Ibett Ortiz

Chapter 29   *Mystery Box Writing* 167
By William Straits

Contents

Content-Specific Activities

Chapter 30   *Nature's Advice Book: Third-Grade Students Examine Their Knowledge of Life Science by Considering the Lessons Learned From Nature* 173
By Kathryn Mahlin and Amy Robertson

Chapter 31   *Ecosystem Journalism: Allow Your Students to Display Their Understanding of Life Science Concepts by Creating an Imaginative Newspaper* 177
By Amy Robertson and Kathryn Mahlin

Chapter 32   *Linking Science and Writing With Two Bad Ants: A Trade Book Inspires Two Teachers to Connect Their Curricula in a Creative Way* 183
By Ingrid Hekman Fournier and Leslie Dryer Edison

Chapter 33   *Partners in Crime: Integrating Forensic Science and Writing* 189
By Erik Hein

Chapter 34   *A Reason to Write* 193
By Peggy Ashbrook

Chapter 35   *A Key to Science: A Simple Writing Technique Helps Students Communicate Understanding of Important Science Concepts* 197
By Jo Ann Yockey

Chapter 36   *Taking a Look at the Moon* 205
By Craig R. Leager

Chapter 37   *Creative Writing and the Water Cycle* 211
By Rich Young, Jyotika Virmani, and Kristen M. Kusek

Chapter 38   *Volcano Résumés* 215
By Sandra Rutherford and Cindy Corlett

Chapter 39   *Reading and Writing Nonfiction With Children: Using Biographies to Learn About Science and Scientists* 219
By Rebecca Monhardt

Part 3: Approaches to Science Journals and Logs

Chapter 40   *Journals of Discovery: Incorporating Art and Creative Writing Into Science Journals Leads to Meaningful Reflections on Learning for Both Students and Teachers* 227
By Cathy Livingston

Chapter 41   *Science Interactive Notebooks in the Classroom* 233
By Jocelyn Young

Chapter 42   *Using Science Journals to Encourage All Students to Write* 239
By Joan C. Fingon and Shallon D. Fingon

Chapter 43   *Learning Logs: Writing to Learn, Reading to Assess* 247
By Daniel Heuser

Contents

Chapter 44   *Using Web Logs in the Science Classroom* 253
By Staycle C. Duplichan

Chapter 45   *Interactive Reflective Logs: Opening Science Notebooks to Peer and Teacher Feedback* 259
By Cynthia Minchew Deaton, Benjamin E. Deaton, and Katina Leland

Chapter 46   *A Laboratory of Words: Using Science Notebook Entries as Preassessment Creates Opportunities to Adapt Teaching* 265
By Jeanne Clidas

Chapter 47   *The Art of Reviewing Science Journals: Questions to Consider When Planning and Assessing Students' Journal Entries* 271
By Daniel P. Shepardson and Susan Jane Britsch

Chapter 48   *The P.O.E.T.R.Y. of Science: A Flexible Tool for Assessing Elementary Student Science Journals* 277
By Jennifer C. Mesa, Michelle L. Klosterman, and Linda L. Cronin-Jones

Index 285

Introduction

As I write this introduction, I am struck by how much this task resembles what we want our students to accomplish when we ask them to write in science class. I sit surrounded by piles of *Science Scope*, *Science and Children*, and research journal articles, as well as pages of scrawled, handwritten notes. Already I have collected, sorted, organized, and reorganized my ideas. As I type them, I will clarify them even further. In short, I am learning as I write.

Why Writing?

There are many reasons to have our students write, but the one that is most powerful for me is simple: Writing helps students learn. While writing, students manipulate and organize their ideas (Langer and Applebee 1987). As they try to explain the concepts they are learning, they may discover gaps in their knowledge (Glynn and Muth 1994). When they use analogies to describe how something new is like something they already know, they link new knowledge to prior knowledge, strengthening both (Rivard 1994). In translating between everyday language and scientific language, they clarify their ideas (Prain 2006). In my classes, I have students write because writing can be a powerful tool for learning.

There are other good reasons to have students put pen to paper (or fingers to keyboard). First, writing is an essential part of the practice of science (Norris and Phillips 2003). Scientists record their findings and interpretations, allowing other scientists to examine their work. This record allows scientists to piece together small ideas, eventually building large theories. Scientists themselves use writing to organize their thoughts and find meaning in their work, reflecting on their own and in communication with peers.

Students' written work also provides a window to their thoughts. Not sure if your students really "get" the molecular nature of matter? Have them write a book that explains the concept to young children (see "Students as Authors," p. 159). You'll spot misconceptions you would never pick up during class discussion. Assessing writing doesn't have to be time consuming. I often have students respond to a question in writing, then quickly scan the answers and sort them into piles based on levels of understanding. This approach lets me know what points need to be addressed and which, if any, students need one-on-one clarification. However, beware of mistaking students' use of science terminology for understanding science material. As Abell points out in "On Writing in Science" (p. 1) students are skilled at throwing around science words to hide their confusion.

Building Basic Skills

You don't have to be trained as an English teacher to integrate writing into your curriculum. However, you may need to practice with students the aspects of their writing that are most important in a science classroom. They may need help learning to put ideas into their own words instead of plagiarizing, or they may require instruction on being specific enough for their readers to understand what they've written. Such skills help students think more deeply about science and enable them to communicate clearly—worthwhile ways to spend class time. Tools for these tasks and more can be found in the second section of this book, "Building Basic Skills."

Writing With English Language Learners

Writing can be an especially important part of the science curriculum for English language learners. Writing not only helps them process the science they are learning, but also gives them needed practice using their new language. Science teachers must ease English language learners into the writing process by integrating it with verbal discussions and drawings to allow ELL students to fully express their thoughts. See the section "Writing With English Language Learners" for more guidance.

The "Write" Way?

What kind of writing should you have your students do? The short answer is that it depends on your goals for the activity. Some teachers want students to replicate reports similar to those found in scientific journals. To generate such lab reports, students need explicit guidance regarding what is expected and how well they are moving toward proficiency (see "Lab Report Blues," p. 111). Learning to write traditional lab reports introduces students to the structure of the formal literature of science. However, the actual practice of science involves many genres of writing, including e-mails, lab notebooks, presentation or seminar notes, and personal writing that helps scientists understand their own research (Yore, Hand, and Prain 2002). In addition, some worry that using formal lab reports as the primary form of writing in science class obscures the underlying thinking involved in developing scientific ideas (Wallace, Hand, and Prain 2004). Resources for both traditional and nontraditional lab reports can be found in the section "Writing in and About Lab Work."

If your goal is to stimulate learning for your students, there are several things to consider (Langer and Applebee 1987). First, think about whether you want students to work on organizing a large breadth of knowledge or if you want them to gain an in-depth view of a smaller subject. They are most likely to learn the ideas directly used in their writing. Second, the more information is manipulated, the better it is understood and remembered. Assignments that help students make new connections include tasks that ask them to reword a text, "translate" an idea into another way of writing, and elaborate and make comparisons (Boscolo and Mason 2001). Finally, keep in mind that if students write about familiar content and they already understand the relationships between the ideas, writing is unlikely to produce new learning.

There are many types of writing that can meet these goals. In part 2 of this book, "Classrooom-Tested Lessons," you'll find examples of different genres of writing that work well in classrooms as well as content-specific activities that you can use right away. You'll notice that these activities require the kinds of thinking described above.

A word on the value of giving students a chance to write for authentic audiences:

Preparing a text for a real person or group, rather than just pretending to do so, is a powerful motivator (Wallace, Hand, and Prain 2004). Students can write for younger children at their school, for visitors to a museum or nature center, for a local newspaper or PTA newsletter, or even for their classmates. For a richer learning experience, students can receive feedback from that targeted group and revise accordingly. Several activities in this book provide suggestions for activities that involve authentic audiences.

Journals and Logs

Many teachers like to have their students collect their thinking and writing in learning logs or journals. When journals are used well, they become an essential part of science class, as integral as the teacher or textbook. Students value their journals because they hold a personal record of learning and ideas. Journals may be primarily focused on investigations, or they may involve reflection on all sources of learning in the science classroom. There are a variety of ways to organize and assess science journals and logs; several systems are described in "Approaches to Science Journals and Logs."

The goal of this book is to provide practical guidance for integrating writing into your classroom. Some articles describe general techniques you can use in any class. Others outline writing activities tailored to a specific topic. Even if you don't teach these topics, you can use such articles as springboards for additional ideas. Whatever science you teach, you'll find strategies and lessons to get you started.

References

Boscolo, P., and L. Mason. 2001. Writing to learn, writing to transfer. In *Writing as a learning tool*, ed. P. Tynjala, L. Mason, and K. Lonka, 83–104. Amsterdam: Kluwer Press.

Glynn, S., and D. Muth. 1994. Reading and writing to learn science: Achieving scientific literacy. *Journal of Research in Science Teaching*, 31 (9): 1057–1073.

Langer, J., and A. Applebee. 1987. *How writing shapes thinking: A study of teaching and learning (Tech. Rep. No. 22)*. Urbana, IL: National Council of Teachers of English.

Norris, S., and L.Phillips. 2003. How literacy in its fundamental sense is central to scientific literacy. *Science Education*, 87 (2): 224–241.

Prain, V. 2006. Learning from writing in secondary science: Some theoretical and practical implications. *International Journal of Science Education*, 28: 179–201.

Rivard, L. 1994. A review of writing to learn in science: Implications for practice and research. *Journal of Research in Science Teaching*, 31 (9): 969–983.

Wallace, C., B. Hand, and V. Prain. 2004. *Writing and learning in the science classroom*. Boston: Kluwer Academic Publishers.

Yore, L., B. Hand, and V. Prain. 2002. Scientists as writers. *Science Education*, 86 (5): 672–692.

Chapter 1
On Writing in Science

By Sandra K. Abell

"**M**y fourth graders write all the time in science. They record purpose, equipment, procedures, and results in their science notebooks for every activity. But lately they seem to resist writing. I'm thinking of dropping the writing—it just takes too much time. After all, they just need to learn science in science class."

Why Use Writing in Science?

Many teachers use writing in science as a recording tool (science notebooks) or to find out what students have learned (constructed response tests). Yet writing experts Judith Langer and Arthur Applebee (1987) tell us that writing to evaluate knowledge and skills is only one of several purposes for writing. According to their framework, writing in science classrooms can also (1) draw on prior knowledge to prepare for new activities, (2) foster new learning, (3) consolidate and review ideas, and (4) reformulate and extend knowledge.

Can Writing Help Students Understand Science Better?

One of the most important reasons for using writing in science is to foster conceptual understanding. Mason and Boscolo (2000) studied Italian fourth-grade student writing in science. Students who engaged in writing to reflect, reason, and compare understood photosynthesis better than students who did not write to learn. Fellows (1994) found that urban middle school students who had more opportunities for writing explanations produced better logical arguments and improved their understanding of matter and molecules. Other studies have shown that students who write to explain their ideas learn science better than students who write only to record or summarize (Hand, Prain, and Yore 2001).

What Supports Do Students Need for Science Writing?

Many students find it easier to express their ideas through talking than writing. In a study by Warwick, Linfield, and Stephenson (1999), 11-year-olds were able to express clear understanding of fair testing and other experimental design ideas in interview settings, but those ideas were less apparent in students' written work. However, teachers can help all students become better writers and better science learners by teaching them how to write scientifically. Warwick, Stephenson, and Webster (2003) found that the writing of fourth-grade students in England reflected high levels of understanding of ideas like variables and fair testing after teachers

provided a writing frame with prompts such as "We are trying to find out…" and "We made the test fair by…." (p. 176). Working with second-grade students in Wales, Patterson (2001) found that when teachers provided explicit instruction in writing, students were able to express greater scientific understanding. For example, when teachers showed students how to use connectives (words like *for, to, when, because*) in their science writing, students moved from descriptions such as "It has dots" to explanations such as "It has got dots for bugs to eat" (p. 9). In other words, teaching writing techniques led students to express more thorough understanding.

How Can Teachers Provide Feedback on Student Science Writing?

Owens (2001) found that elementary teachers are often anxious about how to respond to science writing—Do we respond to the ideas or the writing? If students use the right words, does that mean they understand? How do my comments affect student learning?

How teachers respond to student writing depends on the purpose of the writing. If writing is aimed at building science understanding, then teacher responses need to push for clarity in explanation and point out discrepancies in thinking. Teachers should not accept the right word as a substitute for conceptual understanding. For example, a student who writes, "Things float because of their density" might understand or may just be making "noises that sound scientific" (Osborne and Freyberg 1985) without understanding that an object's mass and volume are both important considerations in sinking and floating. Teacher responses to science writing help students become better writers and thinkers (Spandel and Stiggins 1990). In the density example, responses such as "What do you mean by density?" or "Can you give an example?" or "What about things that sink?" help students move beyond vocabulary to conceptual understanding.

Should All Students Be Expected to Write in Science?

All students can be involved in writing in science. For kindergartners, science writing might include pictures and invented spelling. Even in second grade, students can improve their science thinking and writing when teachers provide writing supports such as concept maps (Patterson 2001).

What Can Teachers Do to Help Students Write to Learn Science?

Instead of merely writing *about* science, students need to engage in writing *to learn* science (Owens 2001). Writing to learn helps students build their knowledge through conjecture, explanation, comparison, and reformulation. Teachers can do the following to help students better learn science through writing:

- Ask students to write in science every day.
- Expect all students to be successful writers in science.
- Provide writing tasks that go beyond recording and summarizing.
- Include writing prompts that help students structure their writing.
- Respond to writing with direct feedback about the science ideas.

In these ways, writing and thinking become essential components of the elementary science classroom.

References

Fellows, N. J. 1994. A window into thinking: Using student writing to understand conceptual change in science learning. *Journal of Research in Science Teaching* 31 (9): 985–1001.

Hand, B., V. Prain, and L. Yore. 2001. Sequential writing tasks' influence on science learning. *In Writing as a learning tool: Integrating theory and practice*, eds. P. Tynjala, L. Mason, and K. Lonka, 105–130. Dordrecht, Netherlands: Kluwer.

Langer, J. A., and A. N. Applebee. 1987. *How writing shapes thinking: A study of teaching and learning*. Urbana, IL: National Council of Teachers of English.

Mason, L., and P. Boscolo. 2000. Writing and conceptual change: What changes? *Instructional Science* 28 (3): 199–226.

Osborne, R., and P. Freyberg. 1985. *Learning in science: The implications of children's science*. Portsmouth, NH: Heinemann.

Owens, C. V. 2001. Teachers' responses to science writing. *Teaching and Learning: The Journal of Natural Inquiry*. Summer: 22–35.

Patterson, E. W. 2001. Structuring the composition process in scientific writing. *International Journal of Science Education* 23 (1): 1–16.

Spandel, V., and R. J. Stiggins. 1990. *Creating writers: Linking assessment and writing instruction*. White Plains, NY: Longman.

Warwick, P., R. S. Linfield, and P. Stephenson. 1999. A comparison of primary school pupils' ability to express procedural understanding in science through speech and writing. *International Journal of Science Education* 21 (8): 823–838.

Warwick, P., P. Stephenson, and J. Webster. 2003. Developing pupils' written expression of procedural understanding through the use of writing frames in science: Findings from a case study approach. *International Journal of Science Education* 25 (2): 173–192.

Chapter 2
Science the "Write" Way:
Nonfiction Writing Activities Help Students Learn Science

By Valarie L. Akerson and Terrell A. Young

Learning to write well is a long process that comes through teacher modeling, instruction, practice, and feedback. Luckily, the writing process can be used to improve science learning, too. Here are a few good writing suggestions that integrate science while helping students develop their informational writing skills.

Science Journals

There is perhaps no better place than a science journal for students to develop informational writing skills. Daily journal prompts are one way to encourage students to write expansively about developing knowledge (see Figure 1 for sample journal prompts).

Figure 1. Sample journal prompts on trees, followed by examples of typical student responses

What do you think is a tree? How is it different from other plants?
I think a tree is wood and leaves. Trees are bigger than plants.

What do you think a tree is made of?
Trees are made of wood and leaves.

What are the parts of the tree? Draw a tree.
Leaves and the wood trunk (Later in the unit they add other parts, such as roots.)

(After we find a tree to "adopt") What is our tree like? What is special about our tree? How do you think our tree might change over time?
Our tree is big. It is special because it is ours! It has big leaves.

Why do you think trees are different shapes? Why do you think their leaves are different?
Because the leaves catch the sun in different ways.

(After several weeks) How does our tree look different? How does it look the same?
The trunk still looks the same. It is getting leaves!

What different shapes of leaves did you find? How can we sort our leaves?
I am putting the big ones together, then putting the spikey ones, and then the skinny ones.

What things can you tell me about a tree now? How do you think it is different from other plants now?
Trees are a kind of plant.

In journals, students make records of what they are doing in investigations—they organize data by creating tables and write observations based on their investigations. They record, via drawing and writing, characteristics of what they observe (e.g., what a pill bug looks like and how it reacts in different settings). In using the journal in this way, students learn that making records of actual observations is something scientists often do and is a useful kind of nonfiction writing.

Beyond recording observations, students can use journals to write inferences based on their observations. For example, if students observe that pill bugs prefer walking on dirt, they could infer that the dirt is similar to the bugs' natural environment—thus making meaning of the observations. Students may find that inferences made from early observations change as they make more observations. This tentativeness in inferences is an intrinsic part of the nature of science, but by making the recordings in their journals, students can track their ideas over time and note any observations that lead to a change in inference.

Observations Versus Inference Charts

Another tool that supports science learning while developing informational writing skills is the observation versus inference chart. We've used this chart successfully to introduce primary students to the distinction between *observation* and *inference*. On the chart, one column is labeled "Observations" and the second is labeled "Inferences." During a class discussion following an exploration, the teacher records student observations under the "Observations" column and then asks students to make inferences about what those observations mean in the "Inferences" column.

For example, after students have had time to observe snails up close, the teacher would collectively record students' observations (e.g., "The eyestalks move when I touch them") on the chart, then ask students to infer the meaning behind the observation (e.g., "They are trying to move them out of my way—to keep them safe"). The teacher can record the response on the inferences side.

After seeing a few examples, students begin making good distinctions between observations and inferences, and they can be given similar smaller charts in which individual or small groups of students can record observations and inferences about other investigations on their own.

Student-Authored Books

To gain simultaneous insights into a content area, research, and literacy, students can research and write their very own book on a theme such as "A Book about Scientists." Individual students or small groups can research subtopics—"What do scientists do?" "How do I become a scientist?" "What do scientists do in their spare time?"—and write

Figure 2. Sample chapter from a student-authored book called "What Is a Scientist?"

Ch. 5 What are Scientists Like?
    They are like regular people. They are smart and good. They learn lots of things. They can be girls and boys. They can be grown-ups or kids.

chapters for the book (Figure 2). The chapters usually begin as notes from research or interviews of scientists.

Afterward the book can be published for classroom enjoyment. Publishing a book is another good place to reinforce accuracy in writing in terms of spelling and grammar conventions and the process of writing. Student can edit their drafts—prior notes that they have taken—as they type their chapters on the computer.

After the chapters are compiled, students create a table of contents and a reference list to demonstrate that nonfiction writing must be based on accurate information. Then students can illustrate the chapters with their own drawings.

We keep copies of our student-authored books in free-reading-time tubs, so students can revisit their work, encouraging both recall of information about scientists and the importance of writing informational text.

Custom ABC Books

For younger primary grades, have students collectively create informational text in the form of an alphabetical or counting book. Students not only practice writing and researching content but also learn how to gain information from nonfiction text and group it into categories.

Start by reading examples—such as George Ella Lyon's *A B Cedar: An Alphabet of Trees* (1989), George Shannon's *Tomorrow's Alphabet* (1996), or Kathy Darling's *Amazon ABC* (1996), then choose a content area or have students pick the own content area. Next assign individual students a letter or a number. Each will research information related to that content and write an informational page that relates to their assigned letter or number.

For example, primary students might study organisms, and each child in the class is assigned a letter of the alphabet and selects an organism to study that begins with that letter. The student who gets *L* studies lemurs. That student then writes and illustrates an informational page about the lemur. When all pages are complete, the teacher compiles the book as a class alphabet book. Teachers can also involve their students with similar projects related to nonfiction counting books (see References and Resources). April Pulley Sayre and Jeff Sayre's *One Is a Snail, Ten Is a Crab: A Counting by Feet Book* (2003) is ideal for intermediate students, as readers are required to count, add, and multiply the feet of various creatures. Using *Counting Wildflowers* (McMillan 1986) as a model, a first-grade teacher can take digital pictures of animals on a class field trip to a farm. Students can then record information about what they experienced on the trip.

E-mails to Scientists

Finally, students can pursue science learning by writing e-mails to real scientists. Most appropriate for older elementary students, this activity provides an opportunity for students to compose their own questions about science content. Or, students can interview scientists about how they became scientists and the kinds of work they do. Students can use these e-mail conversations as a basis for a nonfiction report on that scientific specialty. Students can even be required to ask the scientists how they use writing in their work!

Teachers can find contact information for scientist e-mail pals by contacting local universities and science labs. For instance, Indiana University houses a science outreach office in their college of arts and sciences with staff whose purpose is to make contacts between university science faculty and K–12 educators. A similar office is located in Washington State at the Pacific Northwest National Laboratory's Office of Science Education, which not only arranges for scientists to visit classrooms and interact with students but also provides professional development opportunities for teachers. Teachers can find similar opportunities for contacts with scientists in their own local areas.

Reports and Other Uses

Nonfiction writing can also be used to help students develop understandings of science as inquiry, as students record observations, inferences, and results of investigations, and write formal reports to share with peers. Students can also use writing to design their own investigations, leading to further understanding of investigations as recommended by the *National Science Education Standards* (NRC 1996).

Writings Are Assessments

Incorporating various nonfiction writing activities such as those suggested above not only encourages students to think about science content, but also results in material/work that can help teachers assess student understanding.

For example, observation versus inference charts can be used to capture a picture of what the whole class understands about a given topic. If a student records an observation of an investigation exploring whether pill bugs prefer light or dark environments as "Pill bugs love the dark," the teacher will know that the student is confusing the observation with an inference. The teacher can then ask the student to describe how he or she knows that pill bugs "love the dark." When the student states that it is because pill bugs tend to stay in the dark side of their environment, the teacher can point out to the student that moving to the dark side is the observation and the inference is that they "love the dark."

Similarly, individual journal writings can be used to assess what individual students understand about a science content area. In a unit exploring electrical circuits, students can be asked to respond to a journal prompt of "How do you think electricity works?" several times throughout the unit. Initially the student may respond with something like "Electricity is lightening," whereas later in the unit the student may respond with something like "Electricity makes things work," and finally the student may respond with something like "Electricity works through a complete circle—a circuit." Thus, the teacher can track the development of the student's idea over time, from less informed to more informed views.

Whether supporting content learning, guiding teacher instruction, or furthering the development of students' literacy or science process skills—or all of the above—nonfiction writing opportunities are an essential aspect of science learning from which teachers and students benefit in many ways.

References

Darling, K. 1996. *Amazon ABC*. New York: Lothrop, Lee, and Shepard.

Lyon, G. E. 1989. *A B Cedar: An Alphabet of Trees*. New York: Orchard Books.

McMillan, B. 1986. *Counting wildflowers*. New York: Lothrop, Lee, and Shepard.

National Research Council (NRC). 1996. *National science education standards*. Washington, DC: National Academies Press.

Sayre, A. P., and J. Sayre. 2003. *One is a snail, ten is a crab: A counting by feet book*. Cambridge: Candlewick Press.

Shannon, G. 1996. *Tomorrow's alphabet*. New York: Greenwillow.

Resources

Atwell, N. 1990. *Coming to know: Writing to learn in the intermediate grades*. Portsmouth, NH: Heinemann.

Brown, J. E., L. B. Phillips, and E. C. Stephens. 1993. *Toward literacy: Theory and applications for teaching writing in the content areas*. Belmont, CA: Wadsworth.

Calkins, L. M. 1994. *The art of teaching writing*. Portsmouth, NH: Heinemann.

Chapman, M. L. 1995. The sociocognitive construction of written genres in first grade. *Research in the Teaching of English* 29 (2): 164–192.

Ehlert, L. 1990. *Fish eyes: A book you can count on*. San Diego: Harcourt.

Hadaway, N. L., S. M. Vardell, and T. A. Young. 2002. *Literature-based instruction with English language learners*. Boston: Allyn and Bacon Longman.

Hughey, J. B., and C. Slack. 2001. *Teaching children to write: Theory into practice*. Upper Saddle River, NJ: Merrill/Prentice Hall.

Noyce, R. M. and J. F. Christie. 1989. *Integrating reading and writing instruction in grades K–8*. Boston: Allyn and Bacon.

Pomeroy, D. 1996. *One potato: A counting book of potato prints*. San Diego: Harcourt.

Chapter 3

Unlocking Reading Comprehension With Key Science Inquiry Skills

By Roxanne Greitz Miller

As secondary science teachers, we appropriately focus the majority of our instruction on science content rather than the related subject areas, such as reading or writing, that support it. However, we must remember that scientific literacy cannot be attained without fundamental literacy—the ability to read and comprehend textual information and write competently about the subject under study (Norris and Phillips 2003). As a result, science teachers—schools' resident experts in digesting expository text laden with factual details, processes, and complex vocabulary—must make it our business to instruct students in the fundamental literacy skills that support scientific literacy, especially reading comprehension and writing composition in the expository domain. Fortunately for middle school science teachers, classrooms are a natural laboratory where the relationships between science, reading, and writing can be developed and strengthened to provide a foundation for students' learning and future career success.

The Background

The reciprocal nature of science inquiry and reading is made explicit in the following definition of inquiry:

> [Inquiry is] a multifaceted activity that involves making observations; posing questions; examining books and other sources of information to see what is already known; planning investigations; reviewing what is already known in light of experimental evidence; using tools to gather, analyze, and interpret data; proposing answers, explanations, and predictions; and communicating the results. Inquiry requires identification of assumptions, use of critical and logical thinking, and consideration of alternative explanations. (NRC 1996)

More simply stated, one must be able to read and comprehend to examine science information and must be able to compose (both in writing and orally) to communicate scientific results. On the lesser-known flip side, several research studies have shown the positive effects of science inquiry curriculum on developing students' reading skills and comprehension. On first review, teachers may wonder why this is so. While it is readily apparent that you can gain science knowledge through reading and that you must be able to read and write to "do" science, how do students gain reading skills *through science*? The basic answer may be found by examining what science is really meant to be. The Latin *scire*, from which the English *science* is derived, refers not to a subject area or academic domain, but rather "to knowing" about the world. Students who learn about their world by forming their own questions, comprehending information presented in varied forms, and expressing their knowledge both in writing and orally are better equipped to learn in any subject area. Additionally, four major cognitive strategies are used when effective readers read: (1) They plan, (2) they translate or interpret, (3) they reread, and (4) they reflect upon and evaluate what they read.

To promote the application of science inquiry skills to reading and writing, structured, scaffolded, and explicit instruction in their transference must occur within the classroom. Students who are high achievers or hail from educationally advantaged backgrounds intuitively apply inquiry strategies while reading. To meet the needs of all students, teachers must model and demonstrate inquiry thought during reading, building a tool kit of comprehension activities for students to use when reading in class and independently. These activities should use a common technical vocabulary to describe the similar thought processes between science and reading.

A Framework

What do science teachers need to know to foster development and transfer of inquiry strategies from science to reading? Teachers do not need to know everything about science and reading to raise student achievement. Rather, they need to know a few things well: (1) which cognitive processes are shared in the building of scientific knowledge and the processes of reading comprehension, (2) how these processes can be transferred, and (3) how to promote deep learning through teaching.

I designed the Science-Cognition-Literacy (SCL) Framework (Figure 1) to give science teachers a basis for

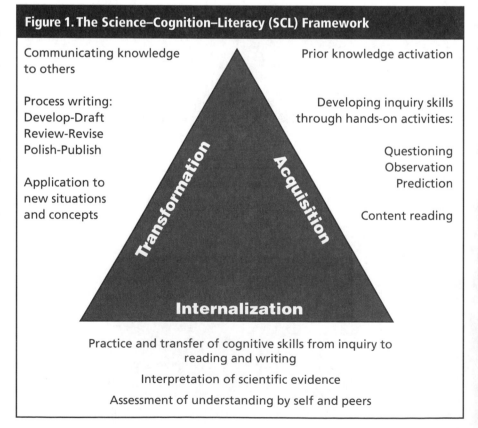

Figure 1. The Science–Cognition–Literacy (SCL) Framework

Communicating knowledge to others

Process writing:
Develop-Draft
Review-Revise
Polish-Publish

Application to new situations and concepts

Prior knowledge activation

Developing inquiry skills through hands-on activities:

Questioning
Observation
Prediction

Content reading

Transformation

Acquisition

Internalization

Practice and transfer of cognitive skills from inquiry to reading and writing

Interpretation of scientific evidence

Assessment of understanding by self and peers

visualizing the sequence of cognitive processes and instructional activities for developing science inquiry skills and applying them to reading (and writing) activities based in science. The SCL Framework is intended to serve as a guide for putting all of the pieces together in a seamless fashion. Rather than treating reading and writing as ancillary activities to support science learning, in this model, the literacy activities are fully embedded into the science curriculum and take on an equally important role as hands-on inquiry experiences.

Within the SCL Framework's cognitive phases of Acquisition, Internalization, and Transformation are embedded activities that address four essential elements in constructivist theories of learning: (1) connecting to prior student knowledge, (2) organizing new topical content, (3) providing opportunities for students' strategic reflection, and (4) giving students opportunities to extend their learning. The effectiveness of this approach arises from cognitive scaffolding that assists students (and teachers) in organizing complex information and connecting it to prior schemata, and from templates that support social interactions around complex topics, interactions that Vygotsky (and others) see as critical to the development of reflective thought (Vygotsky 1978, 1986).

The SCL Framework is best implemented during longer units of study that incorporate science inquiry investigations and reading and writing materials in a project-based format centering on one broad science topic, such as the states of matter. The longer units allow for deeper refection on reading and sharing of student knowledge. However, the individual strategies from the Framework can be applied to stand-alone, single lessons that concentrate on a single reading sample and inquiry experience, and I would encourage you to do this as well. Shorter lessons centered around single reading samples with inquiry can serve as steps to building students' repertoires of reading skills and provide practice in using these inquiry strategies while reading. In addition, such lessons also make apparent for students that these inquiry skills can be used during short reading assignments in other subjects, not only during longer science units.

The activities contained in the SCL Framework's Acquisition phase are aimed at developing student inquiry skills and science content knowledge to serve as connectors to the subsequent literacy activities. To begin this phase, teachers identify the particular science topic for the lesson (for example, phase changes within the states of matter). Teachers activate students' prior topic knowledge by leading them to actively reflect, share with others, and employ prewriting and K-W-L (What I Know/What I Want to Know/What I Have Learned) as generative techniques for individuals and groups. Students write down and share their ideas about the topic, along with predictions and expectations about the upcoming activities. Collaborative sharing of prior knowledge serves not only to enrich students' topical comprehension, but also to assist the teacher in identifying the "knowledge level" of the class as a whole, along with any preconceptions needing attention along the way. These written artifacts are used in later activities and stages to assist in designing the students' investigations, and as resources for students' self-assessments of their thinking.

Students then engage in hands-on science inquiry investigations related to the topic. Extended, reflective investigations are recommended by experts to promote the construction of more meaningful scientific concepts based upon the unique knowledge brought to the classroom by individual learners. The assumption is that when students interact with problems they perceive to be important and connected to their experiences, and when teachers are guided by what is known about learning, students are able to develop scientific concepts in

dialogue with peer investigators. Placement of hands-on investigations at the outset of the units provides students with concrete, first-person experience in applying cognitive inquiry skills that subsequently are tapped in later stages of the SCL Framework for transference to reading and writing.

If the SCL Framework is being applied to a unit, rather than a single lesson, then students read a variety of expository text sources for additional content information related to the science topic in parallel to the science investigation. Ideally, these texts will come from not only their textbooks, but also trade books, magazines, and alternative media such as online text. Students should be taught to use the cognitive strategies of think-alouds, text analysis, graphic organizers, and contextual clues to grapple with unfamiliar reading vocabulary. Specific inquiry strategies and their application to reading are discussed in Table 1.

Table 1. Key science inquiry skills and reading applications		
Science inquiry skill	**SCL phase**	**Reading application to be taught to students**
Prediction	Acquisition	Before reading, students should preview the text and predict what the reading sample is about from the title, illustrations, and other key text components. As students read, students should constantly predict and anticipate what the next points to be discussed in text will be.
Observation	Acquisition and Internalization	Students use their observation skills to take note of key points in text—headings, boldface terms, illustrations, special use of language. Students should use contextual clues from the reading to decode new vocabulary, observing where and how the new terms are used and what supporting vocabulary and ideas are used to extend their meaning.
Questioning	Acquisition and Internalization	The K-W-L technique can be used before, during, and after reading to generate questions related to student knowledge. As they read, students should make margin notes and use the think-aloud strategy to sketch questions on the reading sample (or extra paper) to provide a concrete reminder of points that were not understood and need to be discussed in small groups or with the teacher. During the reflection activities, students must constantly self-assess their understanding of the reading, questioning themselves and posing questions to others as appropriate.
Planning	Acquisition	When students preview the reading sample, they should examine the structure of the text (sequential, descriptive, compare/contrast, etc.) and select an appropriate graphic organizer or other organizing tool (such as a T-chart) to use while reading to organize the points of information in the text.
Reviewing, analyzing, and interpreting data	Internalization	After reading, students should review what they have read and revisit and revise their graphic organizers if necessary, reconstructing their ideas and incorporating their knowledge from the hands-on activities with what they have read.
Explaining and communicating	Transformation	Students should be required to explain, both orally and in writing, what they have read. Doing so strengthens reading comprehension and science content knowledge.

After Acquisition, students move to the Internalization phase, focusing on two activities: practicing science-developed inquiry skills during reading and writing, and developing metacognitive thought about their learning. Sufficient time and opportunities for interaction and reflection are essential for meaningful learning in hands-on science activities. However, students often lack the time or opportunity for interaction with and reflection on central ideas because of time constraints of our regular school day. The Internalization phase aims to address this situation by placing an emphasis on, and deliberately planning time for, reflection and interactions between student groups and with the teacher after the hands-on activities.

In this phase, students critically reflect and share their thoughts on their investigations and reading activities during cross-talk activities, serving to further construct meaning and ameliorate educational differences among diverse students. Teachers facilitate these discussions, acting as inquiry "guides," drawing students' attention to the thinking processes used during inquiry, and explicitly modeling the manner in which inquiry skills acquired during science can be transferred and applied when reading. For example, teachers can explore with students the ways in which observation, questioning, and prediction can be used as effective strategies during reading comprehension. Students revisit their reading, actively applying these inquiry skills to the reading sample. Students then evaluate the scientific evidence from their investigations, interpreting their data, drawing conclusions, and revising initial hypotheses in light of their new knowledge from the reading. Finally, students assess their understanding through the use of metacognitive strategies, the K-W-L technique, and written drafts.

The Transformation phase centers on the communication of student knowledge through composition, demonstrated in both oral and written formats. Writing tasks can be short compositions, longer reports, reader-response journals, scientist notebook entries, or traditional laboratory reports—the key is that the writing assignments must contain specific requirements structured to obtain a new product necessitating the transformation of student knowledge gained from readings and investigations, rather than simply a reiteration of facts and methods. Writing in this manner promotes the reinforcement of reading, capitalizing on the well-known "reading and writing connection" (Nelson and Calfee 1998), as well as serving as a communication tool. Oral reporting in this phase serves to give students the opportunity to share their experiences and also provides students with a gauge of how their work compares to others—a modeling approach crucial to the development of students toward higher levels of achievement.

Key Inquiry Skills to Unlock Reading Comprehension

The previous definition of science inquiry from the NRC provides us with a list of targeted inquiry behaviors that can be applied to reading comprehension. The notion here is that we, as teachers, want to create inquiring students who will apply this model of active learning to science, reading, and all subjects. Table 1 provides a list of inquiry skills and how and when they may be applied to science reading activities.

Closing Thoughts

By strengthening students' science inquiry skills and showing them their applicability to reading, we are introducing students to a new way of thinking about science and text. In essence, rather than teaching them to read, we are teaching them to learn from reading. Doing so in the middle grades simply makes sense—students of this age have reached a level where they are capable of reflective thought and are encountering the significant challenge of multiple teachers, subject areas, and text demands. By providing them with a common and useful strategy for learning from and comprehending text—not just in science, but in any subject area—we are encouraging them to achieve at their highest levels in middle school and beyond.

References

National Research Council (NRC). 1996. *National science education standards*. Washington, DC: National Academies Press.

Nelson, N. and R. C. Calfee. 1998. The reading and writing connection viewed historically. In *The reading and writing connection: Ninety-seventh yearbook of the National Society for the Study of Education*, ed. N. Nelson and R. C. Calfee, Vol. 97: 1–52 . Chicago: University of Chicago Press.

Norris, S. P. and L. M. Phillips. 2003. How literacy in its fundamental sense is critical to scientific literacy. *Science Education* 87: 224–240.

Vygotsky, L. S. 1978. *Mind in society: The development of higher psychological processes*. Eds. M. Cole, V. John-Steiner, S. Scribner, and E. Souberman. Cambridge, MA: Harvard University Press.

Vygotsky, L. S. 1986. *Thought and language*. Trans. A. Kozalin. Cambridge, MA: Harvard University Press.

Chapter 4

14 Writing Strategies

By Thomas Turner and Amy Broemmel

I n 1905, a young scientist named Albert Einstein published a three-page paper presenting his theory of relativity. That brief paper was a major step in revolutionizing how physicists throughout the world thought, and it changed the way the world in general thought about science (Penrose 2005). That a relatively small piece of writing could be so important certainly illustrates the significance of writing to science. Good scientists record what they do—their results, procedures and operations, observations, and hypotheses, as well as their problems and questions.

Scientists need to develop their writing skills for a number of reasons:

- Writing down their ideas and describing what they do and find gives scientists, and those who read and depend on their work, a more accurate record from which to attempt to replicate results.

- Written accounts of what scientists observe that are recorded at the time of their observations help scientists remember more accurately and completely.

- Written summaries of scientific work allow scientists to synthesize bodies of work and look at them holistically so that they or other scientists can extend and develop ideas further.

- Written notes about their work allow scientists to reflect on and mentally process what they have observed.

- Written presentations of their work allow scientists to share and publicize their findings, get credit for their work, and, as a result, claim the benefits of their successes.

- Written descriptions of planned work enable scientists to obtain funding to continue their often-expensive work.

- Written summaries of their ideas allow scientists to share the importance of their work with nonscientists.

Why We Need to Teach Writing in Science Classes

Any science teacher who wants his or her students to be engaged in real science is going to engage them in real science writing. Students do not intuitively know how to do such writing, and instruction in scientific writing is not likely to occur in other school subjects. This writing instruction can serve two purposes: It can increase science understanding and engage students in activities that are useful in the assessment process in science itself. Montgomery (2005, p. 28) points out that student writing provides the teacher with "a tangible demonstration of learning and gives students the opportunity to connect their personal experiences to the content." Montgomery goes on to say that well-crafted, thoughtfully planned writing assignments require the student to do a "deep analysis of subject material."

Well-designed science writing assignments essentially have three critical attributes:

1. They provide authentic purposes for writing.

2. They motivate students to want to write and "do" science.

3. They help students plan and structure both their writing and their science activities.

These attributes are inextricably and symbiotically related. They combine to make the writing assignment comprehensible, authentically important, and feasible. Matsumura and his colleagues (2002) found that the cognitive challenge of the writing assignment had a significant effect on the quality of students' final drafts. That is, when students felt that assignments were cognitively challenging and satisfying to complete, they worked more effectively in producing a finished writing product. Writing experiences should help students feel good about their own writing.

Writing in science should begin with clear, imaginative writing purposes and stimuli that are then scaffolded in such a way that students are able to find an organizational structure for their writing. Writing fluency is often enhanced and supported by experiences like brainstorming or free writing.

Writing Assignments That Work in Science Classes

Writing in The American Scientist, Gopen and Swan (1990, p. 550) assert, "The fundamental purpose of scientific discourse is not the mere presentation of information and thought, but rather its actual communication." Of course, much of the public and many scientists would question this idea because they often think that scientific concepts, data, and analysis are extremely complex, difficult, and abstract. However, like Gopen and Swan, we would argue that what matters most in scientific writing is that a majority of the reading audience accurately perceives what the science writer has in mind, and that when science writing improves, it is a sign that the thinking is better. In the interest of promoting such thinking, we would like to offer 14 examples of different kinds of writing assignments that can provide legitimate, purposeful writing practice while promoting solid science learning and review.

1. Writing Hypothetical Letters

Often scientists share their observations and questions, as well as their differences of opinion, by letter or, in today's world, by blogs and e-mail messages. A very simple, yet effective example of a scientific exchange can be seen in the children's book, *Dear Mr. Blueberry*, by Simon James. In this book, James tells a story through an exchange of letters between a little girl named Emily and her teacher, Mr. Blueberry. Read the book aloud and talk about how Emily seeks help, information, and even opinion but is strongly true to her own observations. Students can work collaboratively to create their own hypothetical exchange of letters between themselves and a scientist or teacher. An important lesson of this poignantly sweet book is that a person should believe in the power of evidence even when it contradicts authority. A second lesson is that it is possible to contradict without being disrespectful to authority. In their letters, students can share observations about some theme or topic. If possible, the return letters by the "authorities" or "scientists" can come from older children or parents with science backgrounds. This activity can also be accomplished electronically in collaboration with university students studying to be science teachers.

2. Process Steps Analysis

After observing and/or taking part in a demonstration of a scientific process, the class could discuss what they saw. After talking the observations through, they can analyze and document the sequential steps that they would need to completely replicate the demonstration. In some cases, where it is safe and feasible, students might even have the opportunity to recreate the demonstration following their own written steps.

3. Identifying Critical Attributes

Small groups of students are asked to look at something. This can be an object of any kind or even a plant or an animal. Each group has a different object. They are given the opportunity to make a thorough examination, and identify its critical attributes. Critical attributes are those observable qualities that make the object, plant, or animal unique, allowing it to be distinguished from all others. The groups can then compile a list of what they believe to be the critical attributes of what they have seen. The lists are shared with the whole class, and students attempt to match the correct item with the critical attribute list. If accurate matching is not possible, students are encouraged to revisit and revise their lists.

4. Collaborative Writing of Scientific Stories

The teacher begins by reading (or having the students read) a science-related trade book. Fiction books, such as *How Groundhog's Garden Grew* (Cherry 2003), and nonfiction books, such as *One Tiny Turtle* (Davies 2001), can be used effectively for this activity. After students have become familiar with the story, the teacher starts a discussion focusing on the scientific content or process described in the book. Once the teacher is satisfied that students understand the science of the book, he or she has the class sit in a circle on the floor. Three clipboards with paper are given to students positioned at equal intervals around the circle. Each student holding a clipboard is asked to think about the science described in the book and then write one sentence that describes the first event in the book. They then pass the clipboards to the right. Students are instructed that when they receive a clipboard, they need to read what has been written up to that point on the paper and then write an additional sentence describing the next event in the scientific process described in the story. Each paper will, in the end, contain a complete retelling of the story in the sequence it occurred. (Three papers are used to provide a means of keeping students actively engaged and to document student understanding of various parts of the content and process.)

5. Chain of Evidence

Because most students have watched many television shows dealing with forensic evidence in criminal investigations, those observation experiences can be used as the basis for writing activities. First the teacher identifies a crime for the team to investigate. Appropriate possibilities include robberies, kidnappings, acts of vandalism, or simple crimes that happen around the school every day. (Avoid scenarios involving violent or graphic crimes.) Begin with a brainstorming session. Have the class create a detailed summary of the chain of evidence leading to the arrest and trial of a suspect in their invented crime. Encourage them to use rich details with leading questions, such as the following: What kind of evidence are we looking for? Where are we likely to find evidence? How do we distinguish evidence related to the crime from what we would normally expect within the crime scene? What are some different ways of reconstructing the crime based on the evidence? What are some possibilities indicated by the evidence?

As an alternative to providing students with only the hypothetical crime, the teacher can also provide a list of "suspects" with a brief introduction to each. Students might then choose a "guilty" suspect and create a well-reasoned written explanation of fictional clues and evidence that could lead to the suspect's arrest. Students then have to learn the difference between being reasonably sure that someone is guilty and having sufficient evidence to bring them to trial, then having enough evidence to convict. Students can assume the roles of judge and jury in response to one another's assembly of evidence, ultimately deciding if the written chain of evidence is sufficient to lead to a trial and subsequent conviction.

6. Accident Report

In this activity, the teacher creates an accident scene by either using photos or actually staging an accident. Examples of cases might include a lunchroom mishap such as spilled trays; a playground incident such as a fall from a piece of equipment, someone being hit by a ball, or a collision between two running students; or a classroom situation such as stacks of papers falling on the floor and getting mixed together. After examining the accident scene and gathering evidence, the investigators are asked to write reports based on their observations. In very small groups, students then read one another's reports, noting inconsistencies or missing details.

7. Label Analysis

The teacher first organizes students into groups and then provides each group with an empty package or label for some product. The products can be foods, medicines, household cleansers, or anything else with a label that lists the ingredients. Each group then writes a description of what they know about the product based on the list of ingredients—in other words, what the contents list tells you and what it doesn't tell you. For example, if something advertised as a juice product has little or no actual fruit juice in it, what does that mean? What does the label tell you about nutrition? What are the risks and benefits of using the product?

8. Technical Directions

The teacher begins by giving students toys or models that require some assembly. Students are then asked to take the role of the marketing staff at the product's manufacturing company. Students must first practice assembling the toy or model, carefully noting the quickest, most efficient steps for assembly. Then they are responsible for writing the directions that will be included on the package. Finally, students attempt to assemble other groups' toys or models using the new directions.

9. Scientific Directions

The teacher organizes the class into small groups and assigns each group a familiar location within a short distance from the school. Each group then discusses the best route to the assigned place and writes directions for getting there using landmarks based on scientific observations taken along the route. For example, the directions could include descriptions of plants, geological formations, or environmental cues. As a follow-up, have students see if they can navigate to a spot using others' directions.

10. Scientific Reporting

After a discussion of the essentials of accurately reporting scientific observations, students are organized into groups. Each group is given a video recording of a scientific experiment and asked to create a detailed list of observations that someone could use to recreate the experiment. The group is allowed to view the video as many times as they like to ensure that their observation list is accurate and complete. (See Resources for recommended video collections.)

11. Proposal Writing

The basic function of a proposal is to describe and pitch to others ideas for projects, papers, and research studies. Proposal writing is an essential activity for many scientists and the skills needed to write proposals should be developed as early as possible. Instead of simply assigning projects and research reports, teachers can provide general parameters for the intended assignment (e.g., research related to rock formation or a project depicting a food chain). Proposal writing activities can begin with a simple brainstorming session for project ideas. The fundamental question is, What do we want to do? After helping generate a list of ideas, the teacher can then lead students through the process of selecting and refining a single idea from the list. The next step is to create a proposal outline. The teacher may choose to have a set of specifications or even provide a simple outline such as the following:

- Title (A proposal…)
- Abstract or summary
- An introduction giving background and explaining the situation
- A statement of the project problem to be solved
- Some suggestion or suggestions about solutions to the problem

■ Some explanation of how you will solve the problem

■ An outline describing the proposed project outcome

■ Step-by-step description of your research methods

■ Conclusions

After the outline is created, assign a different group to write a draft for each part. Finally, piece together the proposal, editing each part so that it is consistent with the rest. The combined class effort can then serve as a model for small groups or individual students to develop their own proposals.

12. Pourquois Story Writing

Pourquois stories are fictional explanations of natural phenomena. They are usually based on definitive descriptions of the phenomena themselves. One example is "How the Elephant Got His Long Trunk." A series of logical plot actions are described, connecting the main characters in the story to the creation of the phenomenon. Provide students with a list of natural phenomena and have them create their own pourquois stories for one of these. Stress the importance of including scientific facts in explanations. Examples of appropriate subjects include why magnets attract, why we have tornadoes, why snakes shed their skin, why hens cackle and roosters crow, why owls hoot, how squirrels got their bushy tails, and why volcanoes erupt.

13. Preparing Descriptive Research Through Web Quests

Web quests are designed to be structured inquiry activities in which information is drawn from the internet. Web quests focus the learners' time on using information rather than looking for it and emphasize thinking at the levels of analysis, synthesis, and evaluation. Essentially, students are directed to a sequenced series of specific websites to solve a structured inquiry problem. A number of websites provide examples of Web quests (see Internet Resources). An example of a teacher-created web quest might ask students to determine which simple machines would be most effective in performing a particular multistep task. The web quest would be designed to lead students to a series of websites that present verbal and/or pictorial information about simple machines. Students would use the information to develop a written solution to the problem. Teachers can also train students to develop their own web quests as an alternative means of demonstrating understanding of particular scientific content or processes.

14. News Clip Observations

The teacher shows a short news film clip without sound. The clip may show a natural disasters the effect of weather, destruction brought about by human effort, or another science-related concept. Students then write descriptions of the event based on their observations. After students have completed their descriptions, replay the film clip with sound and ask students to compare the accompanying news commentary to what they wrote.

Final Note

A science class is not complete unless it helps students learn to think like scientists, and writing is an essential part of such thinking. The 14 writing experiences described here for integrating meaningful, interesting writing into science are not intended to be followed to the letter. Rather, they are all adaptable ideas. Neither are they intended to replace traditional science instruction. However, if we want our students to think like scientists, then it is only logical that we should ask them to observe, document, and write like scientists, as well. We believe that these and other thoughtfully structured writing activities can be integrated into science classrooms in a way that addresses curriculum, provides alternative, authentic means of assessing student understanding, and motivates students to become actively involved in the learning process.

References

Cherry, L. 2003. *How groundhog's garden grew*. New York: Blue Sky Press.

Davies, N. 2001. *One tiny turtle*. Cambridge, MA: Candlewick Press.

Gopen, G. D., and J. A. Swan. 1990. The science of scientific writing. *The American Scientist* 78 (November-December): 550–558.

James, S. 1991. *Dear Mr. Blueberry*. New York: Margaret K. McElderry Books

Matsumura, L. C., G. G. Patthey-Chavez, R. Valdes, and H. Garnier. 2002. Teacher feedback, writing assignment quality, and third-grade students' revision in lower- and higher-achieving urban schools. *Elementary School Journal* 103 (1): 3–25.

Montgomery, M. 2005. Authentic science writing. *Principal Leadership: High School Education* 5 (6): 28–31.

Penrose, R. 2005. *Einstein's miraculous year: Five papers that changed the face of physics*. Princeton, NJ: Princeton University Press.

Internet Resources

WebQuest.org
  www.webquest.org
Teachnology
  www.teach-nology.com/teachers/lesson_plans/computing/web_quests/science
Science Web Quests
  www.can-do.com/uci/k12-lessons.html

Chapter 5

This Isn't English Class!

Using Writing as an Assessment Tool in Science

By Michael Rockow

Our students learn how to write in English class, but they seem shocked when I tell them that they can put those skills to work in science class, too. We know that writing is a huge part of science. It is the way scientists communicate ideas, results, conclusions, and opinions to other scientists. Thus, in my classes students use writing in a number of ways to demonstrate knowledge, and I use their writing for assessment.

Using writing to demonstrate knowledge has a number of advantages. During a writing assignment, students have enough time to gather their thoughts. They often make connections during writing assignments that they had not made before. Another advantage of writing for assessment is, students do not feel as if they are being tested. Students sometimes panic on tests for various reasons, but this does not usually happen with writing assignments. In a writing assignment, students can present all of the information that they know, as opposed to traditional tests where they are only able to show their knowledge of specific questions. Students can also demonstrate their abilities to analyze situations and information better than on a standard paper-and-pencil test. Finally, with tests or assignments from the book, the tasks can become mundane. With writing assignments, you can change the format to make them all seem different and fresh.

Unfortunately, there are a few drawbacks to using writing assignments as assessment tools. These tasks take a lot of class time. Although paper-and-pencil tests can be given in a class period or less, writing assignments will take longer to complete. Time must be taken to explain the assignment and grading criteria, and students must be given sufficient time to complete the writing. These assignments also take longer to grade. Because of these reasons, I do not use writing assignments to assess every unit. I use them primarily with my Earth science units, due to the fact that this part of the curriculum lends itself to science fiction. However, writing assignments like the ones discussed here can be used in any branch of science. There are a wide variety of assignments to choose from when implementing a writing activity for assessment. I most often use the following three types of assignments.

Persuasive Writing

In this type of assignment, students are given a problem that has multiple answers and asked to choose a position and write a persuasive essay to support and explain their point of view. You can have students use their notes or give them study materials to help gather information on the problem and the possible answers. This is done at the beginning of the assignment. Students are expected to support their arguments with facts from either their notes or from supplemental materials. I allow three days for this type of assignment, one day each to plan, write, and revise/finish. You can use their points, facts, and explanations to assess what they know about the topic. Students are graded on the accuracy of their facts and how well the facts support their argument. Our persuasive essays are five paragraphs, although the length can vary.

One example of this type of assignment is to decide whether Pluto is a planet or not (AGI 2003). Prior to the assignment, we discuss the characteristics of the planets, as well as the characteristics of asteroids, moons, stars, and comets. During the assignment, students decide which of those objects is most similar to Pluto and then write a five-paragraph, persuasive essay in class to support their choices. In order to foster creativity, I stress that the assignment has no wrong answers, a point that is easier to make now that the International Astronomical Union has changed Pluto's status as a planet. I make the point here that the case of Pluto illustrates that scientific information can change through time.

The first day of the assignment, students make an outline in which they write down their opinions and three facts that support their opinions. To help them, I have students use their own notes as well as NASA's Our Solar System Lithograph Set. You can download these information sheets at NASA's educational materials website free of charge (see Internet Resources). I collect the fact sheets at the end of each period and students get them back the following day. Students are expected to write their rough draft during the second class period and their final essay during the third class period.

Students use the same format they learn in English class (introduction, three supporting paragraphs, conclusion). This gives me a chance to stress that though they learn writing skills in English class, all other classes, including science, use these skills as well. The first paragraph is an introduction that states the opinion. The second paragraph is structured around one of the facts from the outline and explains how that fact supports the opinion. The third and fourth paragraphs are structured like the second, but with the other facts from the outline. The concluding paragraph restates the opinion. Figure 1 provides the Pluto project assignment, my scoring criteria, and an example of an essay from one of my students.

Because there are no wrong positions, students are graded on their arguments, the accuracy of the facts that they use to support their arguments, and the appropriateness of their explanations. This assignment can assess students' knowledge of the different parts of the solar system, planets, moons, comets, and asteroids, not to mention the characteristics of Pluto.

Role Playing

This is a type of assignment in which students take on a role, such as a scientist writing a letter to a colleague urging support of continental drift or a reporter from a newspaper discussing the effects of a change in hunting laws. Students can use their knowledge in context and not just recite facts. In this type of writing, students demonstrate knowledge by informally

Figure 1. Pluto project

Should we call Pluto a planet? Is it more like an asteroid? Could it be a comet? You decide which you think Pluto is most like and then defend your point of view in a five-paragraph, persuasive essay. You will need at least three facts that support your opinion. You will be graded by how well you use those facts to illustrate and explain your point of view.

Pluto project grading criteria

• Introduction	1 point
• First body paragraph	
• Fact	3 points
• How it supports your point	4 points
• Second body paragraph	
• Fact	3 points
• How it supports your point	4 points
• Third body paragraph	
• Fact	3 points
• How it supports your point	4 points
• Conclusion	1 point
• Writing conventions	2 points
• Total	25 points

Sample persuasive essay

I believe that Pluto is a comet. Contrary to the old belief that Pluto is a planet, I think Pluto should've been classified as a comet. Pluto is made up of some of the same materials as a comet. Also, they are both located beyond the orbit of Neptune, and they both have eccentric orbits. Using this evidence, Pluto can be proven to be a comet.

The materials that make up Pluto's surface are very similar to the ones on a comet. Pluto is made up of ice and frozen gasses; it also has methane, nitrogen, and carbon monoxide. If you take a look at a comet, aside from a few of the materials, a comet has a surface quite like Pluto's. A comet is made up of dust, rock, ice, methane, and ammonia. By comparing the surface of Pluto and a comet, we can conclude that the two share a similar exterior.

Another trait shared by comets and Pluto is that they both are stationed in the same area. This area is home to many icy objects and is beyond the orbit of Neptune. These icy objects are sometimes referred to as Kuiper belt objects, Edgeworth-Kuiper belt objects, or trans-Neptunian objects. Pluto is one of the largest of the bodies lying in the "Kuiper Belt area." By understanding that Pluto is not out of place in this area of icy bodies (not considering size), it is just another fact that points in the direction saying that Pluto is a comet.

Pluto and comets also have "interesting" orbits. Other planets orbit around the Sun with an orbital eccentricity measuring close to 0. Comets orbit the Sun with an orbital eccentricity measuring close to 1. Pluto orbits the Sun with an orbital eccentricity of 0.25. Both these orbits are eccentric orbits, as they are not close to the standard orbit of the planets. This "odd" orbit proves that it would make more sense for Pluto to be a comet than a planet.

With evidence and facts one can most definitely prove that Pluto is not a planet, but a comet. So, Pluto has suffered long enough. It is done being grouped with the nine others whose names we learn in elementary school. It is time we put Pluto in its rightful grouping, up high with the comets.

discussing what they know while pretending to play their roles. They are not only graded on the facts that they put in their work, but also on the proper use of those facts.

In one of my role-play assignments, I have students write to the authors of an old geology textbook (Thurber and Kilburn 1965). Because the book was written before the theory of plate tectonics had been established, it is only mentioned in passing. At the end of our unit on plate tectonics, students write to the authors as if they were colleagues, informing them of this new theory. In this context, students can show off their knowledge of continental drift, seafloor spreading, mantle convection, and the way the theory of plate tectonics explains earthquakes and volcanic activity.

Again, as with the persuasive essays, I allow three periods for this assignment. During the first class period, students write outlines for their letters, complete with the facts they are going to use. Students write rough drafts during the second class period and write their final copies

during the third. In this assignment, students get to use their notes only as reference material. Students use the first paragraph to introduce themselves and their purposes. They explain what is meant by continental drift in their second paragraphs and lay out some evidence that supports it. The third paragraph explains seafloor spreading and discusses supporting evidence. The fourth paragraph discusses the theory of plate tectonics and convection and how the theory explains a type of landform, such as a mountain or volcano. Their concluding paragraphs thank the authors for reading their letters. Figure 2 provides an example of the letter-to-the-author assignment, my scoring rubric, and a sample letter from one of my students.

Figure 2. Letter to the author

The authors of this textbook barely mention the theory of plate tectonics. Maybe that's because they don't know very much about it. You are now experts on the theory so your assignment will be to tell them about it. You are an important geologist, writing to the authors to teach them about this theory. You will be graded on how well you explain the different parts of the theory and the evidence that supports it.

Letter-to-the-author grading criteria

• Introduction	1 point
• Continental drift	
• Explanation	3 points
• Evidence	3 points
• Seafloor spreading	
• Explanation	3 points
• Evidence	3 points
• Plate-tectonic theory	
• Explanation	2 points
• Evidence	2 points
• Conclusion	1 point
• Writing conventions	2 points
• Total	20 points

Sample letter
Dear Dr. Kilburn and Dr. Thurber,

I have examined your book about Earth science and there was very little mentioned about continental drift and plate tectonics. I am writing this letter to inform you about this new theory about the Earth.

I have evidence of continental drift, and that there used to be a super continent called Pangaea. All of the continents almost fit perfectly together. Antarctica does not have many plants, yet there are fossils of ferns found there. This could not have happened unless Antarctica was closer to the equator. Fossils of reptiles were also found on a few continents, which look like they could fit together. The fossils were found on the edges of those continents, which would have been right next to each other if the continents were connected. On some of the continents that would easily fit together, there are mountain ranges that would be connected if they were side to side. These artifacts could only be there if there was a Pangaea.

Seafloor spreading has occurred. The oldest rock is at the edges of the ocean, really close to the side of the continents. The oldest rocks are about 200 million years old. The ocean floor is much younger in the middle, where the mid-ocean ridge is. At the ridge, magma is forced between two ledges, which pushed the ledges away from each other and forced the continents even farther apart. Once the magma hits the water, it cools quickly. Every time the magma came out of the volcano, it hardened, which increased the size of it each time. Every time more magma came out, the continents were forced apart even more. This is why the youngest rocks are at the mid-ocean ridge. Every time magma comes out, it forms new rocks.

You also forgot to include plate tectonics. Plates cover the surface of the Earth. Convection cells are the start of seafloor spreading. Heat is what makes the convection cells move. The plates of the Earth start to move when the convection cells push and pull the plates. It creates them to move. Convection cells also create earthquakes when plates move. The lithosphere is the top of the Earth, where the plates are moving. The asthenosphere is where the convection currents are pushing the lithosphere's continents apart. Mountains are formed when two plates are compressed together. When they are compressed the mountains get taller.

Thank you for listening to my advice. I believe that if you write another book you should include these facts.

Imaginative Writing

Teachers can also use imaginative writing to assess student knowledge. Students are encouraged to write a story, poem, play, song, etc. incorporating facts about the topic in question. Students demonstrate knowledge by the ways in which they use the facts in the story. Students are graded on whether their facts are accurate. I typically assign this type of activity for homework, though it can be done as an in-class assignment. When we do it in class, I give students one period to write outlines and a second period to finish their final copies. Students use their own notes for this type of writing, and I do not give them any extra support materials. However, if they want to do their own research at home on the subject, I do not discourage them. A good source for information on the Earth's structure, which we use as part of our Earth Structure unit, is the online unit Journey to the Center of the Earth, designed by Lawrence and Sheryl Braile (see Internet Resources).

In one of my imaginative assignments, students write a short story, poem, or song about a trip through the layers of the Earth to its core. They are required to include at least two facts about each of the four different layers of the Earth. They are graded on the accuracy of the facts they mention about the Earth's layers. Through this assignment, I assess students' knowledge of the layers of the Earth, including scale, composition, and density. Figure 3

Figure 3. Journey to the center of the Earth

Write a story, poem, song, or rap about a trip to the center of the Earth.

Journey-to-the-center-of-the-Earth grading criteria

- Assignment is in a proper form 2 points
- Facts about each layer   4 points each, times 4
- Writing conventions   2 points
- Total   20 points

Sample story

It was a cold afternoon when my classmates and I found ourselves outside school. We were staring down a hole, which seemed suspiciously large. Out of the hole came a little train, which looked strange. What was even stranger was that our science teacher was riding in the conductor's seat. I guess we were going to board the train and go down the hole to go to the center of the Earth. The teacher told us to get on board, where he told us about sediments.

Then the little train started to head into the dark hole and the next thing we heard was "Next stop… basement." It took about two minutes to get there because the basement is only about a kilometer into the Earth. I looked at the thermometer in my train car and it said it was 20°C. The rocks out our window looked like granite but the info screen that popped up in the car said that they were schist. They looked shiny.

I took a few minutes to get to our next stop… the Moho. We noticed on the info screen that we were 35 km into the Earth here, which I guess is the end of the crust. As we laughed at the name, we noticed that all of the rocks were green. We soon learned that these rocks were made of olivine. We also noticed that it was starting to get hot. The info screen said that it was 600°C. I am glad that we have A/C in this car.

After traveling through the asthenosphere and the upper mantle, we reached the outer core, 2,800 km into the Earth. Instead of going through a hole, we ran into liquid iron and nickel. After traveling through the liquid for a while, we retuned to the hole. We had entered the inner core, which we found out is also made of iron and nickel, except that it is solid here.

We stopped a few minutes later. The info screen read that we were 6,300 km from the surface and that the temperature was 4,800°C. We were told that this was our last stop…the center of the Earth. Pencils started floating off of people's desks because of the gravity down there. Then, the whole train shook. We were going back. Out of nowhere, the train went black and we started spinning out of control. Screams could be heard while we grazed the sides of the hole. After we rolled a number of times, we regained control of the train and started making progress up the hole. It took us 14 hours to get back. What a field trip!

provides an example of the assignment, my scoring criteria, and a sample story from one of my students.

Modifications

In these assignments, it is important to modify the work so students can show the teacher what they know. There are a number of ways to do that. I allow my English language learners (ELL students) to write in their native language if they have trouble writing in English. ELL instructional aides, other teachers, or parent volunteers can help with translations. An alternative is to have an aide work with the ELL students and help them put the ideas on paper in English. For the few students who have trouble writing, I help organize the writing for them. I give them a handout that provides the beginning of each sentence and they finish the sentence by inserting pertinent facts. I call these sentence starters. For example, the opening sentence starter for the Pluto project is "I think Pluto is most like a _____ because _____." Students write that down on their paper and fill in the blanks. A sentence starter for the letter-to-the-author assignment is "The evidence for continental drift includes _____." This approach works well for some of my students because it allows them to concentrate on the facts they know without having to worry about organizing the writing. I use this approach primarily with ELL students, students with writing Individualized Education Programs (IEPs), and students with severe anxiety problems. Students who have trouble with the physical act of writing can either type their work or give their assignment as an oral report. Again, there are many ways to modify these assignments to assess what students have learned.

Conclusions

Writing has many purposes in science, but this article deals only with its use in assessing student knowledge. If you use this approach sparingly and vary the writing assignments, students will be more eager to complete the assignments and will be able to show off their knowledge. There are many other ways to use writing in science classes. It is a great way to turn your science curriculum into an interdisciplinary experience.

References

American Geological Institute (AGI). 2003. *Project CUES: Constructing understanding of Earth systems. Pilot test edition*. Alexandria, VA: AGI.

Thurber, W. A., and R. E. Kilburn. 1965. *Exploring Earth science*. Boston: Allyn and Bacon.

Internet Resources

Journey to the Center of the Earth
    http://web.ics.purdue.edu/~braile/edumod/journey/journey.htm
Our Solar System Lithograph Set
    www.nasa.gov/audience/foreducators/topnav/materials/listbytype/Our_Solar_System_Lithograph_Set.html

Chapter 6

Making Thinking Visible

A Method to Encourage Science Writing in Upper Elementary Grades

By Roxanne Greitz Miller and Robert C. Calfee

What does it mean to "write to learn science," and why should we use writing as a vehicle for science learning when other alternatives exist? Many studies have examined the role of writing in the learning process, demonstrating that writing, in conjunction with other activities such as reading and hands-on experiences, contributes to greater critical thinking, thoughtful consideration of ideas, and better concept learning.

We would like to add a basic and universal observation to the findings supporting the use of writing, particularly in science: *Writing makes thinking visible*. Few activities can achieve what writing can in science. It enables students to self-assess complex content knowledge and allows teachers to evaluate the student in two dimensions: overall writing ability and specific content area achievement.

However, for writing to fulfill these standards, carefully planned and scaffolded writing activities—beyond what we normally see in science classrooms, especially at the elementary level—must be implemented. To illustrate this point, we will describe the *Reading and Writing About Science (RWS) Project* conducted between 2000 and 2003 with support from the National Science Foundation. Twenty-one teachers, with levels of experience ranging from beginner up to 30 years, participated in the project, teaching 587 students in grades 4 through 6.

The goal of the project was to provide upper elementary teachers with the skills to create classroom situations that integrated literacy with science, equipping students to communicate their thinking and understanding through exemplary science reading and writing activities. This approach aimed to produce deeper science concept learning, while also serving as an authentic indicator of student achievements in science and literacy.

A CORE Framework

To make a dramatic change in the way teachers approach science writing, we found it necessary to address both science instruction as a whole and the use of writing during various stages. To guide us in this endeavor and communicate a concrete example of an ideal foundation for highly effective science writing to teachers, we turned to the CORE Model of Instruction (Chambliss and Calfee 1998).

The CORE Model was originally developed as a representation of the manner in which reading and writing can be linked and used to reinforce each other; we saw possibilities to extend this model to experiential learning (such as science inquiry).

The CORE Model incorporates four elements: Connect, Organize, Reflect, and Extend. The elements can be used for designing a sequence of instructional activities. Students first connect what they already know about a topic to new science content or experience. They then organize information from multiple sources into coherent packages. Next they reflect on the collection of "stuff" by discussing it with others in preparation for the writing task. Finally, completion of the project serves to "stretch" or extend the learning.

The following paragraphs expand on each of these elements. The interactive elements serve both teacher and students as lenses (and common language) for thinking about their progress through a unit. In our project, teachers appreciated the logical and easy sequencing of activities; students quickly internalized the complementary nature of the stages and their usefulness as aids in learning and writing.

Connecting Knowledge

During the *Connect* phase, teachers used classroom discussions to determine students' prior topical knowledge. Virtually all teachers are familiar with collaborative activities such as think-pair-share, brainstorming, and hands-on science. A critical strategy in the RWS Project was "wall-papering" the room with written documentation of these activities.

For example, during an initial brainstorming session on earthquakes, the teacher wrote students' comments and shared experiences on flip-chart paper to facilitate the discussion and activate background knowledge. Rather than removing this artifact after the discussion was over, it remained posted in the room for the remainder of the unit, during which it was revisited and revised as necessary by both teacher and students.

This technique was especially important in our local area, where large numbers of students who are at-risk or English language learners benefited from the instant availability of ideas and vocabulary to scaffold subsequent academic tasks. Students quickly caught on to the fact that they could revisit their initial sharings, correct misconceptions, and add new knowledge throughout the unit.

Organizing Information

Information is essential in science but it can quickly become overwhelming; students need to learn strategies to *Organize* and manage their collections. To facilitate organization, the RWS Project taught students to create graphic organizers before, during, and after science reading. (These same organizer structures can also be used for organizing information from hands-on activities.)

We identified five basic graphic organizers as particularly effective for organizing science content. We have found that closely matching the organizer's structure to the nature of the science concept is particularly effective when tasking students with subsequent writing. For example, when studying tsunamis, students were shown how to construct a "falling domino" organizer, a sequential graphic that indicates cause and effect (akin to what happens in a line of falling dominoes), with each occurrence causing something else to happen. The graphics we used with great success include the web, linear string, falling dominoes, branching tree, and matrix. See Table 1 for a discussion of graphic organizers.

Table 1. Graphic organizers used in RWS Project

Name	Use	Science example(s)	Picture
Web (also referred to as the topical net or cluster)	To group similar concepts/ideas related to a unifying theme; may also be used to indicate sequence if arrows are used to connect subgroups	The rock cycle (with subgroups indicating the different types of rock and processes); states of matter	
Linear string	To represent a sequence but with no indication of cause/effect	Food chain; scientific timeline; steps of an experiment	
Falling dominoes	To represent a causal sequence	Tsunami; origin of the solar system	
Branching tree	To represent sequences from multiple perspectives	Parasite/host interaction, each line representing what is happening to one of the organisms	
Matrix	For categorization and classification	Compare and contrast different animals and their characteristics	

In response to post-project surveys conducted one to three years after participation, many RWS teachers commented that one of the most beneficial things they learned from our professional development sessions was how graphic organizers, and specifically choosing a matched organizer rather than a more general one, dramatically improved student writing.

Once students completed their organizers (constructed collaboratively in small groups or in large groups with the teacher, or independently) and thereby had a foundation for writing, they moved onto the prewriting phase. The organizers served a dual purpose here. Not only were they used to organize science concepts *before* and *during* content acquisition activities, but they were used again *after* in preparation for writing.

Reflecting on Learning

Metacognition and self-evaluation are large components of all the CORE Model phases; however, they are most prominent in the *Reflect* phase. During this phase, students reflect on their learning in large and small groups facilitated by the teacher. At this time (prior to writing), students have a final opportunity to correct any science misconceptions and solidify their content knowledge. Cross talk between students and groups extends the experience of the individual student and further lessens academic disparity between diverse students and English language learners.

Table 2. Guidelines for constructing effective writing prompts		
Prompt element	**Criteria**	**Example**
Focus statement	The focus statement has a twofold purpose: It activates students' prior knowledge, and it models implicitly to students that thinking before writing is critical to writing a coherent and interesting essay. Focus statements may be separated from the actual writing directive by placing them in separate paragraphs, folding over the sheet of paper, or using two separate sheets.	You are learning about different kinds of rocks and how they are formed through the rock cycle process. Although rocks can have many differences, they all are related to one another through the rock cycle.
Audience	Tell the students who the audience is for this composition. Giving the students an idea of whom they are writing to/for gives them essential information about tone, vocabulary, and structure. It also makes the writing more real to the students and encourages them to consider audience in their writing and by extension, authorship in their reading.	Suppose you want to explain to your parents about the rock cycle.
Form (type)	Tell the students what form the writing is to take, whether it is a letter, paragraph, essay, or another form.	Write as many paragraphs as you need to explain (1) what the rock cycle is, (2) what the different kinds of rocks formed by it are, and (3) how the rocks can be changed from one kind into another. Be sure that your composition has a clear beginning, middle, and end.
Purpose	Be specific and simple with instructions on the purpose of the students' writing. Use specific phrases and keep them consistent between assignments throughout the year.	General examples: "Write a story that tells …" "Write an essay to explain …" "Write a letter to convince …" "Write a letter to persuade …"
Supporting details	Always remind students to give supporting details. Include a concluding sentence in your prompt directing them to do so.	Use examples from the reading passage (or an alternate/additional source, such as an experiment, if it is appropriate to the prompt) to support your writing.
Planning space and directive	Students should be provided with space to create webs, weaves, or graphic organizers of their own design to help organize their thoughts prior to writing. This space may be provided between the focus and directive statements or on a facing page. A statement directing students to use the space should be included in the prompt (or after it) so that students (1) are encouraged to develop a written organizer and (2) know they are allowed to write in the blank space (obvious to us—but not to students accustomed to being told, "Don't write in the book"). Younger students may be provided with an advanced organizer that accompanies the writing prompt.	After prompt: You may use this space to plan your writing.

At the end of the reflection phase, students in the RWS Project received their writing prompt. We placed the prompt in this phase, rather than the *Extend* phase during which the composition is actually written, because a significant factor in writing success is the ability to effectively dissect a writing prompt by reflecting on the task to be performed, its components, and the knowledge needed to perform the task.

Immediately upon beginning to work with schools, we found drastic inconsistencies between how teachers structure (or do not structure) their writing prompts. RWS teachers were trained to construct their prompts to use five common elements: focus, audience, type, purpose, and supporting details. Guidelines for these elements appear in Table 2.

Teachers guided students through the prompt dissection process, facilitating identification of individual prompt elements, until students were able to do so for themselves. By using a consistent format, students were able, over time, to recognize more easily what they were being asked to do and how to set about doing it.

When first exposed to this method, teachers often said that using a prompt like this was "too long and too complicated" for their students. We persuaded them to try anyway. The overwhelming response was longer and richer student responses, even with students as young as third grade. We believe part of the success of this system is how it not only makes the writing task easier for the student to approach but also scaffolds teachers in creating better-designed writing assignments that assess student thinking and learning.

Extending the Experience

The writing composition is the focus of the *Extend* phase, with students working individually to respond to the writing prompt. Figure 1 (p. 36) features an example of a writing prompt along with an example of a student's composition and graphic organizer.

The traditional "process writing" approach (develop, draft, revise, polish, and publish) was used to guide the steps of the composition process.

Toward our goal of real communication through writing, we attempted whenever possible to target the writing task for an authentic audience, including readers of a school science magazine, pediatric patients, and a younger elementary student. After composing, students were given the opportunity to share their writing with other students and the teacher. In addition to facilitating writing as communication, sharing allowed students to become familiar with how and what other students write, giving them concrete examples of others' work. Without this type of sharing, students have no idea where their work stands in comparison with others; it is essential—particularly for students from diverse achievement levels—to have this type of feedback and examples of outstanding student writing to which they can aspire.

Evaluating the Results

A final challenge for our project was to develop a rubric for scoring science content in student writing. Often we were confronted with a fine piece of student writing, coherent and well written but missing the "meat." The challenge was to design a rubric that would enable teachers (and students) to identify key features distinguishing poor, fair, good, and excellent science content writing from one another.

We aimed to design a generic rubric that could be used with virtually any science writing assignment, while allowing teachers to target specific key ideas and benchmarks within the

Figure 1. A sample prompt and its corresponding student writing and graphic organizer

Teacher prompt
Today you learned about bacteria. You learned some are helpful while some are harmful. Pretend you are a reporter writing an article for a fourth-grade science magazine. The title of this article should be "The Good, The Bad, and The Ugly." In your writing, explain how bacteria are helpful and harmful. Also, explain how they are different and the same. Be sure your article isn't just a list of illnesses or symptoms that are caused by bacteria. Instead, use details and examples from your reading to compare and contrast these bacteria. Use paragraphs to show main ideas.

Student work
The Good, The Bad, and The Ugly
Bacteria can be harmful because it causes illness. It could spoil your food. For example, they make green stuff mold on old bread and it's bad if you eat a lot of mold.

Bacteria can help you by digesting the food you eat. It could be a toxic avenger that means it cleans up oil spills. Bacteria rejuvenates plants to create oxygen. They are decomposers they re-cycle dead things back into the air, water, soil. And they produce food and they help you make food. For example yogurt and cheese. And antibiotics is a medicine made by bacteria.

Harmful and helpful bacteria are alike because they both reproduce themselves. They are both a small size. They live almost everywhere. They are carried by animals, air, and the water. And bacteria come from other bacteria.

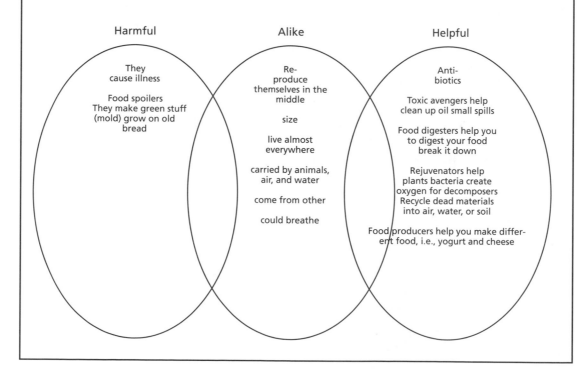

scoring levels. Upon examining many writing rubrics in use in science and other subjects, we drew upon a rubric previously published in *Science Scope* (Harding 2002) and adapted it considerably. See Figure 2 for a science writing rubric.

Score	Description	Criteria
Figure 2. Science writing rubric		
4	Exceeds expectations	Commanding use of key terms with very few or no errors Connections between concepts well developed Concepts presented demonstrate understanding at the analysis, synthesis, or evaluation levels; reflect transformation of content beyond that provided in the text or activities by the student Further examples and extensions provided and illustrate excellent comprehension
3	Meets expectations	Sufficient use of key terms to illustrate comprehension; majority of key terms used accurately Connections between concepts beginning, though may be limited to the applications provided in the text or activities
2	Not yet within expectations	Relatively few key terms present; or a majority of the key terms present used inaccurately Connections between concepts not present; or generally incorrect
1	Below expectations	No examples from text or activities present (text or activities not referenced) However, paper scorable
NC	Not scorable	Unrelated, unintelligible, or length not sufficient to score Copied from board or another student

In addition to this rubric, we also used more traditional rubrics for other traits (such as grammar and mechanics, spelling, and vocabulary) to give us an indication of overall student writing ability as well as content knowledge.

Measures of Success

We addressed success of the project from two perspectives, student and teacher. For students, writing scores on RWS science writing assessments demonstrated growth in all rubric components, with the most substantial gains emerging in length and coherence.

Fourth-grade students appeared to benefit most from the program. This may be due to previous inexperience with exposition and science content; thus, training in expository reading and writing techniques and science content early in grade four may provide students with what they need to succeed. However, additional analyses showed that students who participated in two years of the program (either in fourth and then fifth grade or fifth through sixth grade) continued to increase their writing scores throughout the extended exposure to the program.

Additionally, and of great interest to our region, students who performed poorly at the outset of the program showed the most benefit from participation. Within each classroom, students were divided into tertiles (low, medium, and high) based on the prewriting scores. The writing performance gap between high and low tertile students was reduced by approximately 40–50% as a result of RWS participation.

Teachers' Insights

A major concern of our team was to design a science-writing program that worked in real schools with real teachers. Results from teacher artifacts and discussion sessions showed the design was perceived as effective, efficient, and adaptable. Long-term surveys showed teachers continue to implement the writing strategies outside their participation in the research project. Rather than reverting to prior practices, teachers sustain their changed instructional practices, and their self-perception of knowledge regarding effective writing techniques continues at high levels.

Teacher insights shared with us were especially thought provoking. The following comments emerged during a videotaped discussion near the end of the project when participants were asked, "What do you believe about the most effective ways to teach reading and writing, from your experience in the project?"

- "We [teachers] realize that narrative and exposition share features. But we now prefer exposition over narrative for teaching reading and writing—it's more concrete, and instead of teaching narrative first to students, we think that exposition should be taught first and that read/ write instruction should be content-based."

- "The instructional methods we are using in RWS clue the kids in on what the instructional format is going to be. After doing one unit, the kids know what's coming and prepare themselves along the way. It's creating a reflective student, not just the teacher. Students are 'owning' the instruction and are motivated."

- "Instead of just creating scaffolds for content, we're creating scaffolds for process. We're creating successful practice, and think that it will lead to successful large-scale assessment."

These excerpts must be viewed as testimonials, to be sure, but the substance of the comments also merits attention. These are teachers serving students with significant needs, working with limited resources under extraordinary pressures to increase test scores in all subject areas, discussing curriculum and instruction in language more typical of gifted classrooms. To borrow Neil Armstrong's famous sentiment, while what we have learned in the RWS Project may be viewed by some as a small step toward effective science writing, we believe it was a giant leap for RWS Project students toward their success in science and in future schooling.

Acknowledgment

The work described in this article was made possible by a grant from the National Science Foundation's Interagency Education Research Initiative (No. 9979834).

Resources

Chambliss, M. J., and R. C. Calfee. 1998. *Textbooks for learning: Nurturing children's minds.* Malden: Blackwell.

Harding, T. 2002. Svithjod, stories, and songs: Rewriting Earth science in creative ways. *Science Scope* 26 (1):19–21.

National Research Council (NRC). 1996. *National science education standards.* Washington, DC: National Academies Press.

Chapter 7

Writing to Learn

By Brian Hand, Vaughan Prain, and Keith Vance

Because of time constraints and a crowded science syllabus, student writing is often used only to assess past learning. Writing, however, can provide new avenues for students to understand science. The Writing in Science Wheel (Figure 1) graphically organizes the five elements in writing to learn science—topic, purpose, audience, production method, and format—and the tasks and demands within these five elements (Hand and Prain 1996). We created the following writing activity to

- introduce students to a model for writing about science,

- clarify and consolidate student understanding during a unit on genetics, and

- assess students' research skills.

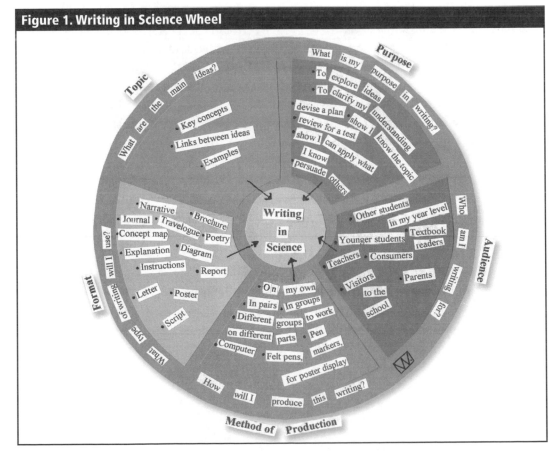

Figure 1. Writing in Science Wheel

Figure 2. Task organization	
Model element	**Task set**
Topic	Student choice (genetic engineering)
Purpose	Persuade audience Demonstrate understanding of concepts
Audience	General public
Method of production	Computer word processing Individually
Format	Letter to editor of the local newspaper (maximum 250 words)

Figure 3. Possible topics

1. Write a textbook explanation for your peers on reproductive processes.
2. Report on the forces that occur in a car accident.
3. Pretend you are an oxygen molecule and describe your journey through the ecosystem.
4. Produce a brochure for the general public to sell a type of clothing that can be worn in all temperatures. Address the concept of heat transfer.
5. Produce a solar system travel brochure for the general public.

We use this activity with two ninth-grade classes over five class periods. Figure 2 outlines the five elements of the writing assignment.

The Write Start

Class 1: To introduce students to the writing model, we have students read a newspaper article outlining the risks and benefits of a new cigarette filter. We then ask students how the writing model could be used to plan a letter to the editor of the local newspaper. Each section of the model is discussed and suggestions are put on the blackboard for consideration. The class then makes a final decision on each part of the model.

We emphasize the necessity for making decisions in all five parts of the model, particularly in defining the most relevant science concepts. A discussion about how to effectively integrate these concepts into a persuasive writing style follows, and we outline an example of a writing plan. We then ask students to form groups of three and allow them 15 minutes to draft a letter, after which we discuss whether the letters satisfy the goals outlined in the model.

This introductory activity provides students with a framework for writing to learn and helps them learn to structure a persuasive letter. It also paves the way for the next writing assignment on genetics. You may use the same activity formats for any science topic (see Figure 3 for a list of possible topics).

Class 2: We hand out the Genetics Assignment Task Sheet (see p. 43), which explains that students are to write a persuasive letter to the editor on a current issue in genetics that they choose and research. This activity assigns four of the five writing model elements: The purpose is to persuade others, the audience is the general public, the production is by individual students, and the format is a letter to the editor.

Students have to select only the topic, but in future assignments, they gradually take control of the decision-making in all five elements of the model. Therefore, we devote class time to discussing the choices available in all five elements of the writing wheel, such as writing journals, concept maps, or poetry for audiences of younger students, consumers, or their peers.

Classes 3 and 4: After choosing their topics from a list of current events issues, students conduct research in the library and organize their information into scientific concepts and sides of the issue to be explained in their letters.

Class 5: Students draft, edit, type, and print their letters.

Write on Target

We found that while most students successfully integrated the science content into their writing, some had difficulty achieving an appropriate balance, placing too much emphasis on either the science or the ethical arguments. Therefore, we also developed a checklist of requirements for students to refer to while working on future writing assignments (see Figure 4). Students indicated that the list helped them check their progress as they produced their letters.

Figure 4. Student check list

- Have you chosen to write about concepts that relate to the assignment topic?
- Have you explained the concepts clearly in your writing?
- Have you researched the concepts you weren't familiar with?
- Are your ideas relevant to the assignment topic?
- Does your writing show your understanding of the topic?
- Are the links between ideas clear?
- Have you used effective examples?
- Have you checked the assignment guidelines to make sure you are on track?
- Is the purpose of your writing clear?
- Have you identified and understood your audience?
- Are the words and style appropriate for the purpose and audience?
- Is the content appropriate for your audience?
- Is the meaning of each sentence clear?
- Are all the words spelled correctly?
- Has the correct punctuation been used?

Genetics Assignment Task Sheet

Many developments in modern genetics are controversial—gene therapy, cloning, and artificial breeding, just to name a few. Some people welcome the new developments, while others warn that they bring potential dangers. Your job is to clearly present both sides of an issue, while persuading readers of one point of view.

Select and research an issue in genetics and write a letter to the editor following the guidelines in the Writing in Science Wheel. You may use information from the internet, the local college library, the school library, science textbooks, or books and magazines from home. Plan your letter carefully. Show in your writing that you

- understand the topic you have chosen,
- clearly understand the arguments for it,
- clearly understand the arguments against it, and
- have chosen an opinion on the topic.

Most important, base your writing on facts and incorporate scientific information.

Your teacher will allow three class periods for research and writing time; you should not spend more than an additional two hours on the assignment. You will have one period to type and print the assignment in the computer room.

Length: about 250 words
Due date: _____

By using the writing process to explore science, students and teachers can find new ways of clarifying, revising, and consolidating knowledge. Using higher-order thinking skills to communicate science through writing helps students refine their understanding of science (Rivard 1994). For teachers, student writing provides a window into students' science understanding and allows misconceptions to be corrected.

References

Hand, B., and V. Prain. 1996. Writing for learning in science: A model for use within schools. *Australian Science Teachers Journal* 42 (3):23–27.

Rivard, L. 1994. A review of writing to learn in science: Implications for practice and research. *Journal of Research in Science Teaching* 31: 969.

Chapter 8

Helping Students Write About Science Without Plagiarizing

By Jodi Wheeler-Toppen

I want my students to have an experience as similar to that of real scientists as possible. And, as I tell my students, real scientists begin with research—reading and talking to other scientists about what is already known in their field. Therefore, I take my students to the library to begin their search. They check out books, copy pages from magazines, and frantically search the internet. To all appearances, they are hard at work. But invariably, despite all warnings about plagiarism, the final papers often contain paragraph after paragraph of sentences copied verbatim from books and websites.

I have realized that many of my students don't plagiarize just because they are lazy. Many of them simply do not know how to write about science. Reading and writing in the primary grades often focuses on stories, which leaves middle level students unprepared to work with expository text (Spor and Schneider 1999).

But why should I have to teach writing in my science class? Actually, writing is an integral part of science. The growth of scientific knowledge depends on scientists' abilities to record their thoughts and discoveries for future scientists to build on. Everyday literacy is the basis of scientific literacy. In addition, writing about science helps students learn science. To transfer science concepts from what they read into what they write, students must build their own representations of the concepts presented in the text.

Writing Isn't Easy

Writing places a heavy load on students' working memory, the part of memory in which they store information for the task at hand. Students must consider their goals for the assignment, find a strategy for organizing the material and structuring the writing process, and generate information to include in the writing, all while translating this information into written text on the page. As teachers, we can help students learn to do some parts of writing automatically, so they do not have to devote as much working memory to those steps.

Writing involves moving back and forth between planning, writing, and revising. Good writers spend a lot of time in the planning stages (Pressley and Woloshyn 1995). Although there are many strategies for helping students plan their writing, I focus here on the Guided Reading and Summarizing Procedure (GRASP), data charting, and discussion webs—three that work well with middle school students. Using planning strategies makes some of the process of writing automatic, which frees working memory to focus on content.

Modeling

The key to teaching any writing strategy to middle school students is for the teacher to model for them the thinking that a good writer uses when approaching a writing task. For example, if a teacher wants students to write conclusions for a laboratory activity, the teacher should model the type of thinking involved in creating conclusions and relay the thoughts aloud as he or she begins the writing process. (It may be useful to organize your thoughts on an overhead or the board as they are spoken to the class.) "Well, I know I want to say that mealworms are attracted to dark places, because that's what we figured out. So I'll jot that down first. But I want to be sure to say how I know that's true, so let me get out the data chart and look at the numbers we got." Think-aloud modeling allows students to see the thought processes that go into a completed piece of writing. Teachers can use think-aloud modeling to show students how to implement any strategy to organize their writing.

In addition, students can model planning and organizing for one another. Therefore, each of the following strategies involves students working together to plan their writing. Peers can be a powerful influence, and working together forces students to articulate their thinking. As students plan with their peers, they become accustomed to the idea that writing is a process.

GRASP

The first difficulty students have when writing about a text is that they do not know how to summarize what they have read. The GRASP strategy helps students focus on critical information and write it in their own words (Hayes 1992). To begin, ask students to read a passage of about 1,000 words from their textbook. Then ask students to close their books and list the information that they remember from the reading. Working with closed books ensures that students do not copy from the book. Next ask the class to generate four to six categories into which students can group the information they listed. If students have difficulty, suggest categories. You may want to suggest subheadings from the text. Students should then work with a partner to sort their lists into the categories (see Figure 1 for an example). Finally, students write one sentence that incorporates the most important information in each category. Model for students how to combine ideas into complex sentences and reassure them that it is OK to leave out details. The sentences from each topic can be combined into a summary of the most important information in the text, written in the students' own words.

Topics	The rock cycle	Igneous rocks	Sedimentary rocks	Metamorphic rocks
Content	Igneous rocks	From cooling magma	Sediment cements together	Pressure and heat create
	Sedimentary rocks	Obsidian and basalt	Layers = strata	Mountains cause
	Metamorphic rocks	Intrusive—under Earth's surface	Rocks broken by wind and rain	Slate and marble
	Change into each other	Extrusive—over Earth's surface	Chalk and sandstone	Come from other rocks
Summary	There are three main types of rocks: igneous, sedimentary and metamorphic.	Igneous rocks, such as obsidian and basalt, form from cooling magma.	Sedimentary rocks, such as chalk and sandstone, form when sediments dislodged by wind and rain are cemented together.	Metamorphic rocks, such as slate and marble, are created from other rocks by intense heat and pressure.

Figure 1. Sample GRASP for types of rocks

Data Charting: Integrating Sources

Ultimately, we want our students to move away from simply reporting what the text says to transforming the knowledge for their own use. At a basic level, this includes using several sources to form a more complete understanding of a topic. The data charting strategy teaches students to do just that.

To teach students this method, select three short sources that discuss a topic under study in the class. Lead the class in generating three or four questions that could be asked about the topic. For example, if you are studying insects, students might ask the following: What makes something an insect? How many insects are there? Where do insects live? Have students create a chart with one question at the top of each column and one source along each row.

Ask students to begin by reading the first source several times and looking for information to answer the questions. They should jot notes related to the questions in the corresponding boxes on the chart. Then students should read the other sources several times to answer the same questions. When students have finished taking notes on all of the sources, review the notes they took as a class. Model writing a topic sentence for a paragraph that answers the first question. Then ask the class to use the notes from all three sources to complete the paragraph. Write the paragraph on the board or overhead as the class composes it. Once again, students may need careful think-aloud modeling to be able to construct the paragraph. Finally, place students in pairs to write topic sentences and paragraphs for the other two questions. The three sections can be compiled into one report.

Critical Thinking: Discussion Web

A more complex level of transforming texts comes when students read and form opinions on what they have read. Discussion webs can help students write about controversial topics, such as environmental debates and the ethics of various genetic procedures (Alvermann and Phelps 2001). In addition to helping students improve their writing, discussion webs teach students to consider both points of view when forming an opinion.

To create a discussion web, students need one or two sources that discuss both sides of a debate. At the center of the web, students write the question that is at issue (Figure 2). Then they read the text to find arguments and evidence for both points of view and record them on the sides of the discussion web. Have students share their findings to complete a class discussion web on the board. Encourage students to discuss the strengths and weaknesses of the two positions. After the discussion, students should be allowed to draw their own conclusions from the evidence and write them in the box provided. Students can then write an essay explaining which point of view they have selected and why.

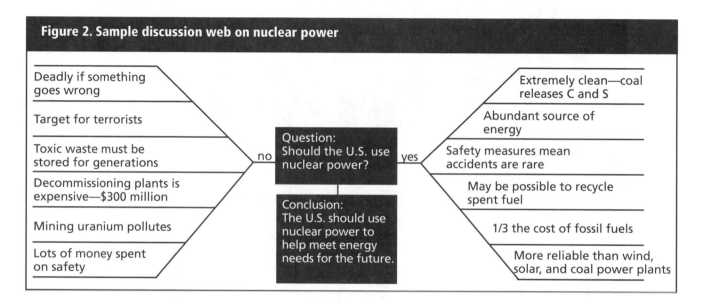

Figure 2. Sample discussion web on nuclear power

No		Yes
Deadly if something goes wrong	Question: Should the U.S. use nuclear power?	Extremely clean—coal releases C and S
Target for terrorists		Abundant source of energy
Toxic waste must be stored for generations		Safety measures mean accidents are rare
Decommissioning plants is expensive—$300 million	Conclusion: The U.S. should use nuclear power to help meet energy needs for the future.	May be possible to recycle spent fuel
Mining uranium pollutes		1/3 the cost of fossil fuels
Lots of money spent on safety		More reliable than wind, solar, and coal power plants

Conclusion

For strategies such as these to be truly useful, students need to understand their purpose and know when to use them. As each strategy is introduced and practiced in class, explain why you are teaching it. Ask students to suggest other types of writing assignments where the strategy might be used. In this way, you not only improve students' writing for specific assignments, but also increase their ability to select strategies for future writing tasks. With practice, strategy selection and the strategies themselves will become automatic. Students who can employ such strategies become confident writers and can tackle a task without resorting to plagiarism. They turn in work written in their own words that demonstrates content they have processed and learned for themselves.

References

Alvermann, D. E., and S. F. Phelps. 2001. *Content reading and literacy*. Boston: Allyn and Bacon.

Hayes, D. 1992. *A sourcebook of interactive methods of teaching with texts*. Boston: Allyn and Bacon.

Pressley, M., and V. Woloshyn. 1995. *Cognitive strategy instruction that really improves children's academic performance*. 2nd ed. Cambridge, MA: Brookline Books.

Spor, M. W., and B. K. Schneider. 1999. Content reading strategies: What teachers know, use, and want to learn. *Reading Research and Instruction* 38 (3): 221–231.

Chapter 9

Learning to Write and Writing to Learn in Science
Refutational Texts and Analytical Rubrics

by Amy Singletary and Victor Sampson

Most middle school science teachers are familiar with the idea of reading and writing across the curriculum. As science teachers, we understand that our students need time, practice, and lots of encouragement to learn how to read and write well. What we also need to remember, however, is that learning how to read and write in science is an important part of scientific literacy, and it can help students understand and retain key science content (NRC 1996; Saul 2004). Here we outline a technique that science teachers can use in middle school classrooms to help students learn to write, and write to learn, in science.

Why Are Reading and Writing So Important in Science?

Science teachers need to help students learn how to read and write in science for a number of reasons:

■ Students need to know how to learn about science on their own if we expect them to be lifelong learners. This requires students to be able to read, understand, and critique academic, nonfiction, and persuasive genres of writing.

■ Reading and writing are important aspects of doing science. Scientists must be able to read and understand the writing of others, evaluate its worth, and share the results of their own research through writing.

■ All students, regardless of their interests in scientific careers, need to be able to read and write about scientific issues so they can make educated decisions and participate in a democratic society.

■ Students who are skilled at reading and writing in science are often able to learn the concepts, theories, models, and laws of science more deeply and retain more information than students who are not. (Shanahan 2004)

It is important to remember, however, that students will not learn how to read or write in science by reading novels or by writing short stories in language arts. Students need to be introduced to the various genres of science writing and be taught how to combine words and symbols to create meaning in a manner that is consistent with the stylistic rules of science. They also need to practice this type of writing and receive good feedback about the quality of their writing so they have an opportunity to improve. It is therefore important for science teachers to engage students in real science writing as part of their science education. One effective way of doing this is to give students opportunities to write *refutational texts* as part of their experiences in science.

Refutational Texts

A refutational text introduces a common concept, idea, or theory; refutes it; offers an alternative concept, idea, or theory; and then attempts to show that this alternative way of thinking is more valid or acceptable. An example of a refutation can be seen in this excerpt below (the key sentence that identifies this passage as a refutational text is italicized).

> Many people believe that a change in the Earth's distance from the Sun causes the seasons to change. *However, this cannot be true, because the seasons are different in the Northern and Southern Hemispheres.* The actual cause of the seasons is the way the Earth is tilted on its rotational axis. When the Earth's axis points toward the Sun, it is summer for that hemisphere. When the Earth's axis points away, it is winter for that hemisphere. This is because the hemisphere that points toward the Sun receives more direct sunlight and has longer days.

A refutational text, such as the example provided here, is one of three kinds of persuasive arguments that are often found in scientific writing (Hynd 2003). A one-sided persuasive argument only presents the concept, idea, or theory the author prefers a reader to adopt. Two-sided arguments can be nonrefutational or refutational. A two-sided, nonrefutational argument presents both sides of an issue, but makes one side seem stronger by presenting more evidence, explaining it more logically, or making the argument more compelling in some other way without explicitly stating that the author prefers it. A refutational argument, in contrast, is more explicit than a nonrefutational argument about which is the preferred side.

Most textbooks and science trade books are written in an expository or narrative style and usually do not include persuasive arguments. When they do, they often use one-sided arguments rather than refutational, two-sided arguments. Thus, students are likely to be unfamiliar with this type of writing and need explicit instruction, a great deal of practice, and good feedback to learn how to write in this manner. Science teachers, however, can help students learn to write high-quality refutational texts (and learn more content as part of the process) by using writing prompts coupled with analytical rubrics that provide students with feedback about their performances and teachers with insight about what students can and cannot do.

Writing Prompts

A well-designed writing task in science essentially has three critical attributes:

- It provides an authentic purpose for writing.

- It motivates students to want to write.

- It helps students plan and structure their writing. (Turner and Broemmel 2006)

These three attributes, when made explicit to students, make the goal of a writing assignment understandable, the writing meaningful, and a high-quality product achievable. One way to ensure that a writing task has each of these attributes is to use a structured writing prompt (Indrisano and Paratore 2005). A structured writing prompt begins with all the information a student needs to write (the topic, the audience, the purpose, the form of the text, and reminders). It then outlines the steps of the writing process (i.e., creating an outline, producing a rough draft, editing, and preparing a final draft) and provides space for the student to complete each step. An example of a structured writing prompt that encourages students to write a refutational text about the concept of condensation is provided in Figure 1. In this prompt, students are asked to produce a one-page essay (the form of the text) that refutes the claim that water from inside a container leaks through to the outside (the topic and the purpose of the text) for a group of people who believe that this claim is true (the audience of the text). The prompt also reminds the writer to state the misconception he or she is trying to refute, to use evidence to support the claim, and to organize the writing in an appropriate manner. These reminders are designed to focus the writer's attention on important components of a quality refutational text that novices often forget or do not pay enough attention to in their writing.

Teachers should keep four issues in mind when designing these types of writing

---

Figure 1. Refutational writing prompt

What causes water to appear on the outside of a container?

People tend to believe that water from the inside of a container seeps through to the outside after a period of time. Write a one- to two-page paper to refute the claim that water from the inside of a container leaks through to the outside to convince someone that this is a misconception.

As you write the paper, remember to do the following:

- State the misconception you are trying to refute
- Include evidence from a lab experiment, research that you have done, topics from the class discussions, and examples to convince your audience to abandon this misconception
- Organize your paper properly and include an introduction with a topic sentence, supporting paragraphs, and a conclusion
- Use vocabulary that we have learned
- Correct grammar, punctuation, and spelling errors before writing your final draft

You will have two class periods to complete this assignment. The first period will be dedicated to planning and creating a rough draft and the second period will be spent revising and creating a final draft of the paper. The paper will be due at the end of the class period on day two.

Outline
Create an outline for your paper explaining the misconception, the evidence against it, and justification for the evidence. Use this to help you write your rough draft.

Rough draft
Write a rough draft of your refutational text. After you complete the draft, use a different color pen to correct your work. Be sure to look for spelling and grammatical errors. You may use a dictionary or a grammar book if you need.

Final draft
Write the final draft of your refutational text.

prompts. First, students need to refute a common misconception related to a big idea in the curriculum. This helps students learn the content required by the district, state, or national science standards, and it gives them an authentic purpose for writing. It also motivates students to want to write. Teachers can find lists of common misconceptions by entering a topic (e.g., condensation) and the terms "misconception" or "alternative conception" into an internet search engine. Teachers can also uncover any specific misconceptions held by their students by simply asking them to explain an everyday occurrence. They could also use students' science journals or bell-work questions as ways for students to explain these occurrences and then as a source for student misconceptions. Second, teachers need to be sure that the "reminders" included in the writing prompt help students plan and structure their writing. These reminders should help focus students' attention on the goal of the writing assignment, the 6 + 1 traits of writing (Culham 2003), or specific writing requirements outlined in district or state language arts standards. Third, teachers need to be sure that students complete each step of the writing process (outline, rough draft, editing, and final draft). This encourages students to keep their thoughts organized and to look over their work before they are ready to submit the final product. Finally, the writing prompt needs to be coupled with an analytic rubric that can be used to inform and improve student performance. This way, both the students and teacher know what is expected and what needs to be done to improve.

Analytical Rubrics

Analytical rubrics are designed to provide information that can be used to determine students' current level of achievement, diagnose their strengths and weaknesses, and allow them to learn more about what they know or can do. Also, and perhaps most important, analytical rubrics show what students need to do to improve (Hodson 1992). Analytical rubrics are matrices that identify what is expected of students by defining important criteria that is used to assess quality and various performance levels. To increase the clarity of this type of rubric, each criterion is "subdivided into more concise statements and then followed by the related performance descriptions" (Luft 1997). An example of an analytical rubric that we developed to assess students' understanding and their abilities to produce quality refutational texts is provided in Figure 2. In this example, the analytic rubric consists of four sections (outline, content, etc.) that are divided into one or more criteria (the misconception is identified, etc.), which are followed by descriptions that illustrate three distinct levels of performance.

The multilevel nature of an analytical rubric can help teachers uncover specific strengths and weaknesses. The rubric can also be used to help students understand the criteria against which they are evaluated. Analytical rubrics, perhaps more important, can also provide detailed feedback to students about their performance. This kind of detailed information about what a student is doing right and wrong is a key component of an assessment that is educative in nature (Wiggins 1998). It also enables teachers to examine the strengths and weaknesses of their curriculum and methods of instruction. Middle school teachers can use all this information to help students enhance their understanding of the important concepts and what counts as quality when writing in science.

Figure 2. Example of a refutational-text grading rubric

Section 1: Outline

Criterion	3 points	2 points	1 point
Topics/Format	Most points are made in a clear outlined fashion. The outline is neat and orderly.	Some points are presented or the format of the outline is missing. Most of the outline is presented in an organized manner.	Outline is incomplete and flawed. The outline is messy and disorganized.

Total: ____/3 points
Comments:

Section 2: Rough draft

Criterion	3 points	2 points	1 point
Editing	The draft is edited in a different color pen. All grammatical errors are highlighted and corrected.	Some errors were missed or the draft is not edited in a different color.	Many errors were missed and the draft is not edited with a different color. Directions were not followed and a revision was disregarded.

Total: ____/3 points
Comments:

Section 3: Final draft

Criterion	3 points	2 points	1 point
Organization/ Grammar	The paper is free of grammatical errors. The flow of the paper has a beginning, middle, and end.	There are few grammatical errors. The paper is somewhat lacking in organization.	The draft is incomplete and sloppy. The draft is disorganized.

Total: ____/3 points
Comments:

Section 4: Content accuracy

Criterion	3 points	2 points	1 point
The misconception is identified	The writer identifies a misconception and explicitly states why it is inaccurate.	The writer identifies the misconception, but fails to explain that the misconception is inaccurate.	The misconception is buried, confused, and/or unclear. The misconception is disregarded.
Reasons against the misconception	The writer provides several reasons why the misconception cannot be true. The reasons are explained clearly.	The writer provides a few reasons that show why the misconception is inaccurate but leaves some reasons out. The explanations may be unclear.	The writer does not acknowledge or discuss any reasons for why the misconception is inaccurate. The writer may also have incorrect explanations.
Evidence and reasoning in support of the scientific conception	The writer gives a clear and accurate explanation of the scientific conception. The writer illustrates why it is more useful than the misconception.	The writer gives a vague or somewhat inaccurate explanation of the scientific conception. There are some reasons provided to support the scientific conception.	The writer makes no mention of the scientific conception. The writer provides no evidence or reasoning.

Total: ____/9 points
Comments:

Final Total: ____/18 points

An Example Lesson

To illustrate how this writing prompt, coupled with the analytical rubric, can be integrated into a science lesson, consider the following example lesson. This lesson begins with the classroom teacher pouring ice water into a drinking glass. Students are then directed to watch the glass and record their observations. After several minutes, condensation begins to form on the outside of the glass. The teacher then encourages students to explain the origin of this water. The teacher writes each explanation (right or wrong) on the board and then leads the class in a discussion that focuses on ways to test the various explanations (such as using hot water instead of cold or colored water inside the glass). These tests are then carried out by the teacher or by small groups of students and the results are used to weed out the inaccurate explanations until the class agrees on the scientific explanation (i.e., water vapor in the air turns back into a liquid when it touches the cold glass).

The next day, students are given the writing prompt (see Figure 1, p. 51) and the analytical rubric (see Figure 2, p. 53) and are told to use their knowledge and the data they gathered to refute the idea that the water leaks from the glass. Students then submit their texts to the teacher or to one or more of their peers for an initial evaluation. This process is guided by the analytical rubric, which, as noted earlier, outlines the criteria that are to be used to evaluate the quality of text and provides space to give feedback to the student. It is important for the evaluators to provide not only information about how the text should be scored (by circling values for each criterion) but also explicit narrative feedback to the student about what needs to be done to improve the quality of the text. This feedback needs to focus on both the quality of the writing (section 1–3 in the example rubric) and the accuracy of the content (section 4 in the example rubric) so the student knows what needs to be revised (e.g., understanding of the content, the organization or conventions of the writing, or a combination of these). The texts and the rubrics are then returned to students with directions to use the feedback to improve their final products. Students then rewrite their texts as necessary and resubmit the assignment for a final grade. This type of review process provides students with educative feedback, encourages students to develop and use appropriate standards for what counts as quality, and helps students be more reflective as they work. This type of feedback also provides a mechanism that can help all students, especially special-needs and ESOL students, improve their abilities to write in science and ensures that all students understand the content. If you have special-needs or ESOL students in your class, you could modify the lesson to allow them more time on the assignment. Since the rubric in Figure 2 is divided into sections, it makes it easy for the teacher to see if it is the content knowledge (section 4) that students don't understand or if they are just having difficulty with the language or the writing of the assignment (sections 1, 2, and 3). This review process requires about five to ten minutes for an evaluator to complete.

Why Is This Important?

This writing process helps students make sense of their experiences by requiring them to explain a phenomenon and refute a common misconception in writing. This promotes understanding and retention of the content (writing to learn) and makes their thinking visible to the teacher. This process also gives them a meaningful opportunity to improve their abilities to communicate through writing (learning to write). The writing prompt provides an authentic purpose for writing, motivates students, and helps them plan and structure their writing.

The analytical rubric then provides students with the guidance and feedback that they need to improve their abilities to write. As a result, this lesson provides a way to support efforts to promote writing across the curriculum (which is clearly needed) in a way that fosters student understanding of important content and writing in science.

References

Culham, R. 2003. *6 + 1 traits of writing: The complete guide.* New York: Teaching Resources/ Scholastic.

Hodson, D. 1992. Assessment of practical work. *Science and Education.* 1 (2): 115–144.

Hynd, C. 2003. Conceptual change in response to persuasive messages. In *Intentional conceptual change*, ed. G. Sinatra and P. R. Pintrich, 291–314. Mahwah, NJ: Lawrence Erlbaum Associates.

Indrisano, R. and J. Paratore, eds. 2005. *Learning to write and writing to learn: Theory and research in practice.* Newark, DE: International Reading Association.

Luft, J. 1997. Design your own rubric. *Science Scope.* 20 (5): 25–27.

National Research Council (NRC). 1996. *National science education standards.* Washington, DC: National Academies Press.

Saul, E. W., ed. 2004. *Crossing borders in literacy and science instruction: Perspectives on theory and practice.* Arlington, VA: NSTA Press.

Shanahan, C. 2004. Better textbooks, better readers and writers. In *Crossing Borders in Literacy and Science Instruction: Perspectives on Theory and Practice,* ed. W. Saul, 370–382. Arlington, VA: NSTA Press.

Turner, T., and A. Broemmel. 2006. 14 writing strategies. *Science Scope* 30 (4): 27–31.

Wiggins, G. 1998. *Educative assessment: Designing assessment to inform and improve student performance.* San Francisco: Jossey-Bass.

Chapter 10

Peanut Butter and Jelly Science

By Donna Farland

I f only middle school students could communicate in writing as well as they do verbally! When I find myself completely frustrated with the quality of my students' writing or lack thereof, I head for the peanut butter and jelly. I begin the lesson by asking students to write out numbered steps for making a peanut butter and jelly sandwich. Most are eager to attempt this and ask if they'll be graded on it. (They won't be!) After giving students 10 to 15 minutes to work, I collect the student directions.

Students laugh and wiggle in their seats waiting with anticipation to see what's next and why on Earth I'd assign them such a silly task. I move about the room with all seriousness as I take out a loaf of bread, one jar of peanut butter, and one jar of jelly. Safety note: Use a substitute, such as honey, if any student has a peanut allergy.) They'll ask me, "What are you doing?" I simply say, "We are going to make a peanut butter and jelly sandwich." Now, they are sure I've lost my mind and move in closer to see what happens.

Next I randomly choose one of the student directions from the pile to begin construction of the sandwich. A typical set of directions might look like this.

1. Get peanut butter.

2. Get jelly.

3. Put them on bread.

4. Pat down.

5. Eat.

As I act out their written directions, there is typically a lot of laughter followed by an immediate realization by students of the level of clarity and description needed to communicate understanding. As I do exactly what the students have written, it becomes obvious that small, yet critical details, such as "Unscrew the lid of the jar," are often overlooked. Once the laughter subsides, we discuss the importance of writing in science, not only in the classroom but in real-world laboratories and other scientific facilities as well. This visual lesson sticks with students like peanut butter to the roof of a mouth.

Students often forget they have to write in science class because they tend to think of writing as a separate part of their education. Although most students are capable of expressing their needs verbally, the majority of adolescents are less likely to express themselves clearly and articulately in their writing assignments. In some cases, it's not as if students don't know or understand the content, but rather they assume the reader knows what they are trying to

communicate. This activity can be extended by having students write out directions for tying shoes, folding a paper airplane, opening a carton of milk, or other similar tasks.

In the end I pay a small price for this dramatic lesson—the cost of the materials and the class time. In return, the procedure sections of student lab reports turned in after this assignment are typically much longer and more detailed than before it. And when students do cut corners and make assumptions about a reader's prior knowledge, I can comment on their papers clearly and effectively with three simple letters—P, B, and J!

Chapter 11

Write It, Do It

By Erin Peters

Effective writing is a keystone in the process of developing scientific knowledge. Scientists must be able to successfully communicate their findings so colleagues can confirm the authenticity of their claims through the replication of experiments. The activity "Write It, Do It" uses peer review to illustrate the need for clarity in scientific writing. In this activity, students write directions to build an original object from LEGO blocks, use another student's writing to build a second object from LEGO blocks, and review that student's written work for clarity and accuracy.

Preparation

Teachers need enough clear sandwich bags for all students in the class and matching sets of LEGO blocks for each pair of students. I purchased a 500-piece LEGO starter set (Imagine and Build Bucket) for $10 at a local toy store that provided enough blocks for my class of 28 students. The bags should contain several colors of LEGO blocks. If the bags have only red blocks, there is not much challenge to writing the directions. You can use any combinations of blocks as long as they are varied in size, shape, and color (maximum two alike or the assignment will be too simple) and there are identical blocks in each pair of bags. To stock the bags, I lay out the blocks so they are grouped together by matching color and size and chose one from each group (up to nine blocks). Once I have two bags that are identical, I put one bag with the blocks inside the other bag with blocks. This saves time so that I don't have to match the bags in between each class. I also ask the students to check that the blocks are the same before the activity begins. It takes me about 15 minutes to create matching sets of blocks for each student pair and seal them in bags. I use 252 blocks to make my 28 sets (14 pairs of bags). Once the bags are stocked, the only other material needed is blank paper for instructions.

Building

To begin the activity, students choose a partner and decide who is Investigator A and who is Investigator B. By the end of the activity, each investigator will have performed all of the objectives, so the only difference between the tasks is who writes first. Each student pair receives one set of bags. Investigator B takes one of the bags and leaves the room to wait in the hallway for his or her partner to finish the task. Using file folders or science fair boards as barriers is a good way to keep the partners from seeing each other's work during the creation without sending kids into the hallway. I usually give a paper-and-pencil activity to the investigators who are waiting. Because I do this activity in the beginning of the year, I ask students to create a concept map (webbing) of their background knowledge of the topics in physical science, but any type of similar task will work.

Investigator A builds any three-dimensional object from the nine LEGO blocks in the bag. I ask students to build a three-dimensional object because stacking the blocks leads to simple directions, and the object should be slightly challenging to replicate. As Investigator A builds the object, he or she writes directions on how to do it. The directions may include diagrams, but the core of the directions should be text. (See Figure 1 for an example.) When Investigator A is finished building and writing, Investigator B can get involved. Investigator A should carefully hide his or her object from Investigator B. It is important for Investigator A to keep the object intact for two reasons: to keep an original for comparison and so Investigator A does not reassemble an object that does not correspond to the directions. At this point, Investigator A hides the original object and begins working on the paper-and-pencil activity where he or she cannot see Investigator B working. Investigator B, meanwhile, should be reading Investigator A's directions. Investigator B then attempts to use the directions to build an object matching the original one. Investigator A and Investigator B are not allowed to speak (or signal) to each other during this process.

Figure 1. Sample student directions (without corrections)

1. Big = Eight bumpy things on top; Small = Four bumpy things on top; One big black block = only one on bottom
2. Connect the big white by four of the bumps like stairs
3. Connect big blue on top using two bumps
4. Connect big red on top of white so that blue and red make an L and only two white bumps are showing
5. Put small blue on top of red lined up with big blue only four red bumps show
6. Put small yellow on big blue
7. Put big yellow across small blue and small yellow—two bumps from small yellow and two bumps from big yellow show

When Investigator B is finished rebuilding the object, she or he goes to retrieve Investigator A. The investigators should show each other their objects and look to see if there are any differences. Some of the more interesting differences occur because of missing instructions regarding left and right orientations and the mirror images of each other. Most students will naturally launch into discussions about the clear parts of the directions and the unclear parts, but sometimes I need to prompt them to discuss the details of the construction. I ask them to make notes about what was unclear in the directions in a different color pen.

When the discussions are over, the team should repeat the process, this time with Investigator B building an object first and Investigator A following the instructions. It is important for students to switch places because they should experience both receiving and writing directions. Effective communication requires skills in both giving and receiving directions. Scientists need to be adept at both writing findings and reviewing other scientists' findings. When both students have edited their directions with help from their partners, they take them home for homework and write a short reflection about their experience and their partners' edits.

Students generally take 10–15 minutes to write the directions, five minutes to build from someone else's directions, and five minutes for discussion—a total of about 40–50 minutes for the whole activity.

Class Discussion

Once students have experienced writing and using the directions, I ask some questions so they can reflect on their experiences and connect those experiences to the nature of science. First I ask students about their perceptions of the purpose of the activity. When students reply with vague statements about communicating in science, I ask them to make their responses more specific. I make this activity relevant by reminding students that when they take a test for me, it often has short-answer questions. If I am at home grading their tests, I cannot ask them what they meant by a written answer, so I have to use what they write to determine if they know the answer. I hold up two objects that don't match and explain that they could be thinking one thing (I hold up one object), but their writing says another thing (I hold up the nonmatching object). Students start to realize that even if they know the answer, they must also be able to clearly explain what they know.

I also ask students if they saw patterns in the way they communicated with their partners. For example, one student's directions may have forgotten to mention size, or another student could have forgotten to mention how to orient the blocks to the left and the right. This discussion prompts students to think about the level of detail that is required in scientific writing. Characteristics, such as "big," need to be more specific in scientific writing because they are a matter of personal perception. Descriptions in science are empirical and have standards of comparison. I explain to my students that they must practice to be good communicators and through practice they can learn to think like scientists.

Before students exit my class on "Write It, Do It" day, I ask them to write one statement about how this activity contributed to their ability to communicate. Overall, students recognize that written descriptions must be as specific as possible. Some students comment on the need to recognize that their partners may not think in the same way that they do, and they must take their partners' perspectives into account. Many students comment that if the process is not described well, other people cannot do the process in the same way. For assessment, students turn in their edited directions with their reflections on (1) the writing of directions, (2) the comments from their partners, and (3) the directions provided by their partners. Completing the "Write It, Do It" activity helps my students recognize several goals in scientific writing: using detail, using empirical descriptions, and writing so the process can be replicated.

Chapter 12

Comments on Students' Writing

By Inez Fugate Liftig

Today teachers in all content areas—not just the language arts—are responsible for teaching writing. In the science classroom, students hone their skills writing lab reports, answering essay questions, and creating position statements on current science events. As science teachers, we must provide feedback on both the science content and the quality of writing demonstrated in their assignments. Unfortunately, our schedules do not always allow us to hold individual writing conferences or ask for extensive rewrites or revisions of papers. Consequently, the comments we include on students' papers are often the only personal feedback we can provide. Therefore, it is vital that our comments are focused and coherent, providing valuable suggestions to help improve students' writing.

Researching Good Writing

When I first committed to improving the quality of my students' writing, I read all the books and articles I could find on the subject. I then met with reading and language arts teachers to develop strategies to help students answer open-ended questions more effectively. I developed a self-evaluation method for lab reports and an extensive set of activities to teach students to recognize and appropriately respond to the key words in higher-order essay questions.

Of course, these instructional strategies require a tremendous amount of time, particularly for grading and writing lengthy, detailed feedback on student essays and papers. Before recommending this approach to others, I had to reflect on some tough questions: Is it really worth all of the time and effort I put into the feedback? Are my comments appreciated? How do the students respond to my comments and what kinds of comments do they find helpful? To answer these questions, I surveyed nearly 200 of my eighth-grade science students. (See Figure 1, pp. 64–65 for summary.)

Figure 1. Student survey and responses

Directions: Think about the comments that you have received on papers that have been returned to you in *all* your classes. Use your observations, thoughts, and ideas about them to help answer the questions below.

1. How often do you read the comments and remarks written on your returned papers?
   55% always
   32% most of the time
   9% some of the time
   3% hardly at all
   1% never

2. Do you prefer comments to be written in red or blue/black ink? Explain if you feel differently about the colors?
   Color preference
   53% red
   8% blue/black
   38% either color
   1% neither/none

   I prefer red for corrections because it:
   - is different from the color I use
   - stands out better
   - is easier to read
   - seems more important
   - is attention grabbing
   - is easy to find the comments
   - makes me more eager to read them
   - catches my eye

   I prefer blue or black ink instead of red for corrections because:
   - red makes it seem like everything is wrong
   - red is only to point out bad things
   - red makes me think all the comments are going to be negative and I don't want to read them
   - teachers circle things when they use blue but they do not when they use red

3. On a returned paper which comments are you most likely to read, those written at various places throughout a paper or those written as a summary at the end?
   53% next to
   28% as a summary
   19% does not matter

4. Do you feel the comments that teachers write on your returned papers help you in any way? Please explain your answer in as much detail as you can.
   73% helpful
   15% not helpful
   12% sometimes helpful
   1% uncertain

Comments written on my returned papers are helpful because:
- I know where I need to do better for the next paper
- they tell me what I should keep doing or stop doing in my work
- I can see where I have to improve on a similar paper
- positive comments encourage me and tell me what I am doing well
- they help me learn a certain way to answer questions
- when I do the next paper, I can look back and reread the comments and try to go from there to do better
- I get the comments stuck in my mind and next time I can do better
- if they say I did something well, I'll try to repeat it
- they encourage us to improve, keep up the good work, and give us hints about how to do so
- if I had not gotten the comments I would not know how to improve
- one bad paper with lots of comments is more helpful than six good ones without comments
- they help me know what the teacher wants and expects

5. What are some examples of comments that you find most helpful to you on a returned paper?

Characteristics of comments that are helpful:
- say where and why points were taken off
- tell exactly what I did wrong and where
- explain in detail what to do the next time
- tell me where to elaborate
- say how to put things in a special order
- are suggestions instead of criticisms
- say something positive but then say "but you could improve by doing this..."
- get to the point
- Written legibly—not scribbled
- Ask a question next to where I did something wrong, which makes me think of an answer myself
- Circle the mistake or put brackets around it so my eyes go directly to where there is a problem

- Clearly identify the section the comments are referring to so I can check what I already said
- Tell how to fix the mistake instead of just stating there is a mistake
- Comment on the content/structure of the piece, not just spelling, grammar, and neatness

Some examples of helpful comments are:

- Needs to be clearer, give more details here
- Elaborate on this, give me more information about…
- Do you have proof of this statement? Where is the support?
- Did you tell the reader how or why…
- This information seems out of order here. Where should it go?
- So, what's next? Haven't you stopped too soon? What else needs to be here?
- Reread this. Does it make sense?
- Next time, do this…
- Great examples of…
- Sentence fragment
- Try this…
- Creative
- Remember to do…

6. What are some examples of comments on returned papers that are not very helpful to you?

Characteristics of comments that are not very helpful:

- Short, one-word comments that do not give any real feedback
- Point out too many things that are negative Sometimes they just pile up and you feel like nothing can be done anyway
- Lists of what you did wrong, such as spelling mistakes or leaving out words. Do not have stuff that will help you on your next paper
- Unclear what the comment is referring to—mistake or problem is not circled
- Handwriting that is illegible
- Doesn't make sense—then you don't know what it is saying or what you did wrong
- Remove a certain number of points but do not tell you why or where
- Do not explain how to avoid/correct the mistake next time

- Mistake circled but no comments provided

Examples of comments that are not very helpful:
good, spelling, incomplete, needs work, Huh?, excellent, too basic, unacceptable, great, I don't like this, not what I was looking for, good job, redo, awkward, wonderful, wordy, rewrite, sloppy, (check mark only), see me, neatness, OK, X, do better next time, bad, wrong, what?, what else?, I don't understand, vocabulary

7. What other comments or suggestions do you have for teachers about grading students' papers? Be as specific as you can.

Student suggestions for teachers about grading student papers:

- Do not grade by how much you like the student
- Separate the students' behavior from their work
- Think about each student's ability when you grade
- Read a paper (or answer) twice and write specific comments. For example, write "explain with more details" instead of "explain"
- Give students examples of good work
- Reread your comments to make sure they are clear
- Talk to the students after giving back papers and tell them exactly what is going on and how the class did on the papers
- Give students a few minutes to look over what is written on the papers and to ask questions about the comments
- Think of the purpose of the assignments and be fair in the number of points you take off for little errors, such as spelling and punctuation. When teachers read every word they get too picky and take off points for little things
- Write comments on *post-it* notes and put on the students' papers instead of marking up what they have worked on
- Make suggestions about how to fix mistakes, but do not rewrite the student's work
- Make at least one comment on every paper so that students know you looked at it
- If a paper is really bad, meet with the student

Survey Says

Overall, I discovered that students do indeed read the comments that are written on their papers, and nearly 75% of those who read them feel they are helpful, especially when teachers pinpoint where improvements are needed and specifically explain how to make them. Comments also seem to make teacher standards and expectations clearer for many students.

Some educators have cautioned against writing comments in red ink because they may be interpreted as punitive, but in my survey, the majority of students actually prefer comments written in red because they stand out. Some students do, however, associate red ink with negative feedback such as "wrong" or "bad." The remaining students reported having no color preference.

Students do have a definite preference for lengthy, specific (formative) comments and are articulate in stating why. Students prefer teachers to be focused, detailed, and prescriptive in their feedback. In fact, more than half of them preferred comments written in the body of the paper adjacent to the area of attention. Students would like the teacher discuss the overall quality of the returned papers, then give students time to look over their individual feedback and ask questions.

It is important to remember that blanketing papers with negative comments often makes students feel overwhelmed and defeated. Moreover, students see little value in comments that only refer to mechanics and neatness, preferring instead substantive responses that focus on content, technique, or structure. Students also express concern about fairness and warn teachers against taking off too many points for "little things." They see a need for teachers to objectively consider student ability levels by putting aside personal feelings when grading papers. Clearly, students are encouraged by positive comments and discouraged by negative ones.

Making the Time

Writing helpful comments is a time-consuming undertaking. Below are some strategies to help streamline the process:

- Don't try to provide extensive comments on every written assignment. Be selective. Set high standards, but be realistic. Decide what the important science writing skills are in an assignment and provide feedback for these. Focus on providing extensive feedback to only a few students each week.

- Don't count on comments alone to teach the necessary science writing skills. Combine your feedback with whole-class writing instruction and practice. For example, break your lab report format into small manageable sections. Perhaps cluster the writing of titles, problems, and hypotheses into one set of activities, and after students have had some practice, collect samples and focus the bulk of your feedback on the skills that were just taught.

- As you grade papers, keep track of the most common writing problems. Review these in class when you hand the papers back to the students, and give examples of how they can be corrected. If the problems are widespread, devise a review assignment.

- Collaborate with the language arts teachers if you feel that mechanics and format are a priority. Keep a list of the most common problems. For example, track which words are misspelled most frequently or what punctuation seems to be most misused. Then ask the language arts teacher to focus on these problem areas.

- Provide students with explicit criteria for writing assignments in the form of rubrics and focus lists. Whenever possible, share examples of excellent work with students. Exact guidelines and top-quality samples make it more likely that students will know what is expected before they begin writing.

Detailed written comments are a vital part of the teaching of writing in the science classroom and students clearly want them. The secret to success is finding the right balance between instruction and feedback. Not only will your hard work be appreciated, but it will also result in substantial improvement in student writing.

Acknowledgment

The author would like to thank Robert A. Liftig, an English teacher at Eastchester High School in Eastchester, New York, for his help in preparing this manuscript.

References

Liftig, I. F., R. Liftig, and K. Eaker. 1992. Making assessment work: What teachers should know before they try it. *Science Scope* 15 (6): 4–8

Liftig, I. F., J. E. Troy, and R. Liftig. 1990. Words into science. *Science Scope* 13 (5): 14–15

Chapter 13

From Speaking to Writing in the Structured English Immersion Science Classroom

By Conrado Laborin Gómez and Margarita Jimenez-Silva

For many years, teaching English language learners (ELL students) was the exclusive responsibility of teachers endorsed for bilingual and English as a second language (ESL) instruction. However, through voter initiatives and legislative decree, the bilingual education and ESL options to educate ELL students have almost become defunct (Crawford 2004). In most cases, structured English immersion (SEI) has replaced bilingual and ESL programs as the preferred method of educating ELL students (Crawford 2004).

Structured English Immersion

SEI is an approach for teaching content to English learners in ways that make the concepts comprehensible while promoting English language development. For example, teachers provide explicit instruction of vocabulary terms that may be new to English learners. This definition implies that subject matter teachers are expected to teach both language and content. Not surprisingly, many content-area teachers feel ill prepared to teach ELL students using SEI methodology. After all, never before have they been expected to incorporate a language requirement into their content teaching (Echevarría, Vogt, and Short 2008).

Several states require that state-certified school personnel receive SEI training. The intent of this policy is to make all teachers responsible for the education of ELL students. Consequently, all teachers in states with high numbers of English learners, including California, Arizona, and Florida, are now required to incorporate language teaching into their instruction, regardless of the content area. Although the goal of the policy is laudable, implementing it has been a challenge for many teachers who in the past seldom had ELL students in their classrooms and who assumed that ELL students were taught English in another class (de Jong and Harper 2005). Science teachers, because of the hands-on, activity-based approach, provide a supportive environment for ELL students. Nonetheless, even science teachers may be apprehensive about working with ELL students because of the additional responsibility to teach language skills.

Developing Content and Language in Science

Science teachers need specific strategies to develop language skills along with content. Fortunately, research has demonstrated that science-teaching methodology can accomplish the teaching of both science content and English language skills. A technique suitable for and used by science teachers is the *mode continuum* (Gibbons 2002), a process that leads students from speaking about science to writing about science. The mode continuum also lends itself very well to concurrently incorporating listening and reading skills. Furthermore, the mode continuum allows teachers to plan science lessons that are situation embedded, providing students with opportunities to use their social English language skills to discuss academic topics. This leads students to the more academic, less situation-embedded written forms of English.

The mode continuum consists of four specific phases:

- experimenting,
- learning key vocabulary,
- teacher-guided reporting, and
- journal writing (Gibbons 2002).

Phase 1

In phase 1, students are assigned to groups and asked to perform experiments in a specific area or topic (gravity is used here as an example topic). It is recommended that the teacher design various experiments that are related to the same concept. There are books that focus on a particular topic and can provide the basis for classroom experiments. For example, VanCleave (1993), in her book *Gravity: Mind-Boggling Experiments You Can Turn Into Science-Fair Projects,* lists 20 different experiments related to gravity, each one covering a different problem. The teacher provides written instructions along with pictures to help students do their assigned experiment. Visual aids assist students in organizing and making sense of information that is presented (Echevarría, Vogt, and Short 2008). The objective is for students to use their current vocabulary and prior knowledge of the topic while engaging in the experiment. Students are told that at the end of the experiment, they will have an opportunity to describe and explain to their peers what they did in their groups.

Phase 2

In phase 2, the teacher introduces key vocabulary verbally and in writing. After students have spent some time developing an understanding of gravity using familiar words and exploratory talk, the teacher spends time with each group and introduces the scientific concepts and vocabulary the teacher has identified in the lesson's objectives. In the meantime, the other groups continue with their experiments and deciding how they will explain their work to the other students in the class. For instance, one of VanCleave's (1993) gravity activities deals with the term *free fall*. After students have conducted two related experiments, the teacher introduces the key vocabulary term *free fall* in small groups and models for students how to use the term appropriately.

Phase 3

Once students are familiar with the vocabulary and have had some practice using terms, they are ready to use them in phase 3: teacher-guided reporting. The overall aim of this phase is "to extend children's linguistic resources and focus on aspects of the specific discourse of science" (Gibbons 2002, p. 45). As ELL students explain to the whole class what they learned, the teacher interacts with students, recasting their attempts at expressing themselves. For example, a student may state, "The thing made the ball do it," after which the teacher can recast the student's response by prompting, "What do we call the force that made the ball fall down?" or stating, "Oh, *gravity* made the ball *fall down*." Thus, the teacher is facilitating language learning by providing support for students to express their ideas. In teacher-guided reporting, the teacher establishes a bridge between describing phenomena in everyday language and the more formal, academic language associated with science content (Gibbons 2002). This prepares students for putting their thoughts on paper during the last phase of the mode continuum, journal writing.

Phase 4

In journal writing, the teacher prompts students with a question such as "What have you learned?" The intent of this phase is for students to use the formal vocabulary terms that the teacher introduced in phase 2 and that the teacher and students used during teacher-guided reporting. VanCleave (1993) recommends that students purchase a bound notebook to write about their science activities as part of a student portfolio. O'Malley and Valdez Pierce (1996) refer to this as a *collections portfolio,* which contains all daily assignments as well as showing evidence of process and product. Vitale and Romance (2000) further discuss the value of using portfolios in science instruction, emphasizing their value as effective tools for instructional assessment in classroom settings. Because the portfolio contains everything produced by the student, it allows the teacher to assess progress in writing as well as content knowledge.

The Mode Continuum in Action

To demonstrate the effectiveness of the mode continuum in meeting the language and science content needs of ELL students, a series of six different experiments focusing on gravity was conducted by students in a dual-language class. The class consisted of 20 students, 10 designated as ELL students and 10 as English proficient. The ELL students in this class were at various levels of English language proficiency. The groups of students were integrated, half ELL and half English proficient. English-proficient students were tasked with reading the instructions. Following the teacher-guided reporting phase, students wrote in their science journals. For this particular lesson, the teacher selected two separate text types for students' writing: procedure and recount. Consequently, the teacher prompted students with the following two questions: "What did you do?" and "What did you learn?"

Joel is an ELL student at the basic stage of English, having been in American schools for a little more than a year. His experiment examined the content objective of how gravity affects the shape of soap bubbles. The key vocabulary for this lesson included the terms *gravity, bubbles, spool, mix,* and *then* (a sequence word to designate the steps of the experiment). Joel was asked to write the steps used for the experiment (procedure text) and what he learned from it (recount text) (see Figure 1).

Figure 1. Joel's writing sample

The assessment-of-text framework assists in determining what kinds of text students are able to handle and any linguistic strengths and difficulties they may have (see Figure 2). We have used the framework to evaluate Joel's writing and how it reflects his understanding of the experiment. Teachers are able to keep individual profiles of learners as well as class profiles to adapt future teaching to specific student needs.

In the procedure section of the assignment, Joel demonstrates that he can write the steps of the experiment in sequence, incorporating one of the key vocabulary words, *then*. He still needs help using complete sentences and with spelling and capitalization. In the recount section, Joel needs help with expressing the main idea (concept) and providing details. In the content-knowledge column of Figure 2, it is noted that although Joel understood the various steps of his experiment, he did not specifically address in his writing the objective of how gravity affects the shape of bubbles. It should be noticed, however, that Joel has some understanding of the concept, as reflected in his drawing. Although he did not incorporate the key vocabulary term *gravity* in his writing, the contour lines in the bubble he drew curved downward and the water droplets demonstrate the effect of gravity, revealing an understanding of the scientific concept of gravity.

Figure 2. Using the assesment-of-text framework to evaluate Joel's writing (Figure 1)						
Procedure	Understood major steps in experiment	All major steps are present.	Used proper connectives	Good; used vocabulary from instructions	Proper use of tense; needs help with complete sentences	Spelling problems; proper use of periods; needs help with capitalization
Recount	The main concept of the experiment is missing. Student did not use the term gravity. Lacks details	Good; expressed the major task and included a personal feeling about the task	Ideas are linked appropriately.	Good; used vocabulary from instructions	Good; complete sentences	Good

Adapted from Gibbons (2002).

With ELL students, it is critical to use multiple forms of assessment to measure the extent to which the students understand the content objective. In Joel's example, only by analyzing his drawing can we determine that he understood the main concept of how gravity affects the shape of bubbles. We recognize that it is a challenge to assess for content knowledge and evaluate whether or not an ELL student has met the national and state science standards. We suggest that science teachers be very clear about the objectives of their lessons and provide the vocabulary and language that the ELL student will need to demonstrate an understanding of those objectives. It is helpful to provide a list of the key vocabulary for the lesson to all students, whether or not they are ELL students. Students who are English proficient can also benefit from such scaffolding of language and reinforcement of key scientific vocabulary. In many of our classrooms, we may have only a few ELL students; while this model of instruction has proven successful for helping ELL students improve their academic writing (Gibbons 2002), it can also help other non-ELL students in the class.

It is critical when addressing the needs of ELL students that science teachers not only assess at the end of each chapter or unit of study (summative assessments) but also incorporate formative assessments throughout the period of instruction. Formative assessments provide a more informal means for checking for understanding and are key for ensuring that ELL students are meeting the content standards (Carr, Sexton, and Lagunoff 2007). Teachers can also check for understanding of content through the use of oral discussions and presentations, such as the language interaction that will occur in the first three phases of the mode

continuum model. Teachers can also check for understanding through the use of pictures and drawings, such as the one provided in Figure 1 (p. 72). Although the focus of this paper is on transitioning ELL students from speaking about science to writing about science, we strongly encourage science teachers to check for understanding of content through a variety of methods and strategies to ensure that students are meeting national and state content objectives.

Conclusion

A science program designed to meet the needs of ELL students must have a number of components. First, it must provide ELL students with opportunities to listen, speak, read, and write English. It also must use a hands-on project approach to science learning. Furthermore, it must provide an opportunity for ELL students to work cooperatively to develop both social and academic language skills. But most important, it must provide the teacher with a framework to address the linguistic and content-area needs of ELL students in the mainstream classroom. The mode continuum provides such a framework. It incorporates all of these components into an organized, meaningful, and authentic approach to teach the language skills needed to communicate in an academic setting (Gibbons 2002).

References

Carr, J., U. Sexton, and R. Lagunoff. 2007. *Making science accessible to English learners: A guidebook for teachers.* San Francisco: WestEd.

Crawford, J. 2004. *Educating English language learners: Language diversity in the classroom.* Los Angeles: Bilingual Education Services.

De Jong, E. J., and C. A. Harper. 2005. Preparing mainstream teachers for English-language learners: Is being a good teacher good enough? *Teacher Education Quarterly* 32 (2): 101–24.

Echevarría., J., M. E. Vogt, and D. J. Short. 2008. *Making content comprehensible for English learners: The SIOP Model.* Boston: Pearson Education.

Gibbons, P. 2002. *Scaffolding language, scaffolding learning: Teaching second language learners in the mainstream classroom.* Portsmouth, NH: Heinemann.

O'Malley, J. M., and L. Valdez Pierce. 1996. *Authentic assessment for English language learners: Practical approaches for teachers.* Denver: Addison-Wesley.

VanCleave, J. 1993. *Gravity: Mind-boggling experiments you can turn into science-fair projects.* New York: John Wiley and Sons.

Vitale, M. R., and N. R. Romance. 2000. Portfolios in science assessment: A knowledge-based model for classroom practice. In *Assessing science understanding: A human constructivist view,* eds. J. J. Mintzes, J. H. Wandersee, and J. D. Novak, 168–97. San Diego: Academic Press.

Chapter 14

Integrated Assessments for ELL

Students—and Teachers—Benefit From Incorporating Writing and Drawing in Science

By Joan Armon and Linda J. Morris

As she circulates, Ms. Adams observes third graders working in three-person teams. Students dig, stir, talk, draw, and write while observing a mix of brine shrimp eggs and sweet pea seeds placed in salt water and in soil. The task during this second lesson of *Investigating Life Cycles* (BSCS 1999) is to gather evidence and determine which objects are eggs and which are seeds.

Although Ms. Adams observes Emil (all names are pseudonyms) engaged over several days with team members, it is not until she reads her students' notebooks that Emil's confusion surfaces. Emil is learning English, and Ms. Adams relies not only on observations of students and conversations with them during investigations but also on her examination of written and sketched notebook entries. By integrating science, literacy, and art, Ms. Adams provides multiple ways for students to communicate understandings and collects rich, ongoing assessments.

We feature Ms. Adams's approach as one example of how teachers can use writing and drawing in science to meet the needs of students learning English and also guide her teaching. We conclude by noting some of the difficulties posed by integration and offer recommendations.

Why Writing and Drawing?

Writing in science notebooks promotes scientific understanding. As they make entries in notebooks, students question, predict, plan, record, explain, and interpret. Teachers read students' entries to guide instruction and assess growth. Science writing is more than a record of procedures, data, and facts; it is a tool for developing and articulating thinking (Vygotsky 1978).

By overlapping literacy and science instruction, teachers and students build on existing knowledge and skills in both subjects (Saul 2002). Precise word choice, for example, is essential in both writing and science reporting. Teachers demonstrate science writing while linking vocabulary to visuals such as photographs and concrete materials, particularly for students learning English (Krashen 2003). As students develop academic vocabularies in content areas, academic achievement improves (Marzano 2004), as does clarification of thinking (Marzano, Pickering, and Pollock 2001). Since drawing requires careful observation of an object's or phenomenon's distinctive characteristics, students attend to details they might otherwise overlook.

Assessing and Responding

The goal of the investigation described in the introduction is for third graders to understand life cycles. Students discover that seeds or eggs are the beginnings of life cycles and that seeds and eggs are alive. Ms. Adams observes students during science investigations and examines their notebooks to assess their understanding and her teaching. Periodically, she questions students, asking them to construct on-the-spot drawings to demonstrate understanding.

Emil's notebook entry at the beginning of the unit in March appears in Figure 1. Emil's writing, "the little seeds are haching," suggests a lack of understanding that seeds grow into plants. No drawing accompanies the text. Ms. Adams is uncertain whether Emil does not understand the science concepts that seeds grow into plants and that eggs grow into animals, or if the English vocabulary is unfamiliar. This is Emil's first year in this country, so he missed the second-grade science unit featuring seeds growing into plants. The writing suggests Emil may not understand the concept that an egg and seed are alive or that they occur at the beginning of the life cycle. Ms. Adams wonders if Emil understands these concepts and related vocabulary in his native language (Romanian) but is unable to express understanding in English. Highlighting specific vocabulary connected to concrete examples would benefit Emil. However, in the crowded curriculum, Ms. Adams lacks time to grow plants with Emil to assess and build background knowledge. Instead, in a one-on-one conference, she reads *From Seed to Plant* (Gibbons 1991), explaining pictures and the vocabulary (seed, grow, root, stem, leaves, plant) of a plant's life cycle. As she talks, she draws the cycle in sequenced boxes on the whiteboard, adds labels, and asks Emil to repeat key words after her.

Next, to stimulate talk among Emil and his peers about the plant life cycle, Ms. Adams rereads *From*

Figure 1. Emil's notebook entry in March

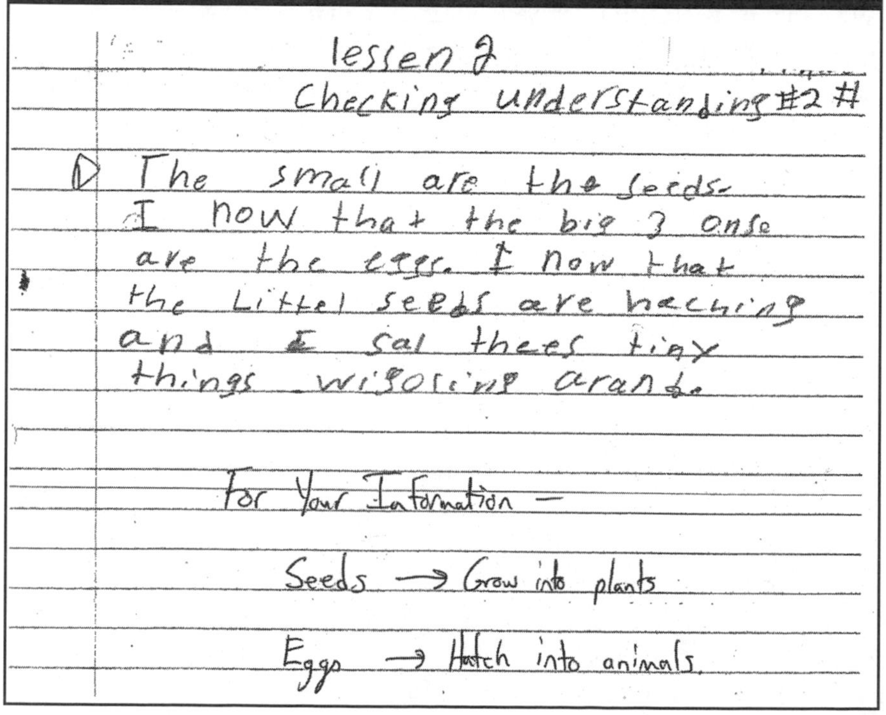

lessen 2
Checking understanding #2#

1) The small are the seeds.
I now that the big 3 onse
are the eggs. I now that
the Littel seeds are haching
and I sal thees tiny
things wigosing arand.

For Your Information —

Seeds → Grow into plants

Eggs → Hatch into animals

Seed to Plant with Emil and his group. Then, at the whiteboard, Emil and his peers collaborate to draw and label a plant life cycle, pronouncing each term several times. The drawings remain on the board.

Then Ms. Adams reads *Where Butterflies Grow* (Ryder 1989), which presents text and images describing the change from a caterpillar to a butterfly. Afterward, the group returns to the whiteboard to add (under their plant life cycle sketches) labeled drawings of the butterfly life cycle (egg, caterpillar, cocoon, butterfly). Ms. Adams emphasizes the egg's development and then compares and contrasts the two life cycles by pointing to and naming drawings in both cycles,

Figure 2. Emil's notebook entry in April

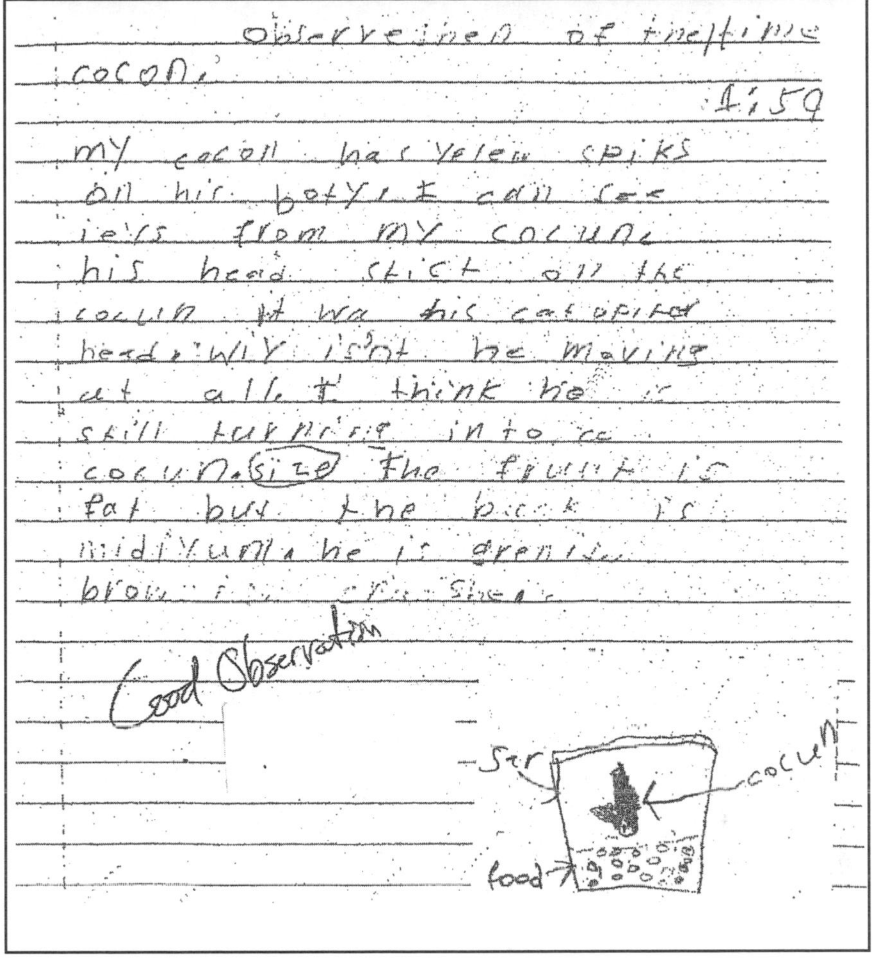

first at the board and then in the two books. She explains the seed growing into a plant and then explains the egg growing into a butterfly.

Ms. Adams assesses Emil's emerging understanding of key vocabulary by asking Emil to point to each stage of each cycle and state the correct term. Ms. Adams notes Emil's growth several days later when Emil completes this task on his own and uses terms correctly during group work.

In April, Emil demonstrates growth in recording observations. A drawing accompanies the writing (Figure 2), and more detail appears both in the drawing and the written vocabulary (*cocoon*). The drawing and the writing include *yellow spikes* on the cocoon, and the drawing includes labels (*jar, cocoon,* and *food*). To build on the strategy of questioning, which students use during reading and writing, Ms. Adams asks Emil to generate a science-focused question about his observations. Emil writes, "Why isn't he moving at all?" and offers an explanation: "I think he is turning into a cocun." The concrete experience of observing a living caterpillar has captured Emil's interest and stimulated more detailed observations, which are evident in this notebook entry. An understanding of the concept that "change occurs in a life cycle" also is evident in this notebook entry.

By May, Emil shows increasing understanding of the life cycle of a butterfly (Figure 3). Three components of the cycle appear, the writing and drawing again include greater detail than in previous entries, and the vocabulary shows more sophistication than earlier entries (e.g., in addition to *caterpillars* and *cocoon* present in the April entry, Emil adds the terms *turned into*, *butterfly*, *drink*, and *net*).

Figure 3. Emil's notebook entry in May

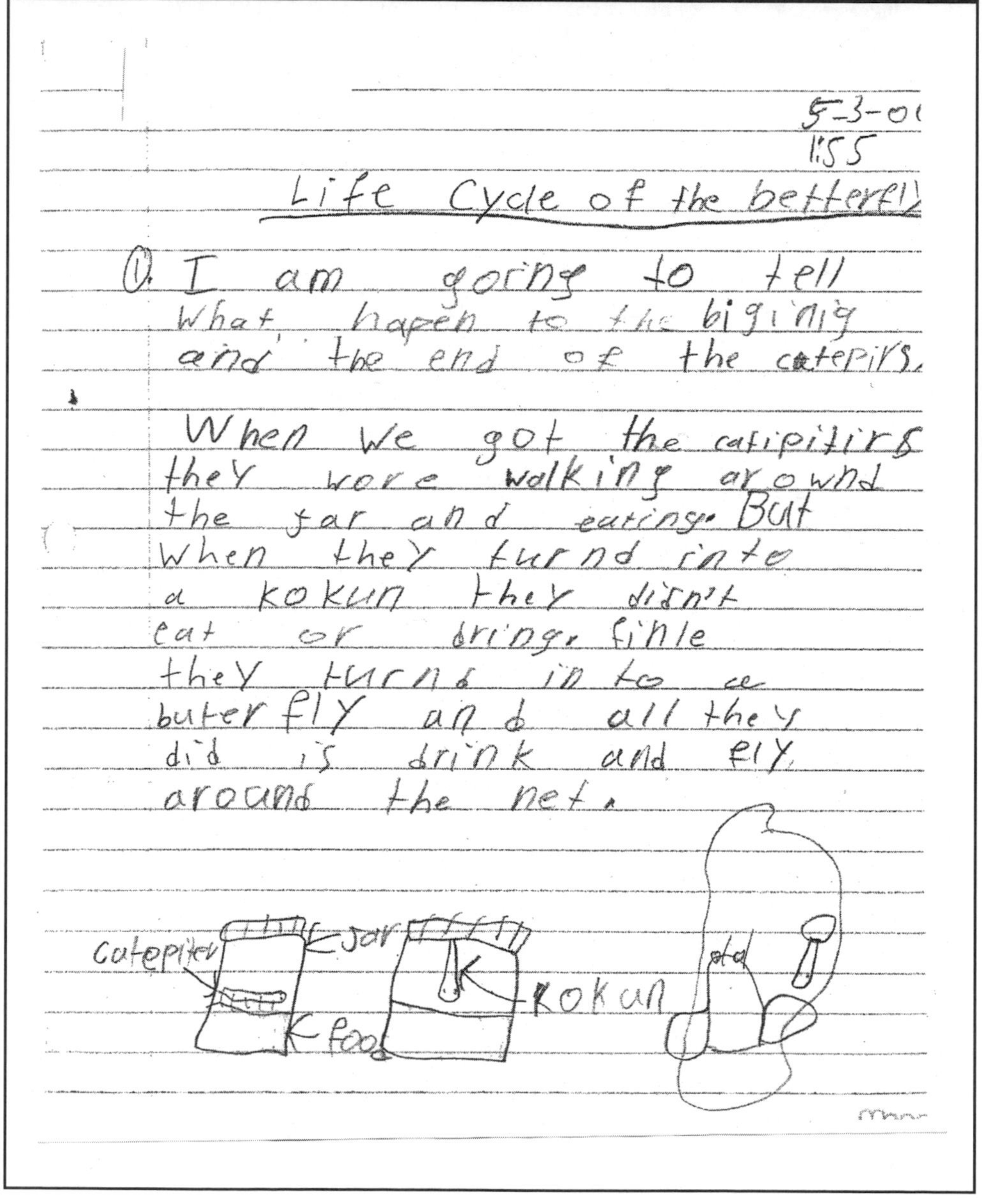

Assessing understanding from this entry, Ms. Adams notes that Emil omits wording or drawing of the egg as the beginning of the life cycle. Experiencing all four stages in a life cycle investigation is essential. In this classroom investigation, actual butterfly eggs are not observed; the investigation begins with caterpillars shipped to the classroom. Although Emil and his peers constructed a simulated life cycle of the butterfly with paper objects representing each component in the cycle, she wonders if Emil may not understand that the simulated paper egg represents the live egg missing in the classroom cycle.

Again, Ms. Adams returns to the whiteboard with Emil to assess his thinking, asking him to draw and label the butterfly life cycle. Building on his previous whiteboard drawings, Emil draws the egg first, and Ms. Adams reinforces the concept of the egg at the beginning of a butterfly life cycle. To provide additional reinforcement, Ms. Adams pairs Emil with Lily, a peer in his group, to reread and talk about the life cycle books.

Strategies to Support Integration

Reinforcing understanding through trade books is just one of many instructional strategies teachers can use to support integration and respond to students' differing needs. Teachers can also

- assess students' understanding before, during, and after investigations, such as using a K-W-L (what I Know, what I Want to know, what I Learned) chart, one-on-one conferencing, or rereading notebook entries, to continuously correct false information and clarify thinking. Ms. Adams and Emil, for example, held several one-on-one conferences.

- deepen students' understanding of science concepts through concrete experiences with authentic materials and complete processes. In the experiences discussed in this article, the students observe, talk, draw, and label the full life cycle of both a bean plant and a butterfly.

- take related field trips, if possible, to complement science explorations. For example, next year, Ms. Adams hopes to raise funds to take students to a local butterfly pavilion during the life cycles unit.

- model the writing techniques that you want students to emulate. Project your own notebook entries on an overhead, read them aloud, and demonstrate writing strategies, such as replacing vague words with more precise ones. Identify any missing or confusing details and clarify them for the class. For example, in the butterfly unit, Ms. Adams writes, "My caterpillar is interesting." She asks the class if this entry creates an accurate picture of a caterpillar in their minds. When students respond that it does not, she erases "is interesting" and writes "has a yellow wormlike shape with fuzz on it." Students agree that these words help them visualize a caterpillar.

- model drawing techniques using line, shape, texture, and color. These techniques foster accurate drawings that reveal specific information valued in scientific drawings. Such drawings rely on close observation but can improve when students build on skills learned in art classes. Teachers who lack knowledge of drawing techniques could involve the school art teacher.

Facing Integration Challenges

Of course, incorporating writing and drawing effectively into your science lessons is not without its challenges. Below we point out some of the main obstacles and suggest some remedies for addressing them.

Time—Adding writing and drawing to science investigations requires more time. To maximize time, include science writing and drawing throughout the day, overlapping strategies used in science, literacy, and art, such as questioning, informational writing with drawings, or inferences based on evidence.

Vocabulary—Some students, particularly those learning English, may not be familiar enough with science, literacy, and art vocabularies to demonstrate understanding through writing and drawing. Supports such as word walls (index cards display words with icons, photos, or drawings) or labeled objects on a table support and cement significant vocabulary.

Balance—One of the integrated disciplines may not be addressed as fully as the others. To avoid potential imbalance, deliberately highlight each discipline with focused instruction on certain days within the integrated study.

Despite the challenges posed by increased time, specialized vocabularies, and balance, integrating writing and drawing with science investigations is beneficial for teachers and students. Students, particularly those learning English, gain multiple ways of acquiring and expressing knowledge in several disciplines, and, as a result, teachers obtain valuable, ongoing data to assess students' understanding and improve instruction.

Resources

BSCS Science T.R.A.C.S. 1999. *Investigating life cycles*. Dubuque, IA: Kendall/Hunt.

Gibbons, G. 1991. *From seed to plant*. New York: Holiday House.

Krashen, S. 2003. *Explorations in language acquisition and use*. Portsmouth, NH: Heinemann.

Marzano, R. J. 2004. *Building background knowledge for academic achievement*. Alexandria, VA: Association for Supervision and Curriculum Development.

Marzano, R. J., D. J. Pickering, and J. E. Pollock. 2001. *Classroom instruction that works: Research-based strategies for increasing student achievement*. Alexandria, VA: Association for Supervision and Curriculum Development.

National Research Council (NRC). 1996. *National science education standards*. Washington, DC: National Academies Press.

Ryder, J. 1989. *Where butterflies grow*. New York: Lodestar Books.

Saul, E. W. 2002. Science workshop. In *Science workshop: Reading, writing, and thinking like a scientist,* ed. E. W. Saul, 1–16. Portsmouth, NH: Heinemann.

Vygotsky, L. S. 1978. *Thought and language*. Cambridge, MA: MIT Press.

Chapter 15

What Writing Represents What Scientists Actually Do?

By William C. Robertson

Often the writing that students in elementary school do in connection with science is their final report of a science fair project. They diligently file a report in the form of the *scientific method* introduction, hypothesis, materials, procedure, results, and conclusion. This form of science writing persists through college courses in science, and it isn't unusual for someone majoring in a science discipline to have lab reports as his or her main writing product in science. Of course, one must do a paper or two based on researching and understanding a particular topic in science, but that's usually the extent of writing that ventures beyond reporting labs.

This situation brings up a couple of questions. The first is whether or not a report based on the scientific method accurately represents what scientists do. The second is what kind of writing do scientists engage in that goes beyond the reporting of conclusions. I'll try to address those questions here. And no, I won't be providing a list of ideas for science fair projects! I know that's a major concern, but it's a topic for another time. For now, just tell 'em to do a baking soda and vinegar volcano (joking!).

First Do, Then Write

Does the reporting of science using the scientific method really represent how scientists do science? The short answer is no. Scientists seldom follow the scientific method, even though the reporting of experiments in scientific journals more or less follows that template. The question that follows is, "Okay, smart guy, what procedure *do* scientists follow?" To understand that process, it might help to consider what most kids do when they get a new video game. Do they read the instructions? Nah. They familiarize themselves with the controls and just start playing. They mess around with the game for a while and see what happens. Only then do they go back to the instructions to learn a few things. The instructions make a whole lot more sense once you are somewhat familiar with the game.

Scientists do something similar to what kids do when they first play a video game. Scientists "mess around" a bit with the subject matter. Of course, messing around in science isn't exactly the same as messing around with a video game. Messing around in science means you become familiar with the research already done in your area, and it means trying out a few experiments (or thoughts, in the case of theoretical science) just to see what happens. You might even try to reproduce what others have done to hone your skills. The main point is, until you become familiar with what you're studying, you can't begin to formulate a hypothesis. Formulating a hypothesis often is a first step in the scientific method, but it is not the first step in doing science.

Just a quick note about how scientists proceed from the point of formulating a hypothesis. A scientist might start with a particular question to investigate and soon realize that the original question was the wrong one or that the original question has led to a more intriguing question. A scientist who is truly interested in his or her field of study soon has more questions than he or she can answer in a lifetime. This is one of the reasons why scientists take on research assistants to help accomplish goals. Plus, graduate assistants are a cheap source of labor!

"Talking" Results

It would be pretty boring if all of science writing involved nothing more than people publishing the results of their experiments. Thankfully for us, that's not all they do. The "scientific community" wouldn't put up with that, anyway. When you make a claim of an experimental result or alteration of a scientific theory, you can expect that others in your discipline will scrutinize your work, looking for errors in procedure or errors in the logic that led you to your particular conclusions. Most science journals publish not just original research but also responses from other scientists to that research. A back-and-forth conversation regarding relevant issues is not uncommon.

A good example of this was the "discovery" of cold fusion a number of years ago. The original research publication on cold fusion sparked a whole bunch of articles in which scientists mostly refuted the original results. Without this written criticism, we would not now know that cold fusion was an unfulfilled dream.

Some of the more interesting historical science artifacts are letters written back and forth between prominent scientists who disagreed on various theories, from the theories of electricity and magnetism to the theories of quantum mechanics. With increased publication in national journals, the increased ease of mobility of scientists, and the presence of the internet, such personal written correspondence among scientists is not as common as it was 100 years ago, but such correspondence established the need to be able to communicate one's ideas and to be able to criticize others' work in a coherent way.

Communicating Concepts

One of the most important uses of writing in science is to communicate the concepts of a discipline to both future scientists and laypeople. Textbooks are one obvious means of doing this, but we should also include synopses of major science ideas intended for the general public as well as magazine and newspaper articles that convey general ideas and recent discoveries.

Although some people who might not be active in research specialize in translating scientific concepts for laypeople, practicing scientists also contribute in this area. Stephen Hawking's books provide an insight into how his mind works; James Watson's *The Double Helix* is a great book that not only explains his and Francis Crick's investigations into DNA, but gives a glimpse into the excitement of scientific discovery.

Science Writing for Students

So what does any of this suggest with respect to students writing while doing science? One obvious place to introduce science writing is in the presentation of science fair projects. Instead of having classmates ask a few questions of the presenter, have them choose one project and write a formal critique of the procedure, results, and conclusion. Where was the procedure particularly good or particularly flawed? Does the conclusion follow logically from the results? You can use this process to teach students how to be critical while not biting the head off the experimenter!

In the realm of reporting science to the public, you could have students compose a column for the school newspaper or bulletin that briefly explains what your class has been doing in science and what conclusions you've reached. You could circulate this column in your class for review and comment prior to submitting it to the school.

Finally, there's the old standby of having kids do a report on some scientific subject. Although it's perfectly fine to have the students report on the adaptations of the red fox or the rings of Saturn, keep in mind that these kinds of reports are not typical of what practicing scientists do. It might be worthwhile to spice up students' science writing with some of the other alternatives suggested in this piece. Now, here's how to create the perfect vinegar and baking soda volcano …

Resource

Watson, J. 2001. *The double helix: A personal account of the structure of DNA*. New York: Touchstone.

Chapter 16

Writing Through Inquiry

By Paul Jablon

The inquiry science process provides a perfect opportunity for students to practice relational meaning in language. As students design their experiments, negotiate their ideas with peers, and share their data and conclusions, they sharpen both their reading and written communication skills. This process needs to be mediated by having the teacher consistently respond to extensive student writing and the concept creation that underlies the writing, thereby supplying scaffolding throughout the whole process.

The following describes how written language acquisition can be embedded into inquiry science. As with all inquiry models it begins with a physical (or modeling) exploration by students *before* new concepts are introduced.

Inquiry and Writing

1. *The students manipulate materials to gain physical knowledge experiences.*

    ■ During this time the student writes the question that she or he is investigating.

    ■ After physically messing with the phenomenon and discussing ideas with team members, the student revises the question to more clearly and concisely state the point of the investigation.

    ■ The student works with other students on a research team (cooperative group) to create initial procedures to be followed.

    ■ Each member of the team writes and revises her or his own procedures and findings.

    ■ Each team member also writes about what she or he was feeling during each part of the investigation, as scientists have traditionally done in their journals, in addition to recording their data. The teacher needs to ensure that students can differentiate between observations and inferences, and between emotions and opinions, and that students subsequently identify and write about them in appropriate places.

2. *Each student discusses findings and relationships between various parts of the system that she or he is investigating with other members of the cooperative science group (negotiates meaning).*

- The student first records her or his ideas for procedures and then works with team members to create a group procedure.

- The student articulates these ideas verbally, modifying her or his understanding, syntactical structures, and sometimes the vocabulary because of verbal interaction with team members.

- The teacher "cruises" the room, reading levels of understanding in groups, and facilitates the direction of each group through fairly open and not-too-leading questions.

- The teacher also asks individual students to verbalize their understandings and then asks them to write down these ideas in their lab notebooks, paying particular attention to see if students include important syntactical structures in their writing. For example, "if-then" phrases occur in everyday speech and writing but take on a special significance in scientific thinking and communication.

- Students begin conducting the investigations they have at least partially, if not completely, designed, and team members begin creating and sharing naive conceptual understandings, enrich their process skills, and may learn from other team members.

- During this process, students are practicing clearly communicating their ideas, using language structures that they hear from team members, and organizing their investigations by creating sequenced oral and then written descriptions. This nonthreatening, small-group modeling of language, and the subsequent chance to rehearse this language, is especially important for second language learners (Krashen 1982).

- While moving from group to group, teachers assess student understandings and skills and their abilities to communicate those skills both verbally and in rough form in their science notebooks. This is also formative assessment for science learning and allows for appropriate and differentiated instruction the next day.

- Teachers urge all students to write data and understandings in a fairly shorthand, but syntactically accurate, manner.

3. *The teacher facilitates a more logical and richer creation of meaning.*

- Reporters from student research teams report back to the larger "whole-class scientific community." This early process of "meaning-making from our results so far" allows students on a team to begin organizing and synthesizing data and making preliminary conclusions based on evidence from investigations in progress. Thus, students begin learning and using strategies for organizing ideas into a logical argument.

- Students from other teams are critical friends, seeking evidence for claims and procedural descriptions from other groups reporting their findings for data that contradict their own.

- The teacher writes the ideas of various groups on posted chart paper and then asks teams to go back and to seek out similarities, differences, and inconsistencies in procedures or reasoning that might result in the differences.

- The teacher, using questions, seeks to have reporters from these teams clarify and expand their descriptions and analyses. The teacher does not accept answers but rather focuses on the explanation of the thinking that leads to the answer. This starts students on the path toward meta-cognition, as they focus on their thinking and thinking strategies.

4. *Each student creates concepts (relational meaning) and creates language (common vocabulary and syntactical relationships between words) to express the concept.*

   - As students in their teams continue their investigations, the teacher needs to continue to circulate throughout the room and help students make rich and accurate verbal syntactical structures that describe the scientific phenomenon, as well as the procedures, that lead to that understanding. As before, the teacher needs to check that the written notes in science journals contain rich syntax similar to the students' oral language.

5. *The teacher then substitutes the more accurate scientific terminology for the common vocabulary since the students have already created the meaning.*

   - If most students are getting reasonably clear conceptual understandings and are using fairly appropriate process skills in their investigations, then the teacher may introduce both scientific and richer generic vocabulary for students' original correct, but less technical, and universally agreed upon words. That is, vocabulary is introduced at the end of the week after students have already created the conceptual understandings.

   - At this time, if students have worked enough days on honing their original naive conceptions, the teacher may let students in on what the larger scientific community understands about the conceptual phenomenon in students' investigations. Students can now compare their naive understandings with this.

   - Whether the teacher first tells students or students first read a textbook or use library research skills to find out what scientists now know about the topic under study, reading shouldn't occur until students have long engaged in their physical or modeling exploration of the phenomenon. When students have created this mental landscape of the natural world

phenomenon, moderated by various syntactical structures that communicate fairly accurate (but not necessarily totally quantitative) relationships, then they are prepared to have a meaningful reading experience.

6. *The students then attempt to take these oral descriptions and translate them into symbolic (written) language (words and numbers and their relationships).*

    ■ While students engage in the investigation, homework should be to organize and synthesize ideas in a written form from the day's classroom investigation, rather than read a text and answer questions. This provides daily scaffolding for thinking and writing in the final lab report.

    ■ If the investigation is mainly finished, students take the cumulative and scaffolded work of the past few days and shape it into a rich and well-written document with a particular format—a lab report. In many ways, the structure of a lab report mimics the five-paragraph essay that the English teachers are using as a written communication model.

    ■ This is also the appropriate time for students to read trade books or various texts, to use the internet in a supervised and scaffolded fashion, or to speak to outside experts who might suggest sources to increase their understanding of the phenomenon being studied. Students can use these understandings from the scientific community to help them uncover the inconsistencies in their own investigations and include these in their reports' conclusions and interpretation of data sections. Teaching students the strategy of comparing their way of expressing an idea with how professionals are expressing similar ideas, gives them the tools for seeing the structures for clear communication. Again, the process is that students have first had a chance to have an informed naive conception so that written work can now have deeper meaning as they attempt to read and translate its meaning based on the mental landscape they have already created.

7. *The teacher then responds in writing to these writings and has students revise them until the students clearly can explain conceptual relationships in a written symbolic form.*

    ■ If the teacher has modeled writing partners (Calkins 1994), then students first critique (critical friends) each other's written work, both for scientific accuracy and literary clarity. Students then rewrite their reports or daily work based on the feedback from their rotating writing partners.

    ■ Once these revisions are completed, or if students do not yet have writing partners, then the teacher responds at length to the daily work or written lab report in writing. These responses suggest areas that need clarification or expansion, rethinking, or reorganization. This is usually done with nonleading but carefully considered questions. However, some direct instruction can also occur in these writings.

- A "grade so far" is given. Students then have an opportunity to edit their work, both for scientific understanding and clarity of communication, to raise their grades.

- This process is repeated as many times as necessary until students are satisfied with their grades (understanding and written communication ability). If students have never engaged in this process, then at the beginning of the school year there are usually many extensive revisions and exchanges of papers between the students and the teacher. However, as the year progresses, students begin to acquire both the scientific reasoning abilities and the writing structures and strategies to clearly communicate this reasoning for each new conceptual understanding that they encounter.

It is this apprenticeship of the novice scientist student to the master scientist teacher that is missing in much of inquiry science teaching. When the teacher is responding both orally and in writing to the students' reasoning about how the natural world works, then the teacher is simultaneously teaching science concepts and process skills and writing and reading strategies within the context of science. Although students initially work in teams to share insights and negotiate meaning, the final translation of the individual student's understandings of the scientific process and the conceptual understanding needs to be negotiated between the teacher and student through a written Socratic dialogue. It is truly an apprenticeship as the student creates and communicates meaning, synthesizing her or his personal scientific investigations with what is known by the larger scientific community.

References

Calkins, L. M. 1994. *The art of teaching writing*. Portsmouth, NH: Heinemann.
Krashen, S. D. 1982. *Principles and practice in second language acquisition*. Oxford: Pergamon.

Resource

Jablon, P. 2002. Alignment of instruction with knowledge of student learning. In *Learning science and the science of learning*, ed. R. W. Bybee, 65–76. Arlington, VA: NSTA Press.

Chapter 17

Getting Students to Become Successful, Independent Investigators

By Jeffrey D. Thomas

Doing inquiry with my sixth- and ninth-grade students has always been a challenge. This is particularly true when implementing student-centered labs, because the process can discourage some students. My students struggle when writing testable problems, planning valid and reliable procedures, and drawing meaningful evidence-based conclusions. To address this issue, I created a student-centered lab handout to facilitate the inquiry process for students. This handout has reduced students' frustration and helped them become more independent and successful investigators.

Student-Centered Labs

Student-centered labs are guided inquiries that require students to (1) pose their problem, (2) plan their procedures, and (3) formulate their results (Llewellyn 2005). During this process, I expect students to make observations, identify variables, ask questions, hypothesize, conduct experiments, organize data, draw conclusions, infer, and share results (NRC 1996; AAAS 1993). In general, I implement five to eight formal, student-centered labs per school year.

First, students choose a related set of variables to develop testable questions that interest them. Generally, this process is guided and relates to the curriculum. To facilitate students' work, I offer starter questions, use technology (such as YouTube or digital images), and conduct demonstrations that illustrate discrepant events, all of which I attempt to make meaningful and relevant (Llewellyn 2005).

Second, to test their questions, students plan and carry out their experimental designs. I guide students to make thoughtful decisions about what materials they will use for their experimental procedures; to determine how to measure the variables accurately, precisely, and safely using the SI system; and to work and communicate effectively and efficiently in their lab groups (Llewellyn 2005; AAAS 1993; NRC 1996).

Third, students create an appropriate graph for interpretation. They use the data to draw evidence-based conclusions that answer their problem and evaluate their hypothesis. Students judge the validity and reliability of their experiment by determining what they did to improve it and any limitations, based on variables and processes, they may have overlooked (Llewellyn 2005).

Finally, students decide how to communicate their work with others (e.g., posters, PowerPoint). I expect students to synthesize the results from other groups and show interest in and demonstrate understanding of the nature of science.

Students use the lab handout to conduct these lab investigations about various topics, including air quality, rocks and minerals, and electricity. The Solar Cooker lab is an example of students doing guided inquiry with the lab handout.

The Solar Cooker Lab

The Solar Cooker lab is a modified version of a curriculum-embedded performance task from the Connecticut State Department of Education (2006). This student-centered lab is the first activity done by students in a unit on alternative energy. The objective of the lab is for students to design a solar cooker that efficiently uses the Sun's energy. A fossil fuel and nuclear energy unit precedes this one.

Prelab Investigation (Day 1)

The goals of the prelab investigation are to engage student interest, brainstorm ideas about ways to capture the Sun's energy, and construct a general class question.

Brainstorming

Students are initially shown a digital image from the Environmental Protection Agency (EPA) website of a cartoon dog in a warm bathtub, with the Sun shining through a large window. This image also depicts a solar water heater, implying that the bathwater is heated by this means. This image helps students brainstorm ways we can use the Sun as an energy source. Students brainstorm independently and then share their ideas with the class. Afterward, students are shown another digital image, this one of a book called *Cooking With the Sun: How to Build and Use Solar Cookers* (see Resources). In pairs, students brainstorm three questions based on the title of the book. The intent is to direct the focus of the lesson to solar cookers, specifically to guide students to pose questions related to how they might cook with the Sun.

Constructing the Class Question

Each student group is asked to write on the board their best question related to the book title. Once all group questions are written on the board (about 10–12), similar ones are combined, which usually leaves four to six questions. Then students vote on the best question to be the class inquiry question. An example of a class question is "How can we effectively cook with the Sun?" This process allows me to focus on a required content standard and gives students more ownership of the inquiry process. Students record this class question on their lab handouts (Figure 1). Generally, we spend approximately 10 minutes introducing and reviewing the topic, 15 minutes brainstorming, and 20 minutes discussing group questions and constructing the class inquiry question.

Figure 1. Class inquiry question

Write the general class inquiry question in the space provided below. We will answer this question after the results from every lab group are shared with the class.

_____
_____
_____

Posing the Problem (Day 2)

Students use the class question from the previous day—"How can we effectively cook with the Sun?"—to begin the process of posing their own testable problems. Because most students do not know what a solar cooker looks like, I conduct an online search and use the class projector to show images of several solar cookers. These images help students visualize how solar cookers can effectively be used to cook food. I then explain that using food in class is not an option because it would be a safety issue; rather, we can use the heating of water to test the effectiveness of the solar cooker. Students then record "the heating of water inside the solar cooker" as the class dependent variable (DV) on their lab handouts (Figure 2).

Students are then asked to get into their lab pairs to identify factors that could affect the heating of water inside a solar cooker (their DV). Thinking about the effectiveness of a solar cooker, students identify eight factors that could affect the water temperature (DV). In general, many students struggle with identifying possible factors; therefore, I circulate among the groups, assess their progress, and provide guiding questions and prompts to assist them. Some factors students identify include (1) type of lining inside the solar cooker, (2) shape or size of the solar cooker, (3) color of the solar cooker, and (4) angle at which the Sun's rays are concentrated inside the solar cooker. Students recorded this in the handout (Figure 2). This strategy of students brainstorming variables has been an effective scaffold to improve students' understanding of inquiry. Prior to this strategy, students have tremendous difficulty identifying a related set of variables (the IV and DV), understanding the IV and DV, writing testable problems, posing the same testable problems among groups, brainstorming constants, and writing procedures (to improve the validity of the results). By using this scaffold technique, most of these issues are resolved.

> **Figure 2. Listing the variables for the experiment**
>
> Based on the class inquiry question, what variable identifies what you want to study? This will be your dependent variable. Review the inquiry question to come up with concrete ideas.
>
> Dependent variable (the factor that you want to investigate):
>
> _____
> _____
> _____
>
> Creating a list of variables:
> Once you identify your dependent variable, make a list of all the possible variables/factors that could affect the dependent variable. List them in the following space.
>
> _____
> _____
> _____

Once students list all of the variables that could affect the water temperature inside the solar cooker (DV), they chose one variable from their lists to be their IV. Once students identified their IV and DV, they independently pose their testable problems, and the remaining variables become their constants (Figure 3, p. 94). One example of the diverse testable problems students pose is "How does the color of the lining inside a solar cooker affect how quickly the water will heat up?"

After students identify the variables, they develop their testable questions (Figure 4, p. 94). Then students write their hypotheses. A common scaffold used by teachers is the "if-then-because" statement. However, I feel this can be limiting for students at times. Therefore, I

Figure 3. Choosing a related set of variables

Choose one of the variables as your independent variable (this is what you will intentionally change). Write this, along with the dependent variable, in the space below.

Independent variable:

_____
_____
_____
_____

Dependent variable:

_____
_____
_____
_____

All of the other variables you listed will be the variables held constant. Please list them below.

Variables held constant:

_____
_____
_____
_____

Reflection: Why do you feel it is important to keep these variables constant when you conduct your experiment?

_____
_____
_____
_____

Figure 4. Writing a testable problem

Write a problem that clearly identifies what you will investigate and include the independent and dependent variables. Your problem should emphasize a cause-and-effect relationship between the two variables and be measurable.

_____
_____
_____
_____

Reflection: Why did your group decide to do this experiment?

_____
_____

do not require them to do this, but it is there to assist them if needed. When students write their hypotheses, they must include a measurable prediction that demonstrates how the IV will affect the DV (Figure 5). For example, one student writes, "If the lining inside the solar cooker is darker, then the water will heat up more quickly." In general, once students have a clear understanding of their problem, few have difficulty writing their hypotheses.

Planning Procedures (Day 3)

Before students begin planning their procedures, I explain that their designs must include (1) a materials list, (2) experimental procedures, (3) safety procedures, and (4) cleanup procedures (on handout, Figures 6 and 7, p. 96). I specifically include questioning scaffolds for the experiment and safety procedures on the lab handout (Figures 6 and 7, p. 96). Then students work in their lab groups to complete these tasks. I also circulate around the room, rephrasing student questions (so they could answer their own questions) and providing prompts instead of answers.

As students plan their experimental procedures, they answer guiding questions from the lab handout to help them (1) think about how they can measure their IV and DV variables concisely and accurately, (2) use their list of constant variables (and control group, if necessary) to write their procedures to improve the validity of their experiment, and (3) write reliable sampling techniques (Figure 6). Once I approve this, students write a complete step-by-step experimental procedure. In my experience, these guiding questions improve the quality of their experimental procedures.

Students also complete guiding questions in their lab handout to write their safety procedures (Figure 7, p. 96). Students use their safety contract, which helps them be more aware of safety issues related to the lab.

As students complete their experimental procedures, they receive feedback from me and revise accordingly. Feedback includes reminders to accurately measure their IV and DV that test their problem and to include variables held constant to improve the validity of the experimental procedures. In addition, I review their safety procedures, such as not using food, wearing chemical splash goggles when using glassware or fluids, and refraining from looking directly at the Sun when outdoors.

Conducting the Experiment (Day 4)

For most student-centered labs, students carry out their procedures in one class period. However, because students have to design and create their solar cookers, then collect their data, an additional two days are usually needed. Typically, students conduct and complete their experiments at varying rates. As a result, groups who finish collecting their data before the end of class begin to construct their graphs while other lab groups finish collecting their data. This allows students who need more class time to complete their procedures without feeling pressure from other students or me. During this time, I circulate around the room and assist all groups.

Figure 5. Hypothesizing

Write a hypothesis that predicts a plausible outcome to your problem; please use the guidelines below:

- Consider the "if-then-because" format (not necessary, but helpful).
- Identify the independent and dependent variables.
- Identify a measurable cause-and-effect relationship.

Example: If there is an increase in the voltage, then the current will increase because…

_____
_____
_____
_____
_____

Figure 6. Guidelines for experiment procedures

When writing your experimental procedures, you must measure all variables accurately using the SI system, including the independent and dependent variable, and variables held constant. Whenever possible, include a control group. Below are guiding questions to assist your group.

- How will you accurately measure your independent variable? What SI units will you use? Explain fully.
- How will you accurately measure your dependent variable? What SI units will you use? Explain fully.
- How will you make certain that all constant variables will be identified to improve the validity of your experiment?
- Describe each constant variable and your plan for keeping it constant.
- Will you collect enough data to make the experimental data more reliable? Do you have enough samples? Trials?

Figure 7. Safety procedures

Safety is of the utmost importance. Please use these guidelines to ensure safety when you conduct your experiment.

- Identify with your teacher a clear set of laboratory safety rules and procedures. Please use your safety contract as a guide.
- Rules should address clothing, what to do in case of accidents or injuries, eyewear, handling chemicals, glassware, equipment, heating substances, and other general safety guidelines.
- Check with your teacher to be sure all safety issues are addressed before you begin.

Formulating the Results
(Days 5 and 6)

Students have considerable difficulty deciding what kind of graphs they should construct. They read a table from the lab handout that compares the two most common graphs, line and bar (Figure 8). Students justify their choices based on this information and on the data they have collected. For example, if their IV is changing the color of the lining of the solar cooker, they create a bar graph because it compares items. However, if they have changed the angle at which the Sun's rays strike a water sample, then they construct a line graph because the change in angle creates continuous data as it relates to the temperature of the water sample.

Figure 8. Deciding on the type of graph to construct

Line graph	Bar graph
A line graph shows data continuously (e.g., 1, 2, 3, 4…), including time, distance, and temperature. The intent of the graph demonstrates a direct relationship between the independent variable on the *x*-axis and the dependent variable on the *y*-axis. Line graphs are useful for understanding trends and estimating points outside of the plotted data. Double line graphs can compare sets of continuous data (two or more lines on a graph).	A bar graph shows data in categories, such as student hair color, levels of air pollution per state, or number of hurricanes per season. The intent of a bar graph is to compare items, usually along the *x*-axis. However, bar graphs can show trends in the data, too.

The type of graph I should use based upon the data I collected is a _____ graph because…

Once students construct their graph(s) by hand, they answer the guiding questions in the lab handout to self-evaluate the quality of their graphs (Figure 9). Then I review their graphs and provide feedback. Students revise their work at home.

The next day I move around the room as students write their findings using the guiding questions in the lab handout (Figure 10). At this time, I pose prompts such as "How does the evidence support your claim?" and "What constants did you overlook?" to clarify student questions and ask follow-up questions to students' responses. I also provide an example of a student lab report (a different lab from a previous year) and review the qualities that made it a model lab report.

As a result, the quality of students' work improves, especially when students evaluate the validity and reliability of their experiments. For example, in a lab that did not use the lab handout, a student writes, "The validity of my experiment was good because I followed all my steps carefully and I measured the independent and dependent variables." This statement contrasts with that from a student who did use the lab handout: "The angle of the heat lamp that was heating the water source was kept the same because a more direct angle would give more energy and a less direct angle would give less energy." Students are given time to write an outline using the guiding questions during class as I circulate around the room providing prompts and guidance.

Communicating Results (Day 7)

In the solar cooker lab, students share their results with the class using poster paper.

Figure 9. Evaluating your graph(s)

Answer the questions below to assess whether you constructed the graph accurately.

- Did you use graph paper and a ruler to construct the graph?
- Did you plot the IV on the *x*-axis and the DV on the *y*-axis? Was this done accurately?
- Did you include the IV and DV in the title?
- Did you label both your *x*- and *y*-axes? Did you use appropriate SI units with your labels? Did you choose an appropriate scale (range 1–10) and intervals (e.g., 2, 4, 6, etc.) on the *x*- and *y*-axes?

Figure 10. Writing the findings

Analysis of the data:
Describe the trends in your data. What do they mean? How do they relate to the variables you investigated?

Conclusions:
- What is the answer to your problem? What evidence supports your claim(s)?
- Evaluate your hypothesis. What possible reasons can explain why the results turned out this way?

Validity:
- What variables did you keep constant in your experimental procedure? How did this improve the validity of the experiment?
- What constant variables did you overlook? How might this have affected the validity of your results? How would you change your procedures?
- How could you have measured the IV and DV variables more accurately?
- Did you collect enough data? How do you know?

They present their problems, data, and bulleted lists of their key findings. Students hang their posters around the room, then circulate to collect and analyze other groups' results. I also use this as a last opportunity to provide students with feedback before they hand in their final lab reports. Because students' testable questions vary, they use the class results to synthesize the best way to capture the Sun using a solar cooker while answering the initial class question.

Before the end of class, I review the lab assessment list and rubric (see Figure 11, p. 98) and give students five days to submit their final lab reports. Students are encouraged to hand me a draft before the due date.

Extensions

To further student inquiries, I align the next investigation of studying solar cookers to science, technology, and society. Students investigate methods to improve the design of their solar cooker so they could theoretically sell it to communities that lack sources of energy to cook their food. Students conduct these investigations based on class lab results and web sources such as Solar Cookers International (*http://solarcookers.org*).

Figure 11. Assessment list and rubric for lab reports

3: Excellent	2: Very good	1: Satisfactory	0: Redo
Element complete, possible minor technical error and/or interpretation	Element complete, a few minor technical errors and/or interpretations	Element incomplete and/or includes major errors/misinterpretations	Element missing or has many major errors and/or misinterpretations

Element	Possible points
Problem/Investigative question	6
____The problem statement relates/aligns to the bigger lab question (class question).	
____The dependent and independent variables describe a cause-and-effect relationship.	
Hypothesis	6
____The hypothesis predicts a measurable outcome of the problem statement.	
____The DV and IV describe a cause-and-effect relationship.	
Experimental design	30
List of variables and materials	
____Lists the variables, including the IV, DV, and all variables held constant.	
____ Lists the choice of materials to test the problem/hypothesis.	
Safety procedures	
____The safety procedures explains ways to reduce risk of injury when conducting the experiment.	
Experimental procedures	
____The experimental procedures test the problem/hypothesis.	
____The procedures follow an orderly sequence that is easy to follow and implement.	
____The independent variable is measured accurately to test the problem/hypothesis.	
____The dependent variable is measured accurately to test the problem/hypothesis.	
____All variables held constant are identified (listed) to improve the validity of the experiment.	
____All variables are measured in the metric system.	
Clean-up procedures	
____The cleanup procedures describe strategies to safely put away/store all lab materials.	

Element	Possible points
Data table and graphs	21
____A data table organizes and presents the data from the experiment so that it is easy to read and interpret.	
Graphs(s)	
____Correct type of graph is used (line, bar, etc.).	
____The title describes the relationship between the IV and DV.	
____Descriptive labels are included on both the *x*- and *y*-axes.	
____Appropriate metric units are described on both the *x*- and *y*-axes.	
____Even spacing and appropriate range are used on both the *x*- and *y*-axes.	
____Data are organized and plotted accurately.	
Results/findings	36
____x 3 ____ A complete discussion of the results is included.	
____x 3 ____ Conclusions are drawn from the results and answer the problem and evaluate the hypothesis.	
____x 3 ____ Conclusions are elaborated upon by making inferences/possible explanations to explain the results.	
____x 3 ____ The validity of the experiment is evaluated (procedures, measurements, variables held constant, etc.) and recommendations are made for improvements.	
Other	1
____Lab report is typed, organized, neat and includes names of all lab partners.	

Total possible points: 100
Total earned points: ____
Comments:

Conclusion

Doing student-centered inquiries using the lab handout increases the amount of class time required to conduct these labs. However, the quality of lab reports and student understanding of the nature of science greatly improves when using the lab handout, as compared to not using it. Once students become more familiar with the process, I modify the lab handout and remove some of the scaffolds. This reduces the amount of class time needed for these labs. Overall, my students are more successful investigators, which gives them the confidence to do more student-centered inquires, more independently, over time.

Acknowledgment

The idea of investigating solar cookers as the context for describing the lab handout was from the Connecticut State Department of Education.

References

American Association for the Advancement of Science (AAAS). 1993. *Benchmarks for scientific literacy*. New York: Oxford University Press.

Connecticut State Department of Education. 2006. *Connecticut Academic Performance Test (CAPT): Third-generation handbook for science*. Hartford: Connecticut State Department of Education.

Llewellyn, D. 2005. *Teaching high school science through inquiry: A case study approach*. Thousand Oaks, CA: Corwin Press.

National Research Council (NRC). 1996. *National science education standards*. Washington, DC: National Academies Press.

Resource

Halacy, B., and D. Halacy. 1992. *Cooking with the Sun: How to build and use solar cookers*. Lafayette, CA: Morning Sun Press.

Chapter 18

Kinesthetic Writing, of Sorts

By Kirstin Bittel and Darrek Hernandez

The ability to clearly communicate what was learned as the result of an experiment is a key component of science in general, not just science in the middle school classroom. The trick in the middle school classroom is teaching students how to write while making that writing meaningful and part of the everyday science experience, but not too time-consuming. Once that happens, it opens the door for students to see themselves as scientists communicating their ideas to others.

In our eighth-grade classrooms, we have focused on our students' ability to write quality conclusions at the end of every laboratory investigation. We have tried several strategies to help our students clarify their writing. The activity that follows has proven very successful with not only our mainstream students but also our English language learners (ELL students) and special education (SPED) students. In fact, our ELL and SPED students are writing significantly better using this tool than they did previously, bringing up their scores on the now-common six traits of writing rubrics by one or two rubric points in both the Ideas and Content and Organization categories (see Internet Resource).

The Flipbook

As students enter the room, they are given three half sheets of letter-size paper. These are used to make the flipbook (see Figure 1, p. 102, for additional instructions). First, students take the three sheets of paper and place them the on the desk vertically. Next, students pull each sheet down so the top edges are about 1–2 cm from the top of the preceding page (Figure 1A). Students then carefully hold the paper and fold the entire stack up so that the bottom edge rests about 1–2 cm below the top edge (Figure 1B). Finally, students rotate the entire set of folded pages vertically and staple in the center (Figure 1C). The flipbook is now ready to use and should have six flaps (one title page and five usable flaps).

The Conclusion Criteria

Students label the top flap of the flipbook "Scientific conclusion." The second flap is labeled "What was the objective?" The third is "Briefly, what did you do?" The fourth is "What evidence do you have?" The fifth is "What did you learn?" The final flap is labeled "Sample conclusion."

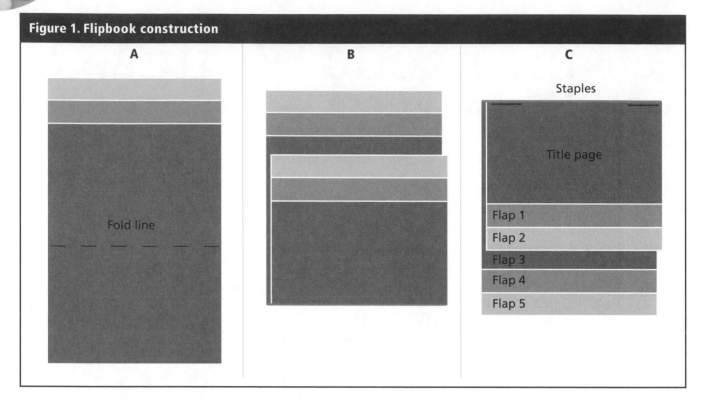

Figure 1. Flipbook construction

After students label each flap, they brainstorm sentence starters for each flap. This helps our ELL students, SPED students, and struggling writers. Students who constructed flipbooks in the past are encouraged to share sentence starters they have used in the past. You can also suggest sentence starters if your students have trouble generating their own.

As a class, we use the sentence starters students just identified to create a quality conclusion. We describe this conclusion as meeting the standard expected and merely a starting point. The information from a sample flipbook is shown in Figure 2. We wrote our sample paragraph about an investigation where students were identifying the characteristic properties of metals because we had just completed this investigation. Any laboratory experience will work to create the sample conclusion for the flipbook.

Conclusion

Having the opportunity to manipulate a tool, in this case a flipbook, creates an opportunity to use a reference guide the students actually enjoy. These flipbooks help all our students, especially our ELL students and SPED learners, as they can more easily communicate their understanding of concepts learned in science class. As students improve their writing skills, they are encouraged to break away from the flipbook and use more complex, less formulaic paragraphs to demonstrate their understanding of the investigations from class.

As a result of using this tool, we are able to spend less time reminding students of what belongs in a conclusion and more time evaluating student understandings. Writing is now a more natural part of the learning process. It is vital to our students' ability to create a strong foundation for constructing meaning and integrating new concepts into their schemas correctly.

Figure 2. Flipbook text example

Tab title	Text written under each tab
What was the objective?	• The objective for today was … • Turn the objective statement into a question, or vice versa. • Scientists can use _____ to help them _____. • In order to _____, you first need to _____.
Briefly, what did you do?	• Today in lab we … • In this activity we … • In order to answer our objective we … • To test our hypothesis we … • To collect evidence we … • We calculated … • We measured … • We tested …
What evidence do you have? Be specific!	• For example … • For instance … • At station 1 … • Take _____, for example, … • We found … • We calculated … • We measured … • We tested …
What did you learn?	• I learned … • I discovered … • I now understand … • In conclusion, …
Sample conclusion	Identifying the characteristic properties of metals can help us make better uses of our resources. In this activity, we observed the characteristic properties of copper, aluminum, and steel. We found that copper is malleable and does not react to acid. Aluminum is even more malleable and very lightweight, and also does not react to acid. Steel is a strong and dense metal, but it will rust. By looking at the characteristic properties of metals, I now understand how different metals can be used in different ways.

Acknowledgments

We wish to extend our gratitude to Kathie Dosh and Rachel Hughes for their helpful comments on earlier drafts.

Internet Resource

Writing assessment rubric
  www.cyberspaces.net/6traits/rubric2.html

Chapter 19

Multigenre Lab Reports
Connecting Literacy and Science

By Leonora Rochwerger, Shelley Stagg Peterson, and Theresa Calovini

The development of communication skills is a key component in any science program. However, I have often found that students do not see the connections between writing and science. In particular, I have experienced students' lack of enthusiasm when the time comes to write lab reports. Students say that they do not see why they should have to write dry, boring lab reports following an enjoyable hands-on activity or lab. This deepens the perceived disconnect between writing and science.

Recently, we conducted an action research project that provided students with alternatives to traditional lab report writing. Students used whatever genre they thought would best communicate what they had learned in a science unit. Basing our project on the work of Grierson, Anson, and Baird (2002), we called this project "multigenre writing" because students chose many different formats, such as comic strips and stories, to show what they had learned in a catapult unit.

The Hands-on Activity

I adapted an activity that had been used by other science teachers in my school as part of the Structures and Mechanisms strand of the science curriculum. In groups of four, students designed and built a popsicle-stick catapult that launched small chocolates (Hershey's KISSES) as far as possible—an assignment we call Throwing Kisses. Students had to maximize distance and accuracy because their catapult needed to knock down a LEGO prince sitting on a card board castle. After five catapult attempts, students received a number of chocolates to take home equal to the number of successful hits.

All hands-on work was done in class. We used one class period to form the groups of four, introduce the project, and explain how the evaluation would be done. As a way to add excitement and help visual learners, I also showed videos with catapults in action (see Internet Resources). This was followed by a computer-lab period in which students did research on catapults (see Internet Resources), then four, 50-minute class periods for the construction and testing of the catapults.

For the construction, students were only allowed to use popsicle sticks, white or wood glue, rubber bands, plastic spoons, and one additional element of their choice. All construction was done in the classroom with simple hand tools. Students were required to use safety goggles throughout the building activity. Students had been introduced to safety considerations using hand tools at the beginning of the year.

The catapults are tested in the hallway and a tape measure is used to measure the distance traveled by the chocolates. Because the catapults are not very big, they can be easily manipulated and stored.

The Multigenre Lab Report

To introduce students to the concept of *multigenre*, I brought in examples of different approaches to communicating information (e.g., newspaper articles, recipes, letters, and postcards). After students became familiar with the concept of multigenre writing, we discussed what a multigenre lab report might look like. Together we came to the conclusion that although it did not have to take the form of a lab report, their multigenre writing should include information that would normally be in a lab report. I then distributed the lab report handout (see sample).

Throwing Kisses Lab Report

Because this is a multigenre lab report, you may choose any style (i.e., cartoons, comic strips, storyboard, or newspaper article) to communicate what you did. You may use more than one style. There will be bonus marks for creativity, so be as creative as you can! The following must be included in your lab report:

- Title—In big bold letters; a cover page wouldn't hurt
- Purpose (or Question or Problem)—What you wanted to find out
- Hypothesis—What you thought would happen and why
- Procedure—Materials (what you used to build your machine and measure the results) and method (what steps you followed to build and test your machine; diagrams with labels should be included)
- Observations—Charts and tables with the results obtained and graph(s)
- Conclusions—Include answers for the following questions: What type of simple machines are included in your catapult? If a lever is part of it, which class is it? Why? Calculate the mechanical advantage of your machine and show the calculation. How did the class of lever you chose and the mechanical advantage of it affect the results you got? Was your hypothesis supported? How? What would you do differently if you had more time?
- Sources—Where did you obtain information about the topic? List books and websites you consulted.

One report per group must be submitted. I suggest that you divide the work among group members. You will have three, 50-minute in-class working periods to complete this lab.

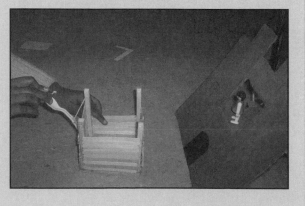

Demonstrating Learning

While I wanted students to enjoy and be motivated by this project, the critical part was that they clearly and accurately represented the science involved. I evaluated the students' learning on the final project using multiple forms of assessment: checklists of individual participation, group and peer evaluations, and a rubric based on the necessary information about catapults and student creativity (see rubric in Figure 1).

Figure 1. Rubric for multigenre lab report				
Category/Criteria	**Level 1**	**Level 2**	**Level 3**	**Level 4**
INQUIRY PROCESS Problem	• not clearly stated	• stated vaguely in teacher's words	• stated briefly in student's words	• stated precisely in student's words
Hypothesis	• poorly stated	• general hypothesis stated	• general hypothesis stated and "if/then" format used correctly	• general hypothesis stated and "if/then" format used correctly with a reason given
Materials and method	• very incomplete	• somewhat complete but not detailed	• complete	• complete and very detailed
Observations	• very incomplete	• somewhat complete but not detailed	• complete	• complete and very detailed
Conclusions	• shows understanding of few of the basic concepts • gives explanations showing limited understanding of the concepts	• shows understanding of some of the basic concepts • gives partial explanations	• shows understanding of most of the basic concepts • usually gives complete or nearly complete explanations	• shows understanding of all the basic concepts • always gives complete explanations
COMMUNICATION Communication of required knowledge	• communicates with little clarity and precision • rarely uses appropriate science and technology terminology	• communicates with some clarity and precision • sometimes uses appropriate science and technology terminology	• generally communicates with clarity and precision • usually uses appropriate science and technology terminology	• consistently communicates with clarity and precision • consistently uses appropriate science and technology terminology
MAKING CONNECTIONS Relating of science and technology with the outside world	• shows little understanding of connections between science and technology and the world outside the classroom	• shows some understanding of connections between science and technology and the world outside the classroom	• shows understanding of connections between science and technology and the world outside the classroom using one or two examples	• shows understanding of connections between science and technology and the world outside the classroom using several thoughtful examples
CREATIVITY	• poor creativity in the use of the genre of choice	• some creativity in the use of the genre of choice	• good creativity in the use of the genre of choice	• outstanding creativity in the use of the genre of choice

Students' multigenre writing took the form of comic strips, video scripts, fiction stories, and even a puppet show. Students were clearly proud of their final work, and we all laughed and enjoyed listening to these presentations. The purpose of these presentations was to provide an opportunity for students to share and appreciate one another's work. They were done in a rather informal way, with no specific guidelines other than the time, which had to be within 5–10 minutes. Students varied in how well they were able to articulate the science of catapults. For example, one group, in their earliest discussions, clearly stated that the purpose of the project was to "show the use of the catapult." This group decided to build a news report around the three musketeers and an evil King Hershey. This group incorporated many aspects of the traditional lab report into the final piece. After introducing the characters—the evil, chocolate-loving King Hershey; the tax-burdened villagers; and the three musketeers who assisted in killing the evil king—the students described how the catapult was made from "low-tech materials such as glue, giant popsicle sticks, and massive iron strings." The musketeers donated elastic bands, magnets, and gravity. The group described in detail how the catapult was constructed and how it was tested. They included a table and graph of the test results. In the end, the villagers lured the evil king into an abandoned castle with chocolate, which the musketeers catapulted with a "giant shower of rocks," and "the abandoned castle quickly fell apart."

In comparison, another group did not incorporate the science into a story. This group spent most class periods creating characters, such as Glueman and Popsicleman, from the in-class materials. Their final project had two distinct parts. The first part was a video of the student-generated characters helping a prince catapult his way into a castle where a princess was being held captive. There was no explicit direction on how to build or test a catapult. The second part was a traditional written lab report with sections on materials, methods, and data. This group failed to interpret the data both in the video and the traditional lab report.

Assessing the Success

In response to student feedback, we continue to consider these questions:

- How can a teacher encourage students to expand their thinking about catapults beyond the classroom activities?

- How do we help students articulate their ideas in writing?

- How do we help students clearly and accurately represent science in their stories?

Time was the biggest obstacle for students and for teachers. To help students with time organization in the future, we plan to provide checkpoints along the way to monitor progress. Either peers or teachers need to give feedback on a regular basis to students' first drafts, especially on how well they are incorporating the science information into their writing.

This project made us look more deeply at the issue of written communication in science, and the role of science teachers in helping students write more effectively. In their projects, many students successfully showed the science of catapults through creative, innovative, and imaginative writing. Students appreciated the opportunity to choose the format they used to show what they had learned in the unit. They were able to draw on the various talents of their group members to create the catapults. Students had opportunities for physical activity, creative expression, and positive social interaction with peers while working in their small groups on both the hands-on activity and the multigenre writing activity. Being able to resolve the catapult problem in their own way and to choose the genre for their reports gave students a sense of competence and achievement. Developing their science knowledge and writing skills through open-ended activities with clear limits allowed students to participate in the group activities in meaningful ways.

Students reported, "By using this approach, I actually learned that science is in almost everything, all the way from history to geography," and "The multigenre writing is funnier and not less work but it feels like it pays off more when you finish because it seems like you did more." Isn't this what every science teacher would like to hear her students say?

Acknowledgments

We thank Juan Cruz for sharing the Throwing Kisses assignment and the International Reading Association for an Elva Knight research grant to conduct the study.

Reference

Grierson, S. T., A. Anson, and J. Baird. 2002. Exploring the past through multigenre writing. *Language Arts* 80 (1): 51–59.

Internet Resources

Mangonel catapult
  www.mangonel.com
Trebuchet catapult
  www.trebuchet.com

Chapter 20
Lab Report Blues

By Andrew Diaz

For middle school students, writing a formal lab report can be challenging. For middle level teachers, reading students' lab reports can be overwhelming. After grading report after report with incomplete procedures, incorrect graphs, and missing conclusions, my frustration level was at an all-time high. I was ready to try anything.

Why not try peer editing? My hope was that by having students critique each other in a constructive, nonverbal manner, they would produce better lab reports. The peer-editing process took about a week and a half to complete (see Figure 1, p. 112).

First, I discussed with the class that they needed to improve their lab reports and gave them an outline of the peer-editing process. Each student wrote a problem statement, hypothesis, and procedure for the lab exploring how the angle of inclination of the Sun affects the temperature of an object. Students then performed the experiment, recorded their results, made a graph, and wrote their conclusions.

The students were each given a code name to keep the reports anonymous and prevent any bias in peer editing. The reports were collected and then redistributed to be graded and edited by a classmate using a rubric (Figure 2, p.113). I showed the students a sample lab and completed rubric using an overhead projector as I explained how to use the rubric as a grading tool. Keeping the labs organized was a challenge, as I had to keep track of the students' code names and who their peer editor was. As the labs were collected, I stapled the editor's rubric to the lab to prevent any of the sets of papers from getting mixed up. I graded the labs to ensure that the peer editors were accurate, and then returned them to the authors for revision. The editors received a grade on their rubric based on how closely their grade matched mine. I was quite pleased with the students' ability to accurately grade their classmates' labs. Many of the editors received an A for their accuracy and none received lower than a C. Once students made their revisions, they resubmitted the reports and then I graded them again.

How well did it work? While there was some improvement in the total average of the lab scores, there was significant improvement in the final copies. But there is more to the story: For many, it was the first time students actually used the rubric! I heard comments like "Oh, no! I didn't know we had to do that." In addition, they had a lot of questions about the content of the rubric, indicating that either they had never read it before or just never understood what they were supposed to do.

Figure 1. Anonymous peer-editing lab

Day 1
Step 1—Students develop a hypothesis and detailed procedure to solve a given problem.
Step 2—Procedures are checked by the teacher for safety.

Day 2
Step 3—Students perform lab according to their procedures. Results are recorded in an appropriate data table, observations are recorded.
Step 4—Students type up a second draft of their reports including the conclusion. Students make a graph using a computer or graph paper and ruler. (Students do not put their names on the reports! Each student receives a letter to put on the report instead of a name.) Due two days later.

Day 3
Step 5—Anonymous labs are collected by instructor then redistributed to the class for editing.
Step 6—Peer editors use rubric provided to edit and grade the labs.
Step 7—Teacher collects peer-edited labs and rubrics and checks the accuracy of the peer editing (peer editors will receive a grade based on their accuracy).

Day 4
Step 8—Students receive their original peer-edited lab back to make revisions for a final draft. Due two days later.

Day 5
Step 9—Final drafts are graded by teacher. Compare grades from this lab with the grades from previous labs for individual students and averages for groups of students.
Step 10—Survey students on the effectiveness of peer editing. Was it helpful and could it be improved?

Students recently completed another lab since this peer-editing experiment, and the majority of students referred to the rubric while writing up their labs! Prior to this, no matter how many times I would say it, most students did not use the rubric at all. This made all the difference, as the reports were vastly improved. They were more complete and had much better detail, with the conclusions showing the most improvement.

Overall, the peer-editing experiment has resulted in higher lab scores, and students are completing their labs with a lot less assistance from me. Best of all, students are using the rubric. After the peer-editing process, I surveyed the students and received excellent feedback—students loved having a second chance to improve their grade!

Figure 2. Lab report rubric

Name: _____   Date: _____

	Points possible	Peer	Teacher
Title	1	_____	_____
Problem			
In the form of a question	1	_____	_____
Variable(s) included (what is being tested/measured)	1	_____	_____
Hypothesis			
Written in the "if, then, because" format	1	_____	_____
Includes variable and measurable result	1	_____	_____
Related to the problem	1	_____	_____
Experimental design			
Materials are listed (quantity and sizes)	2	_____	_____
Procedure is written as a numbered list	2	_____	_____
Procedure is specific (reproducible)	3	_____	_____
Control is identified	1	_____	_____
Variable is identified	1	_____	_____
Constants are identified	1	_____	_____
Results (data table, graph, observations)			
Titles on all results	3	_____	_____
Table of all trial results included	2	_____	_____
Appropriate graph	1	_____	_____
Graph on graph paper or computer generated	2	_____	_____
Graph and table have specific labels and keys	3	_____	_____
Paragraph of detailed observations	1	_____	_____
Conclusion			
Conclusion is in paragraph form	1	_____	_____
Problem is restated	1	_____	_____
Hypothesis is summarized	1	_____	_____
Hypothesis was supported or rejected	1	_____	_____
The data—averages of trials are used to defend reasons of support or rejection	2	_____	_____
Factors or errors that may have affected the results	2	_____	_____
Patterns or trends	2	_____	_____
Answer to your problem is included	2	_____	_____
What your experiment taught you	2	_____	
Neatness	2	_____	_____
Total possible points	44		

Chapter 21

The Nature of Haiku

Students Use Haiku to Learn About the Natural World and Improve Their Observational Skills

By Peter Rillero, JoAnn V. Cleland, and Karen A. Conzelman

Would you like your students to learn about nature and improve their observational abilities? Incorporating haiku into your curriculum can help meet these science goals and give children a positive writing experience as they learn about the world around them. We have helped fourth- and seventh-grade students understand nature through writing haiku.

Haiku is a succinct form of writing that originated in Japan in the 17th century. It focuses on nature and requires keen observation. Many U.S. elementary teachers know about haiku and may even have their students write haiku. In our opinion, however, many teachers have seized on one feature of haiku—the five-seven-five syllable pattern of the three lines—as the only significant characteristic. This singular focus may obscure the beauty and power of describing nature with an economy of words.

There are two reasons why the five-seven-five syllable pattern should not be the emphasis in haiku writing. First, substance matters more than form. In haiku, the succinct description of nature is far more important than the number of syllables. Second, Japanese and English have different language structures. Use of the five-seven-five syllable pattern in English produces wordy haiku that diminish the intensity effected through conciseness (Higginson 1985). For these reasons, five-seven-five has ceased to be a fundamental criterion; haiku are best described as concisely written observations of nature.

Benefits of Haiku Writing

Haiku takes advantage of children's curiosity and interest in nature. The open-ended nature of haiku writing is motivational and student centered. Also, the simplicity of haiku allows children to have successful writing experiences.

At the same time, haiku writing advances many goals of elementary science education. Science and haiku both focus on the natural world, and looking more closely at nature helps students learn about nature. Their observations of nature may bring to mind previous learning, incite curiosity, encourage reading, or create interest in an upcoming lesson. Haiku is a vehicle for bringing children to observe and reflect on the natural world.

We believe observation is the most critical science process skill because other process skills are dependent on it. Haiku writing helps children develop this skill. Children learn to differentiate observation and inferences in some classrooms; however, with haiku, not only is there a reason to learn the difference but there also is an immediate application that reinforces learning.

Other skills important in science and life are developed through haiku. Figure 1 lists National Science Education Standards (NRC 1996) content standards that the haiku writing process meets. Students also learn concise writing, sequencing, and evaluation. In science publishing and haiku writing, communication with an economy of words is valued. To write effective haiku, children need to evaluate their observations, judge those that are most interesting, and sequence their observations in a logical order.

Figure 1. Haiku writing and the National Science Education Standards

Haiku assignments can advance the following *National Science Education Standards'* content standards. (Letters indicate content standards.)

As a result of activities in grades K–4, all students should develop abilities
- necessary to do scientific inquiry (A)
- to distinguish between natural objects and objects made by humans (E)

As a result of activities in grades K–4, all students should develop an understanding of
- properties of objects and materials (B)
- position and motion of objects (B)
- characteristics of organisms (C)
- life cycles of organisms (C)
- organisms and environments (C)
- properties of Earth materials (D)
- objects in the sky (D)
- changes in Earth and sky (D)
- types of resources (F)
- changes in environments (F)

Children Writing Haiku

Children seem to have an easier time writing haiku than many adults. Curious about the world, most children are eager to observe nature closely and describe what they have observed. Simple haiku are the most powerful, and children are neither confused by nor afraid of this simplicity. Nevertheless, a methodical approach to teaching about haiku can facilitate haiku-writing experiences and help students develop keen observation skills. After reading haiku to children and helping them recognize the common features, we recommend the following seven-step approach to help children write haiku.

1. Stay with observations. Three key things to remember in writing haiku are observation, observation, and observation. The power of haiku comes from careful observation and artful reporting of these observations in each line. The following tips may help children stay with their observations.

Children should differentiate observations and inferences. People gain information about an object, a scene, or an event through their senses. These are observations. Inferences are statements that seek to explain observations. A girl observes a deer running. She infers that the deer is afraid. Haiku stays with the observations.

In most forms of writing (including haiku), it is better to show rather than tell. Authors usually do not write "It is a scary night"; instead, they describe aspects of the night—it is dark, the wind howls, a cat shrieks—so readers feel the frightening scene. A child may look at a flower and be tempted to write "It was beautiful" or "I feel wonderful." In haiku, however, he or she should describe the flower so readers can experience its beauty and their own sense of wonder.

Some types of writing value flowery metaphors such as "The path unfolded ahead like a garter snake moving through grass." Although this might help the reader visualize aspects of what the writer observes, it also puts a picture of a snake in the grass in the reader's mind. Haiku, on the other hand, describes a single scene in nature. Because metaphors transport readers to different scenes, they are a distraction to avoid.

Another lure when observing is the use of personification—giving human characteristics and feelings to nonhuman organisms or objects. The "sad, wilting plant" and "happy, singing birds" are examples of personification. The tendency to personify is powerful—children often overgeneralize their experiences of the world to other living things. Personification should and can be avoided by reminding students to stay with their observations.

2. Setting in nature. Interesting haiku come from interesting observations. Taking children to places where they can make interesting observations improves haiku writing. These places can be on or off school grounds; however, trips to exotic places, such as rain forests, are not required for children to discover fascinating intricacies of nature. The beauty of haiku writing is its ability to help children observe the ordinary and see extraordinary things.

As children are increasingly surrounded by the world of people, we believe it is important to move their observations to nature. Providing a few examples of the natural world along with things that don't belong to the natural world is a quick method to encourage children to discover fascinating details in nature.

3. Observation lists. In a natural setting, students can work in pairs and record observations. The observations should not be limited to vision—smells, sounds, and textures can produce wonderful haiku. For safety reasons, the sense of taste should not be used.

When children write their observations, it is best to use present rather than past tense. For example, there is more immediacy to "the grasshopper jumps" than "the grasshopper jumped." The writer should also focus on one entity, which could be as narrow as a flower or as wide as a landscape.

Having students remain quiet prevents chatter from interfering with observing. In pairs, one partner can quietly point out things that he or she finds interesting. The first time children are taken to a place in nature, they may need other prompts to look purposefully—they may have never been asked to just take a close look. With multiple opportunities, however, they gradually feel comfortable observing intently, and then the writing flows.

It is acceptable to have children write in sentence fragments. This helps them write observations faster, and these sentence fragments are easily incorporated into haiku. In as few as 15 minutes, children can produce a good list of observations.

4. Interesting observations. The process so far has been somewhat like brainstorming—getting as many ideas as possible—but at this point, the writers must select the most interesting observation from their lists. We find it helpful to ask each writer to get input from other children. The ultimate evaluation of interest, however, is up to the writer.

5. Three lines. The third line of a haiku should contain the most interest; it should amaze, startle, or make the reader think—but it should be an observation. This helps ensure that the poem builds to a powerful, observation-based ending. Using a sheet of paper with three dark lines, children should

- write their most interesting observation on the third line,
- look at their observation lists and find two observations that build toward the third, and
- write these observations on the first and second lines.

6. Conciseness. The power of haiku flows from an economy of words. Unnecessary words, such as articles, can be deleted. Items unrelated to the central focus can be eliminated. Notice how three observations are stripped down in the following example.

~~The~~ Monarch butterfly
~~It~~ flutters to a soft stop ~~on a thin branch~~
~~It~~ closes its ~~orange and black~~ wings.

Some words are removed because they do not contribute. The writer feels that the most interesting observation is that the butterfly closes its wings when it rests. Observations that don't contribute to this are removed. The goal is to produce three short lines—the first with five syllables or fewer, the second with seven syllables or fewer, and the third with five syllables or fewer.

7. Rewrite. The final step is to rewrite the lines without the crossed-out words. Here, editing can take place. Because the third line is the most powerful, the reader pauses after the second line to set up the third line. Thus, punctuation is often included after the second line to indicate a pause.

Monarch butterfly
flutters to a soft stop;
and closes its wings.

It is up to the writer if the haiku will have a title. In most cases, haiku do not have titles.

At this stage, teachers should acknowledge the accomplishment of writing haiku. Teachers praise the work of the writers, and the haiku can be shared with the class.

Haiku Assignments

After their first successful haiku experiences, children are ready for more. For example, an assignment to write five haiku in a two-week period can help them develop their observation and writing skills and learn more about the natural world. In any long-term assignment, it is generally a good idea for the teacher to check students' progress along the way. This helps children pace themselves and avoids a wait-to-the-end-rush-to-completion work habit. It also allows the teacher to make sure children are on the correct path. Thus, the teacher may decide to have children submit two haiku every few days.

It is hard to know when an exciting observation of nature will happen. Sudden thunderstorms, a mouse running into a hole, and a bird catching a worm are all interesting events. Haiku are usually most powerful when the observations are written immediately rather than from memories; thus, in our haiku assignments, we require the observations to be current, not memories. We also encourage students to carry haiku notebooks with them so they can capture scenes in nature as they happen. Oftentimes, having the notebook is like having a camera; it helps writers observe nature in new ways.

Student Perspectives

Surveys and interviews revealed children's perspectives of haiku. On the written survey, the most common benefits volunteered were ones related to observing, understanding, and appreciating nature. One fourth-grade girl wrote, "Well, you get to look at nature in a different way. It is different than looking out your window. You look at it for a long time and you just get a picture in your head of … and it is so cool."

This benefit is revealed in the detail students report when asked for an interesting observation they made while writing haiku:

"Well, I saw a little ant with fur on it. It had red fur on it. It was like somebody had stuck fur on it and dyed it red." (fourth-grade boy)

■ "I looked at a seashell and it was pretty dull and then I found something about [it] and I wrote all about [it] and it turned out to be good. … The inside and the smoothness and the roughness on some parts." (fourth-grade girl)

These descriptions suggest that haiku helped children notice nature's exquisite details. Objects of nature that might have been stepped over or cast aside quickly became subjects of careful observation and recording in the context of composing haiku.

Extensions

A natural extension to this Japanese style of poetry is the incorporation of graphics. Children can enhance their work with black, brushstroke drawings created with paintbrushes or computer-drawing programs. These simple visual representations are a good match to poems that emphasize economy of words to convey highly focused ideas.

Frequently, children suggest writing their haiku in calligraphy or with a computer font that emulates calligraphy. Jotted notes can be transformed into pages children are eager to display. The natural result can be the creation of a class book. What pride children feel when sharing their collaborative project with family, peers, and the school library!

It's Only Natural

In the elementary years, firsthand experiences should incite children's curiosity and be a starting point for learning about nature. Haiku writing is an effective way to achieve these goals. In the haiku-writing process, children observe, choose an object of interest, record, and observe more. They then reflect and write about nature. As you read their haiku, you will have the wonderful experience of seeing nature through the eyes of children.

The authors would like to thank Linda Thompson and Patty Weikart and their fourth-grade students at Orangewood Elementary School in Phoenix, Arizona, for their work on this project.

Children's Haiku

The flavor of haiku from children is best revealed through these samples from fourth-grade students.

A small spider weaves
in and out he makes his web
it shines in the sun.

Roses are blooming.
The dew is starting to drip
as the sun rises.

Curly seed pods grow.
They fall to the ground and wilt
and make room for more.

Multiple flowers,
sway with gentle wind.
Violet hyacinth.

Spider looks at prey
a few seconds before death.
The spider ends life.

Birds high in the sky
glide down and have a good feast
on the mesquite pods.

References

Higginson, W. J. 1985. *Haiku handbook: How to write, share, and teach haiku.* New York: McGraw-Hill.

National Research Council. (1996). *National science education standards.* Washington, DC: National Academies Press.

Resources

Atwood, A. 1977. *Haiku-vision.* New York: Charles Scribner's Sons.

Atwood, A. 1973. *My own rhythm: An approach to haiku.* New York: Charles Scribner's Sons.

Behn, H. 1964. *Cricket songs.* New York: Harcourt, Brace & World.

Behn, H. 1971. *More cricket songs.* New York: Harcourt, Brace, Jovanovich.

Clidas, J. 1996. Personal plot journal. *Science and Children* 34 (1): 22–25.

Fowler, B. 1997. Take a leaf from our book. *Science and Children* 34 (6): 18–19, 51.

Glatfelter, P. M. 1997. Making observations from the ground up. *Science and Children* 34 (8): 28–30.

Gustafson, J. 1991. A poetry nature trail. *Nature Study* 44 (4): 4–5.

Hamill, S. 1995. *The sound of water.* Boston: Shambhala.

Huevel, C. 1974. *The haiku anthology.* Garden City, NY: Anchor Books.

Painter, A. 1988. *A coyote in the garden.* Lewiston, ID: Confluence Press.

Rillero, P. 1999. Haiku and science: Observing, reflecting, and writing about nature. *Journal of College Science Teaching* 27 (5): 345–347.

Rosenthal, V. 1987. Haiku: The process of creation. *Journal of Poetry Therapy* 1 (1): 31 37.

Ross, B. 1993. *Haiku moment: An anthology of contemporary North American haiku.* Boston: Charles E. Tuttle.

Shannon, G. 1996. *Spring: A haiku story.* New York: Greenwillow.

Strickland, D., and M. Strickland. 1997. Language and literacy: The poetry connection. *Language Arts* 74 (3): 201–205.

Internet Resource

History of Haiku, by Ryu Yotsuya
   www.big.or.jp/~loupe/links/ehisto/ehisinx.shtml

Chapter 22

Keeping Science Current

By Barbara Timmerman

It does not take long for new teachers to realize that their textbooks are 1, 5, or even 10 years old. As soon as a textbook is printed, it often contains information that is obsolete or in need of revision. I remember that my college geology textbook spent one paragraph on the new theory of plate tectonics. Today, the theory of plate tectonics is integral to the understanding of Earth dynamics.

You can use current events to bridge the gap between book knowledge and real-world science. Science is not static, and students benefit from interacting with science as it is happening, even if their involvement is indirect. When students are able to explore science topics that interest them—such as a drug, health condition, or some other phenomenon that they or a family member have experienced—they see that science can be personally relevant and applicable to real-world situations. Through current events, you can lead students to examine various societal issues (such as cloning) that will affect their decision-making abilities, quality of life, and impact on society.

At the beginning of each school year, I present a yearlong activity in which each student keeps a current events journal. Every week, each student chooses one science article from a daily or weekly newspaper or magazine. After students read their articles, I ask them to

1. highlight important information from the article,

2. attach it to the current events journal,

3. summarize the article's salient points in writing,

4. write an additional paragraph about why they chose the article and how it is important to them or to society, and

5. circle five unfamiliar words and define them (the words need not be scientific—the purpose is to expand each student's vocabulary).

Before beginning the activity, I distribute the activity sheet on page 124 and discuss it with the class. I ask each student to get a parent or guardian to read and sign the form. Additionally, I encourage the adults to work with their children and to call me if they need more information.

Figure 1. Current events journal activity sheet

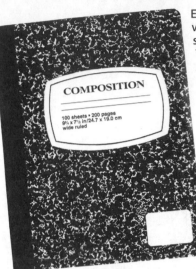

Each week, choose a science article from a daily or weekly newspaper or magazine (online or printed), such as the *New York Times, Newsweek, Newsday, TIME Magazine, U.S. News* and *World Report,* and *Science News.* You may choose any science topic, but you must get your teacher's approval to use any publication not listed above.

Using a bound notebook, create a current events journal according to the following guidelines:

1. Write your name and science period on the first page (the cover page).
2. On the next page, start a table of contents, which lists the name of each article in the order it appears in your journal.
3. Each week, attach your article to its own journal page and record the source and the date of publication.
4. On the back page of that page, write a summary paragraph, in your own words, about the article's content and its main points.
5. Beneath the summary, write a sentence or two discussing why you chose the article and how it is important to you or to society.
6. Find five words in the article that are unfamiliar to you and define them.

At the end of each marking period, your teacher will collect your current events journal and grade it for completeness and organization using the following rubric:

Grade	Number of requirements missing
10	none (journal is complete)
9	one
8	two
7	three
6	four

If your grade is less than 6, your teacher will send home a letter asking your parents or guardians to help you complete your current events journal each week.

You will receive additional points for presenting your article to the class. You may receive extra points for completing more than the required number of journal articles.

Parent/Guardian please review and discuss this assignment with your child, sign the line below, and attach this sheet to the back of your child's current events journal.

Thank you for your support.

Parent/Guardian's signature _____ Date _____

For the first several weeks, I check the journals to ensure that students are following instructions and keeping their entries up to date. I also reward students for presenting their articles to the rest of the class. (Students who feel uncomfortable presenting to a group may present to me alone or to a small group of friends—this generates the self-confidence needed to stand before larger groups.) Depending on the topic, presentations often generate questions, discussions, and lively debates. Students learn to listen to the opinions of others without making value judgments. Although I do not require student presentations, by the end of the year, nearly all of my students opt to present.

At the end of each marking period, students hand in their journals for grading. I assess each journal using the rubric on the activity sheet.

At the end of the year, students write an essay describing the one or two science topics that they found to be most important, enjoyable, interesting, or meaningful. Some students choose to write about the article they found least enjoyable. Nevertheless, the point of view taken is less important than the progress in self-expression and critical thinking that students achieve as they read about current events.

The current events journal activity also has been successful with my inclusion students and students with learning disabilities. I help them choose articles that are appropriate for their level, which eliminates frustration, and students feel that they are equal members of the class.

In summary, keeping a current events journal is a valuable activity because

- students choose topics that they feel are important,
- the information updates textbooks,
- students improve their reading and writing skills,
- students improve techniques for determining what information is important in a reading assignment
- students increase their vocabulary, and
- students develop their communication skills by sharing their articles and opinions.

Ask your students to keep a journal and help keep your classroom current.

Months before the project begins, students review the best practices for implementing scientific investigation strategies. For example, doing research prior to beginning an investigation, making sure data collected from an investigation is quantifiable, conducting multiple trials, and articulating the science outcomes are all important factors (Sumrall and Schillinger 2004). Students obtain their own data using either an observation inquiry assignment or an experimental inquiry assignment (Sumrall and Halpin 2000). Figure 2 (p. 130) shows two assignments that students can do to gather ample data for reporting. Students should be trained in the processes of investigation prior to beginning the development of the newspaper.

Day One

Arrange for the class to take a tour of a newspaper office and interview a reporter to learn how to develop a topic when writing, but prior to visiting the newspaper, give students newspapers to explore. In pairs, students look through the newspapers and gather information about writing style, photograph format, local and national news, and layout format. After 15 minutes, allow students to discuss what they discovered in the newspapers. Students the write results on a transparency to share with the class. Topics such as bird flu, baseball, high gas prices, and comics are often mentioned. Student pairs then generate two questions they want to ask the reporter when they visit the newspaper.

Day Two

After touring the newspaper and interviewing the reporter, students begin training on the writing process (Graves 1990). (It is recommended that teachers in a departmentalized setting work with language arts teachers on the understanding of the writing process.) In pairs, students pretend they are newspaper science reporters who are going to report on the newest trends in science. Like good reporters, students should demonstrate excellent writing skills, so they study the steps in the writing process—prewriting, drafting, revising, editing, publishing, and sharing—in conjunction with creating the scientific newspaper.

Begin with the prewriting step. In this step, students research, use their imaginations, or use prior knowledge or experiences to decide what they want to write about. Students brainstorm ideas they want to research and include in the scientific newspaper. Figure 3 (p. 131) can be used to assist students in topic choices. Local issues such as recycling programs, water treatment, and electricity production should be considered. Then, students write down several ideas that interest them. Some suggestions are given to students, such as weather, inventions, interviewing a scientist, and so on. Students can also review science journals, books, and the internet for ideas. A great resource, with a list of teacher-approved and safe websites to use, is *www.kids.gov*.

In addition to investigating science topics, students begin to create a report that relates to their own investigations. Merging spreadsheets into their word-processed documents is one of many tasks that a teacher will need to facilitate in the development of a data-driven article. Including correct units and awareness of significant figures are other possible data-reporting concerns that a teacher should be ready to address when students are preparing the newspaper.

Figure 1. Science newspaper task sheet

Teacher informs the class that data and results from classroom investigations, including inquiry and experimental inquiry, will be incorporated into the newspaper assignment.

Review various scientific investigation strategies.

Day 1

Look through newspapers to gather information on writing style, layout format, news information.

Come up with two questions to ask the reporter.

Take tour of newspaper office.

Interview reporter.

Day 2

Review the writing process.

Begin writing process

- Prewrite.
- Brainstorm ideas to write about.
- Review science journals, books and internet for ideas.

Divide into groups of four or five.

Discuss and choose two topics to write about. (Research, Interview Scientist/Engineer, Investigate science or engineering careers)

Choose a graphic organizer that best depicts the concept. (Use *www.eduplace.com* or *www.enchantedlearning.com*)

Day 3

Drafting

- Review the guidelines for the article.
- Review inverted-pyramid writing technique.

Day 4

Revising

- Read what your peers have written.
- Refer back to their data to clarify the information.
- Replace overused or unclear words.
- Add or take out parts.
- Conference with peers to receive feedback.
- Ask yourself several questions (Figure 5, p. 132).

Day 5

Editing

- Switch copies of article with another group.
- Read copy of other group's article and look at punctuation, spelling, grammar, sentence structure, subject/verb agreement, consistent verb tense, and word usage.

Day 6

Sharing (teacher tasks)

- E-mail newspaper to students.
- Upload newspaper to teacher's personal website.
- Print out limited number of newspapers for each classroom.

Figure 2. Inquiry assignments

Observation

1. Develop and implement a science observation activity.
2. The instructor must approve your plan of observation before you begin.
3. All group members should be involved in data collection.
4. Each student must spend at least one hour making observations.
5. Do not manipulate what your group observes.
6. Do some counting or measuring, so that the data can be graphed.
7. Graph your results and explain in your graphic organizer why you chose a certain graph.

Experiment

1. Develop and implement an experiment. Group members do not have to perform the experiment together. However, like scientists, compare results and data to see if your group members' results are similar. Similar results from group members makes it easier to see if your hypothesis is or is not supported by evidence.
2. Designate dependent, independent, and control variables.
3. Present a hypothesis, collected data, graphed data, and a conclusion.
4. Turn in one data sheet from each member of the group.
5. Make your experiment different from experiments conducted in class.
6. Photograph your activities during the experiment.
7. Describe in your graphic organizer how you might improve your experimental process, how you might develop another experiment based on this experiment's results, and why you selected a particular type of graph.

Students are divided into cooperative learning groups of four or five. The groups then decide upon several topics and discuss them. Then, each group decides on their top two topics, in case their first choice has already been chosen. During the prewriting step, students also choose a graphic organizer that best depicts their concept. Students are shown websites such as *www.eduplace.com* and *www.enchantedlearning.com* so they can see different examples of graphic organizers to help them with their decision. Students use concept maps, cluster maps, spider maps, and Venn diagrams to map out the information they retrieved on their topic. Groups are given the option of producing graphic representations by hand or by computer.

Day Three

Now that students have their topics, groups, and graphic organizers, it is time for them to begin their first rough drafts. This step is called the *drafting* step. Explanations of the importance of this step, along with comments from the newspaper reporter about how not even the best writer uses his or her first draft, are discussed. Groups are reminded not to pay attention to mechanics in this step. I provide guidelines for the article, which include the following: name, class, and date on top right-hand corner of all pages; page numbering; pages stapled at the top left-hand corner; double-spaced pages; and use of pencil, pen, or computer.

Figure 3. Newspaper content ideas

Science/ engineering careers	Science events	Scientist interview (possible questions)	Recent scientific discovery in
Chemical	Volcano eruption	How do you become a scientist?	Botany
Aeronautical	Tsunami	Who influenced your career?	Zoology
Mechanical	Earthquake	What education did you receive?	Astronomy
Civil	Hurricane	What skills do I need to do your job?	Chemistry
Electrical	Tornado	Who was the most influential person in your life?	Physics
Genetic	Comet	Who do you communicate with in your job?	Engineering
Environmental engineer	Local recycling program	What made you choose this career?	Environmental Science
Biological	Local electricity program	Who is your favorite scientist and why?	Paleontology

Before students begin, they discuss how newspaper articles are written by using the inverted-pyramid writing technique (see Figure 4). An illustration on the board is used to demonstrate how newspaper articles are written, beginning with the most newsworthy information and continuing on to the least newsworthy information. Starting with the most interesting bits of information hooks readers into reading the rest of the article. Students are told not to worry about revising and editing at this stage.

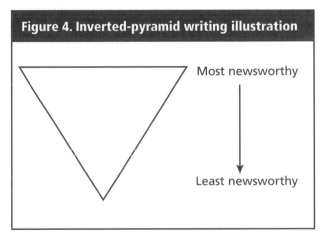

Figure 4. Inverted-pyramid writing illustration

Most newsworthy

Least newsworthy

Day Four

After completing their rough drafts, students move to the next step, *revising*. During this step, students read what they have written and refer back to their data to clarify information, replace overused or unclear words, and add or take out parts if needed. Students conference with peers, who make suggestions as to how to improve the writing (evaluate the arrangement of the sentences, examine repetitiveness and clarity in the wording) and whether the graph is beneficial to the reader. While reading the articles, students should ask themselves several questions (see Figure 5). The questions in Figure 5 relate to the articles students develop that

---

Figure 5. Checklist

- Does the article flow when read out loud? (ST/IA)

- Are descriptive words used to describe the experiment or demonstration? (IA)

- Does the article stay on the topic? (ST)

- Does your first sentence hook the reader into the article? (ST/IA)

- Are transitional devices used throughout? (ST/IA)

- Does your article follow the inverted-pyramid writing format? (ST/IA)

- Are all sentences complete or are there sentence fragments? (ST/IA)

- Is a vivid mental picture created in the reader's mind? (ST/IA)

- Do you repeat words unnecessarily? (ST/IA)

- Does the article have accurate graphical representation? (ST/IA)

- Does the article have inquiry procedures for conducting good, thorough experiments? (ST/IA)

IA= Inquiry Assignments (Figure 2, p. 130)
ST= Science Topics (Figure 3, p. 131)

---

are based on either data they collected through hands-on inquiry assignments (Figure 2, p. 130) or science topics chosen from Figure 3 (p. 131).

Days Five and Six

The next day, students give copies of their articles to the other groups, for the *editing* step. Group 1 gives each member of group 2 a copy of its article, and group 2 does the same for group 3, and so on. Students review "Everybody's a Critic" and the "Peer Editing Guide" for editing tips (*www.tnellen.com/cybereng/peer.html,* and *www.lawsoflife.org/pdf/teachersguidenew/ Peer%20Edit%20Pg23.pdf*). Students give and receive constructive criticism and help with spelling, capitalization, punctuation, grammar, sentence structure, subject/verb agreement, consistent verb tense, and word usage.

Days Seven and Eight

After the groups have reviewed and edited each article, students' papers are returned so they can make minor changes prior to final publication. If available, students use the classroom computer and printer to publish their newspaper using a trifold template. Microsoft Publisher is an example of a software program with this capability. However, newspapers can be sent via file attachments or uploaded to the classroom teacher's website. A limited number of hard copies could be distributed (e.g., principal's office and school bulletin board).

Conclusion

The goal is for students to publish two newspapers every nine weeks. This activity is advantageous for students because the science and language arts content they learn is hands-on and relevant. Students' investigations around recent topics and inquiry assignments are invaluable learning experiences. Through these activities, students are able to attain a true understanding of the nature of science. Furthermore, through students' scientific investigations and interviews with scientists that are published in the newspaper, they address the National Science Education Standard (NRC 1996) that relates to science as a human endeavor.

References

Anderson, A., J. Hattie, and R. J. Hamilton. 2005. Locus of control, self-efficacy, and motivation in different schools: Is moderation the key to success? *Educational Psychology* 25 (5): 517–535.

Graves, D. 1990. The process-writing model. Paper presented at OKTAWL Conference, Norman, Oklahoma.

National Research Council (NRC). 1996. *National science education standards.* Washington, DC: National Academies Press.

Sumrall, W., and R. Halpin. 2000. Integration and presentation. *Science Scope* 24 (1): 68–71.

Sumrall, W., and D. Schillinger. 2004. Non-traditional characteristics of a successful science fair project. *Science Scope* 27 (6): 20–24.

Chapter 24
Science Newsletters
By Melissa Nail

Having students write and publish their own newsletters is a great way to integrate reading and writing, infuse technology, and build home-school relationships. These newsletters can be used to keep parents informed about what is being taught in class, important test dates, homework and project due dates, and any other information you would like to share. Involving students in the creation of the newsletters increases their feeling of ownership and reduces the chances that the newsletter will end up in a wastebasket or forgotten in a locker.

Getting Started

My students write their articles using Microsoft Word and lay out the newsletter using Microsoft Publisher. Publisher, which is included in the Microsoft Office suite of programs, is helpful because it provides a Newsletter Wizard tool that walks students through the steps of setting up a newsletter. All you really need, however, is some kind of word processing software. Today's software allows you to set up columns, place text, import images, and change the type and size of fonts to create a very attractive newsletter. Your students probably are already familiar with how to set up and use word processing software, but you should allow time for a review of the basics. Before they can create their newsletters, students will need to know how to open, edit, and save documents within the word processing program. They will also need to know how to copy and paste text and place graphics in their documents.

Putting It All Together

Once students are familiar with the software, the focus can turn to the content. To get things started, I ask students to brainstorm topics for articles. If they need some guidance, I suggest a few topics, such as explanations of content studied in class, reports on class activities, or summaries of experiments. Topics also can include reminders about upcoming holidays and school closings; reports on new equipment, animals, or other resources in the classroom; and news about the science club, field trips, or after-school events. I contribute a piece to each newsletter called "Teacher's Corner." I distribute it electronically, and each group incorporates the column into its newsletter. I use this column to communicate with parents regarding dates of exams, topics for home study, requests for parent speakers or presenters, and suggestions of ways parents can participate in their child's education.

The internet is the primary source of graphics used to accompany the articles, but students can also create their own figures and illustrations using drawing tools included with the word processing software or other programs. Inexpensive collections of images on a disk can also be found at your local computer or electronics store. If a scanner is available, students can also scan in images they have drawn freehand or found in books or magazines. When a particularly good graphic related to a topic is identified or created, such as a student's illustration of a plant cell drawn using Paint, students are encouraged to share it with the other groups.

There are a number of options available to classroom teachers for putting together the student-created newsletters. If wireless laptops are available in the school, the teacher can simply check out the laptop cart for this project. If the school has a computer lab, the classroom teacher can schedule the lab for the creation of the newsletters. The newsletters can also be created in classrooms with only one or two computers available. This option might require more planning and time because the students would have to alternate and rotate use of the available computers, with only one group at a time publishing a newsletter while other class members work on other exercises. Some schools now have classroom sets of PDAs that teachers can check out and use. If this is the case, students could use the PDAs to individually input their articles using a program such as Word to Go, transfer the articles to a desktop computer with HotSync, and quickly and easily insert the individual articles into their group's newsletter. Some teachers may also wish to collaborate with colleagues within the school so that the students are writing the articles during a language arts lesson and putting together the newsletters during a technology or computer lesson.

Figure 1. Sample student newsletter

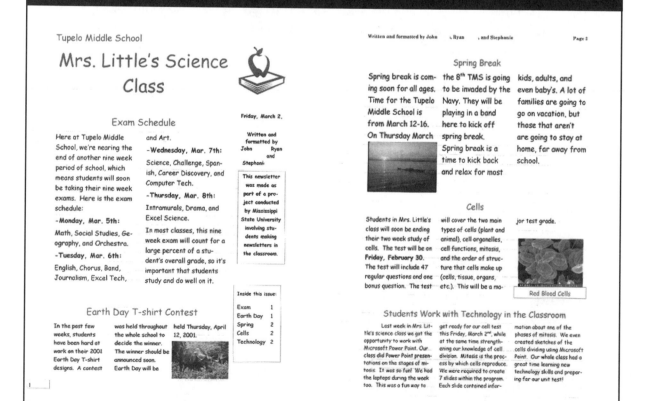

In most cases, a cooperative team of students can create a two-page newsletter in only three class sessions (Figure 1). One session is used for brainstorming, planning, and initial prewriting activities. The second session is used for writing and editing articles, and the third session is used for final editing and inserting the articles into a newsletter template. The most time-consuming part of the process seems to be finding appropriate graphics. Selecting one member of each team to be responsible for illustrations or compiling a shared library of appropriate illustrations seems to be a beneficial strategy for speeding up the production process. Another time-saver (especially as students are initially learning to produce their own newsletters) is for the teacher to either create or designate a particular newsletter template to be used.

Each group's newsletter is printed on the school's printer and duplicated on the school copier to make a copy for each member of the group. Unfortunately, our budget does not allow for each student to get a color copy of the newsletter. However, students can take the original file home on a disc and print their own color copies if they have access to the necessary software and hardware. The file can also be e-mailed home for students and parents to view in color onscreen. Many students will have their own personal e-mail addresses you can use. Permission should be obtained in advance, however, before you collect and use any parent's e-mail address. Before making copies of the newsletter for distribution, I review the content of each one. This usually takes me about a day.

Final Page

The student newsletter project proves to be very successful. Students are actively involved in the publication of the newsletters, displaying more excitement for writing articles than they had ever demonstrated for merely writing reports on topics studied. When the finished newsletters are distributed each quarter, students receive them excitedly. They show off their finished products to classmates, then carefully put the newsletters in folders and book bags to take home and share with their families.

Chapter 25

Scientific Journals
A Creative Assessment Tool

By Larissa Beckstead

"In this investigation, I discovered that the ecosystem is more than just a bush. It is a life cycle … ," reported one of my students in his article for the class science journal. That issue of *Beckstead Heights' Science Journal* contained articles about the bush outside our classroom. The conclusion the student drew was from three months of observing the bush and recording data in his science notebook. By creating a science journal, my students are able to publish their findings like a real scientist while practicing writing skills, and I am able to assess their science and literacy learning.

Science notebooks are typically used for students to record information as they complete an investigation, writing down their procedure, observations, data, results, graphs, and any other factual information pertaining to their experiment. Our class did the same, but I incorporated specific writing assignments to prepare students to publish articles about their science investigations in a class science journal. During that school year, we published eight science journals, all based on investigations or special projects the students completed. In this article, I describe how I integrated language arts and science throughout the school year.

Essays

Having my students create science journals doesn't happen during the first week of school. The students need to have data and other information recorded in their science notebooks to be able to create science journals. A good place to start is our rocks and minerals unit. During this unit, students observe different types of rocks; do different tests on the rocks; go on a rock hunt; and make igneous, sedimentary, and metamorphic rock models from food. All observations are recorded in their science notebooks.

But we are still not ready to create the journal. Not only does the science have to be taught, but certain writing and grammar skills also have to be taught and developed before students write articles, stories, or poems for a science journal.

I do not introduce the science journal until a few months into the school year. This is after I have taught the first three essays in the book *10 Easy Writing Lessons That Get Kids Ready for Writing Assessments* by Mary Rose (1999). This book provides a teacher with well-structured lessons that teach students how to write a five-paragraph essay. Narrative, expository, and persuasive writing lessons are outlined in the book.

I also have students develop their vocabulary. I give them a list of words that they may not use in their writing, such as *good, nice, fun,* and *cool*. They must use a dictionary or thesaurus to find synonyms to use instead.

The final piece to the writing puzzle that helps develop students' grammar skills (subordinate clauses, correct use of adverbs and conjunctions, and paragraph structure) is *Elementary, My Dear! Caught 'Ya! Grammar With a Giggle for Grades One, Two, and Three* by Jane Bell Kiester (2003). (Kiester has also developed *Grammar With a Giggle* books for grades 4–12.) This is a daily oral language practice that has students adding a sentence to the story each day. All of these tools help students be successful when they begin writing articles for our class science journal.

I am now ready to introduce the first article that students will write for our science journal. This article is about the three types of rocks told from a rock's point of view (Figure 1). Its structure is similar to one of the essays from the writing book, which allows students success in their first attempt in scientific writing. In this first science journal writing, I provide students with most of the first paragraph and the last paragraph. They will fill in the blanks with information they want to include in those paragraphs. The second, third, and fourth paragraphs are each about a different type of rock. This is where students will use the information they have recorded in their science notebooks. I tell my students that if they wrote an interesting sentence in their notebook about igneous rocks, for example, they are allowed to copy that sentence because it is their original work. I also allow students to use different science books that were read during the unit of study to help them with their writing.

Figure 1. Rock essays example

Rock Tale
By
Alexa

Splash! Splash! That's the sound of me jumping on top of the water because I am being thrown by children. What am I? I'm a rock. There are three types of rocks: igneous rocks, sedimentary rocks, and metamorphic rocks. I am here to tell you all about them.

Igneous rocks are formed from magma and lava. When the magma and lava are hardening it has an odoriferous smell. When it cools and hardens it forms into an igneous rock. Igneous rocks are rough. Obsidian is an example of an igneous rock.

Sedimentary rocks are constructed by layers of sediment. Sedimentary rocks are located in the Grand Canyon. An example of a sedimentary rock is sandstone.

Metamorphic rocks are constructed by heat and pressure. The metamorphic rocks are made under the ground. An example of a metamorphic rock is a rock named slate. Some rocks are shiny and smooth.

Which type of rock am I? I will give you two clues. I'm one of the three types of rocks. I look like an igneous rock but I am not an igneous rock or a metamorphic rock. I have sparkles on me. What am I?

Along with providing the structure of this first science journal writing, I give students a rubric of what is to be included in the essay (Figure 2). I also include in the rubric the writing strategies I will be grading so students are sure to include those strategies in their writing.

Do I provide this kind of structure for every other science journal article? It really depends on the students. For most of the class, once I have taught a format that can be used when writing an article for our science journals, I only provide some basic structure. I give them the topic of each paragraph, but I don't tell them what should be written in the paragraph. After having written the first essay and using their science notebooks to retrieve information, most students are able to do the process on their own. Some students do require more guidance than just being told the topic of each paragraph. For these students I provide the same kind of help that I did on the first essay. These students receive a more detailed rubric to guide them during the writing of the article. I also provide more one-on-one instruction for these students.

This allows all students to write each science journal article successfully.

Once students complete the article, I make multiple copies of each article so students have a full copy of our class's science journal to take home to share with their family. Students also read their article aloud to the class, which is enjoyable for everyone.

Letters

I have students write their first letter after we complete the volcano investigation in our unit on the changing Earth. In this investigation, students simulate volcanic eruptions with baking soda and vinegar, but I add a twist. After making clear that our classroom eruption is caused by a chemical reaction and is therefore not an accurate model of a volcano, students use colored modeling clay to cover the areas where the "lava" flowed. Students repeat these steps three more times. Each time, they use a different color of clay. Students then use a clear straw to take a core sampling off the side of their volcano to see the different layers of "rock." This investigation shows one way that mountains can be formed.

After completing a volcano investigation, reading books about layers of the Earth, and designing a model of the layers of the Earth, students write a letter to someone as if they are volcanologists who have been studying the volcano on the island of Hawaii (Figure 3, p. 142). Before letting students write their letters, I do three things. First, we review how to write a personal letter. I write a sample letter on the board so students have a model of a letter to help them during the letter-writing process. Second, I have the class brainstorm words they can use to explain what happens during a volcanic eruption, such as *rumble, splash, bubble,* or *spill.* I leave the list up for students to use during the letter-writing process. Finally, I review the science concepts we covered in the unit. Magma is liquid rock located under the Earth's surface. When the magma erupts out of the volcano, it is called *lava.* Lava cools and hardens into igneous rock. Then I tell students that I expect to see those concepts in their letters, and I again provide a rubric to remind them of these expectations.

After the reviewing and word brainstorming has been done, I have students select the recipients of their letters. Many students like to write to their former teacher. If they do, I make sure to make a copy of the letter for that teacher to read.

Figure 2. Rock essay rubric

Paragraph One
Four sentences 5 points_____
Onomatopoeia 5 points_____

Paragraph Two
Igneous rock 2 points_____
How is it formed? 5 points_____
Give an example of an igneous rock. 2 points_____

Paragraph Three
Sedimentary rock 2 points_____
How is it formed? 5 points_____
Give an example of a sedimentary rock. 2 points_____

Paragraph Four
Metamorphic rock 2 points_____
How is it formed? 10 points_____
Give an example of a metamorphic rock. 2 points_____

Paragraph Five
Two clues about which kind of rock is narrating the essay 5 points_____
Ends with a question 5 points_____

Sentence fluency 10 points_____
Word choice 10 points_____
Organization 10 points_____
Presentation 18 points_____
Total points 100 points_____

Grade_____

Again, the science notebook plays an important part in the students' writing. The information they gather during the volcano investigation helps them write interesting details in the body of their letter. Students also find that the books we read help them provide accurate information about a volcanic eruption.

Figure 3. Volcano letter sample

September 27, 2006

Dear Mr. Palamores,

I have been studying an active volcano located on the "big island" of Hawaii. The magma was bubbling for a long time. Inside the volcano the magma looks like blood. Then the volcano rumbled and made a loud boom. The volcano made the lava fly out. The lava was running down the side of the volcano. I saw a river of fire. The lava cools and hardened to become igneous rocks. I had a fantastic time exploring about volcanoes.

Sincerely,
Carlos R.

Poetry

Because poetry is part of our third-grade language arts standards, I also have students write the following types of poems about nature:

- haiku
- tanka
- cinquain
- lantern
- acronym

I have found that Robert Frost's poems provide students with excellent examples of how a poet has written about the world around him. This past school year, I had my class write poems about the bush outside our classroom. As mentioned at the beginning of the article, my class spent three months studying the bush as an ecosystem during our unit of study on ecosystems. Students were able to observe the bush in its dormant phase in winter and watch it come back to life in the spring. The flowers on the bush that grew during springtime later turned into berries, providing food for birds and squirrels. When the flowers started to bloom, bees came to the flowers to collect nectar. This was a wonderful opportunity for urban schoolchildren to observe the interactions of an ecosystem as well as see the life cycle of a plant.

Before students wrote their poems about the bush, I had them read a few of Robert Frost's nature poems. When it came time to write their poems, some students did find it easier to write the poems by sitting outside by the bush for inspiration. I believe having students read and write poems helped them do better on the poetry section of the reading assessment at the end of the year.

Assessment

Because every writing assignment occurs at the end of a science unit and requires inclusion of scientific concepts covered in that unit, our science journals are an excellent form of assessment. Through these types of writing, a teacher can learn many things about a student's understanding of the concepts covered in a unit of study. By reading a student's essay, poem, or letter, a teacher can determine if a student needs clarification of any misconceptions they may have. These articles also help a teacher determine if a concept needs to be retaught. An example of this is the following excerpt from two students' letters:

"I have been studying the active volcano located on the 'big island' of Hawaii. The lava splashed out of the volcano. The lava splashed in the water."

When this letter is compared to the following letter, it is obvious the student missed the concept that lava hardens and cools into igneous rock.

"I have been studying an active volcano located on the 'big island' of Hawaii. The volcano was rumbling. Then I heard a loud *boom*! The lava was all over the place. It looked rusty. When the lava cools and hardens, it turns into igneous rocks. I had a fantastic time in Hawaii studying the volcano."

Spending a few minutes during science reviewing what happens to lava when it cools can help the first student remember concepts he forgot to include in his letter. This can be done through oral review, having students draw the steps of igneous rock formation, or small-group discussions.

Of course, science journal writing is not limited to only the types of writing mentioned in this article. All of the writing genres can be used in science journals. In whatever format you choose to have your students write, I am sure you will find this helps improve their writing skills as well as their scientific literacy skills. Improving test scores is not the only reason I incorporated science journals into my curriculum. Having my students develop an interest in science and hearing the excitement in their voices when they say they are being real scientists is reason enough!

References

Kiester, J. 2003. *Elementary, my dear! Caught 'ya! Grammar with a giggle for grades one, two, and three.* 2nd ed. Gainesville, FL: Maupin House Publishing.

National Research Council (NRC). 1996. *National science education standards.* Washington, DC: National Academies Press.

Rose, M. 1999. *10 easy writing lessons that get kids ready for writing assessments: Proven ways to raise your students' scores on the state performance assessments in writing.* New York: Scholastic.

Internet Resource

Science Notebooks in K–12 Classrooms
   www.sciencenotebooks.org

Chapter 26

A Natural Integration
Student-Created Field Guides Seamlessly Combine Science and Writing

By Tracy Coskie, Michelle Hornof, and Heidi Trudel

"Your ivy is climbing all over my western red cedar!" exclaimed fourth grader David as he pointed up the trunk.
"Yeah, I know. My English ivy can kill your tree!" came Ron's confident reply.
"Who the heck takes care of this place, anyway?" grumbled David.

This conversation highlights some of the student learning that occurred during an integrated science and writing unit that we developed and implemented in a combined third-and-fourth-grade class. Our five-week study taught students how to write a field guide that identified the plants in a small, wooded area they passed through on their way to their school playground. By creating original science writing, students came to understand and care for the natural world in their immediate environment. They also developed important science, reading, and writing skills through purposeful work. Here we describe the process we used to develop a field guide unit (see unit overview in Figure 1, p. 146). We chose to have the students write a field guide about plants because they were easily accessible at their school, but we designed the curriculum to work for a wide range of items, such as animals, rocks, seashells, or other readily available materials. Writing field guides that focus on local features provides students with science and writing curriculum that is both concrete and relevant.

Figure 1. Unit overview				
April 2006				
Monday	Tuesday	Wednesday	Thursday	Friday
17	18	19	20	21
Immersion Use field guides to try to identify a variety of objects—small group exploration stations	Immersion Model the identification process—getting beyond the pictures	Immersion Outdoor scavenger hunt. Work with partner to identify "marked" plants in schoolyard	Immersion Field guide vocabulary with hands on application. I Spy game	Immersion Plant selection. Visit assigned plant and have picture taken
24	25	26	27	28
Gathering Sketch and think—sketching a leaf	Gathering Sketch and think—sketching another aspect of the plant (Zoom-ins)	Gathering Observe and think—using all senses	Gathering Observe and think—coming up with similes and metaphors	Gathering Observe and think—zoom in with your senses
May 2006				
Monday	Tuesday	Wednesday	Thursday	Friday
1	2	3	4	5
Gathering Research and think—kids gather information on their plant	Gathering Research and think—kids determine important information	Drafting Write leaf description. Describe the leaf using new vocabulary	Drafting Fun facts. Look through research to find interesting facts	Drafting Write whole plant description, including where to find it
8	9	10	11	12
Drafting Trying out different introductions	Revising Revising the introduction and fun fact	Revising Revising the leaf section	Revising Revising the plant description	NO SCHOOL
15	16	17	18	
Revising/Editing Refining sketches. Fact-checking with editor	Editing Editing your pages with a partner. Use the editing checklist	Publishing Shared writing—introduction to the field guide	Publishing Finishing Touches—group work on cover, dedication, table of contents, etc.	Celebration – [Following Week] Parent/student scavenger hunt!

Immersion and Exploration

Before students can begin writing field guides, they need to learn how to read them. In this phase, students develop an understanding of what field guides are, how they are organized, what they might find in an entry, how to use a field guide, and so on. We start by creating several identification stations, each including a different collection (potted plants, seashells, rocks and minerals, etc.) and a few relevant field guides, including some written for adults and some for children. Students rotate through the stations with a partner, trying to identify as many of the items as they can.

As students begin trying to tell the difference between two seashells or two rocks, they also begin to notice and describe different properties: size, shape, color, hardness, texture, and so on. Students find they need to refine their descriptions to be more specific, such as "Well, this rock is more like dark gray than black" or "I think this shell is striped, not spotted." Our students also start noticing vocabulary: "What's *foliage*?" and "What do they mean by *range*?"

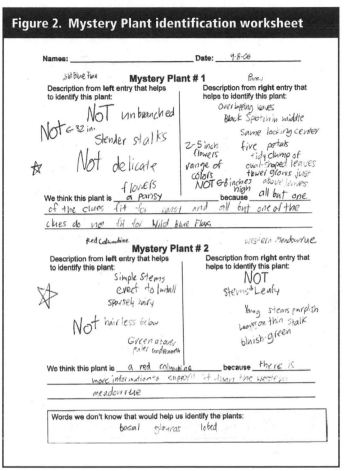

Figure 2. Mystery Plant identification worksheet

These explorations also lead students to new understandings about the texts. They begin giving each other hints: "Look, it's organized by color," or "First you have to figure out if it's a snail or a bivalve." We encourage students to use what they already know about reference books, such as using the index or table of contents, to help them make sense of how field guides worked.

We provide partners with a simple recording sheet to log their "best guesses," and at the end of the session we ask them to reflect on their strategies. Together, we create a list that includes using your senses, looking at details, using background knowledge, using both pictures and writing, and being persistent.

One thing we noticed during this phase was that our third and fourth graders over-relied on pictures for making identifications. To help them see the importance of using the text, we designed a Mystery Plant lesson in which students had to identify a plant using two entries that had very similar photographs, and we modeled for the students how to use the text as well as the pictures. The students had to keep track of what information from each entry was helpful, which they thought was the correct identification, and their reasoning behind their decision (see Figure 2).

Finally, we sent students on a scavenger hunt in the area of the school grounds where they would be making their field guides. This helped them use their newfound field-guide

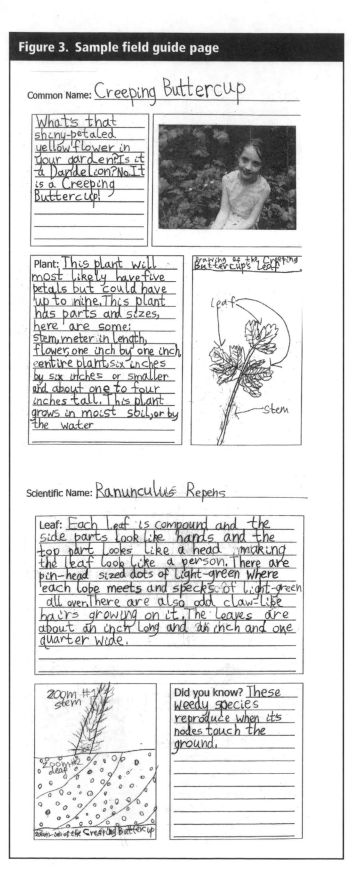

Figure 3. Sample field guide page

Common Name: Creeping Buttercup

What's that shiny-petaled yellow flower in your garden? Is it a Dandelion? No. It is a Creeping Buttercup!

Plant: This plant will most likely have five petals but could have up to nine. This plant has parts and sizes, here are some: stem, meter in length, flower, one inch by one inch, eentire plant, six inches by six inches or smaller and about one to four inches tall. This plant grows in moist soil, or by the water

Drawing of the Creeping Buttercup's leaf

leaf

stem

Scientific Name: Ranunculus Repens

Leaf: Each leaf is compound and the side parts look like hands and the top part looks like a head, making the leaf look like a person. There are pin-head sized dots of light-green where each lobe meets and specks of light-green all over. There are also odd claw-like hairs growing on it. The leaves are about an inch long and an inch and one quarter wide.

Zoom #1 stem

Zoom #2 leaf

Zoom-in of the Creeping Buttercup

Did you know? These weedy species reproduce when its nodes touch the ground.

skills in the real world and also familiarized them with the plants they would later describe in their own guides. Prior to the unit, we worked with a local naturalist to identify both native and invasive plants that were present near the classroom. We tagged the plants we chose with numbers and created a scaled-down field guide that students could use to find and identify the plants. On the last day of the immersion part of the cycle, students were introduced to and photographed with their assigned plant.

Check your district's policy on taking students outside during the school day or away from the school grounds before doing the outdoor activities. If poison ivy or oak is present in the area you are working, teach students how to identify and avoid it first. Also be aware of any other safety hazards.

Gathering Information

Seven days were spent gathering information, through both direct observation of the plant and research. For the final assignment, we required four written sections on a two-page spread: an introduction, a description of the whole plant, a detailed description of a leaf, and a "Did you know?" section. Students also had two blank boxes in which they could draw pictures of their plant. We reserved one space to include a photograph of the student with his or her plant (see Figure 3), which encouraged students' sense of ownership in the process and also provided a sense of plant size. These decisions helped us plan lessons for the gathering-information phase by giving us a focus for what students would need to be prepared to write.

Students completed lessons that supported their investigation of their assigned plants. Lessons included how to observe carefully, how to sketch realistically, and how to paraphrase when researching in a written resource. For example, as we watched students sketching their plants, we realized they were having trouble noticing and recording details, so in one lesson we showed them how many field guides include "zoom-ins." We created a recording sheet for them and modeled how to zoom in to draw different parts of the plant by creating a page that had one large box and three smaller boxes next to it. Students drew the whole plant in the large box, then zoomed in by choosing a small part of the plant, setting it in a new box, and making it much larger. As we modeled, we used half of the sheet to record our thoughts, such as connections, inferences, and questions. Throughout each of the lessons, we continued to encourage students to stop and record their thoughts about their discoveries. One student, for example, said, "On my first zoom in, I saw that the buds looked like baseball bats."

When students began thinking and talking about their plants, asking questions about what they saw, and locating information in books and on the internet, we realized that they needed some basic scientific vocabulary. We created our own vocabulary guide, using examples from field guides on online resources, which helped students learn the words for leaf arrangements (e.g., *whorled* and *alternate*) and leaf shapes (e.g., *palmate* and *toothed*). Students also needed a chance to practice using the vocabulary, so we provided each with a field guide vocabulary booklet in which they could draw pictures and try out sentences using their new words. This booklet was useful during the writing stages.

Using the Writing Process

During the next stage of the project—writing—we guided students through the process of organizing and refining the information they had collected so that it looked and sounded like a real field guide. We scaffolded the student writing (and sketching) by breaking down the process into manageable steps. Students wrote only one section per day, and they wrote each section in a text box that exactly matched the final project's text box. For each section, we modeled writing by displaying the text box on the overhead projector and thinking aloud as we determined what to write. We showed the process of referring back to the notes from the gathering stage to find the information we needed for each section. For example, we showed students how we went into our notes and highlighted any information that specifically described the color, shape, or size of the leaf.

When students finished their draft, they spent several days revising. During this time, we taught specific skills such as re-reading for clarity, using accurate vocabulary, and eliminating redundant or extraneous information. We returned to the lessons students had learned as *readers* of field guides during the immersion stage and reminded them of the advice they had suggested for *writers*, such as "Be very descriptive" and "Give specific information."

After revising, the class spent two days editing the conventions of their writing. Students used a checklist to edit their work, then edited a peer's paper as well. Finally, the teachers took the papers home and did a final proofread so that the published version would be fully

edited. As we were proofreading the students' final work, we realized that we also needed to be fact checkers to eliminate inaccurate or questionable information. Checking students' facts, however, turned out to be a challenge because we did not know everything about the plants. We found ourselves referring back to the students' written resources as well as referencing adult field guides and even visiting the students' plants in the field to make sure their writing was accurate. Often we found that what students had written was surprising but true. Did you know that the berries of the mountain ash have been used as a treatment for dandruff and lice?

Figure 4. Sample field guide rubric			
	3	**2**	**1**
Inquiry skills	• I asked questions while observing my plant. • I recorded my observations and thoughts. • I used additional resources to learn about my plant.	• I asked few questions while observing my plant. • I recorded only observations and no thoughts. • I used only one additional resource to learn about my plant.	• I didn't ask questions while observing my plant. • I didn't record my observations or thoughts. • I used no additional resources to learn about my plant.
Plant vocabulary	• During vocabulary lessons, I took notes in my word book and did all the practice pages. • In my field guide entry, I accurately used at least 3 specific plant vocabulary words.	• During vocabulary lessons, I took few notes in my word book and/or didn't finish all the practice pages. • In my field guide entry, I accurately used at least 1 or 2 specific plant vocabulary words.	• During vocabulary lessons, I did not take notes in my word book or do the practice pages. • In my field guide entry, I didn't use specific plant vocabulary words, or I used them inaccurately.
Communication	• My entry included all necessary information for identifying my plant, including helpful sketches. • I used my introduction and fun fact entry to interest the reader.	• My entry included some necessary information for identifying my plant, including helpful sketches. • I am missing an introduction or fun fact, or they were not interesting to the reader.	• My entry did not include necessary information for identifying my plant. • I did not include an introduction or fun fact.
Conventions	• My entry is neat and easy to read. • There are no spelling or grammatical mistakes.	• My entry is mostly neat and easy to read. • There are no more than 3 spelling or grammatical mistakes.	• My entry is illegible. • There are many spelling and grammatical mistakes.

In addition to each individual plant entry, the class decided to compose a few additional parts for their field guide: an introduction, a dedication page, a table of contents, and an author's note. Some of these sections were written as whole-class shared writing lessons, while others were written by small groups of students who had already finished their entries and had extra writing time. These parts added the class's unique voice and personality to the field guide.

Sharing and Reflecting

Finally, publication day arrived! A note was sent home to families inviting them to a publication party, which was planned for the end of the school day. Parents and other guests arrived and sat near the children. After a welcome, students explained the project to guests and one child read the field guide introduction to the group. Then we organized groups of guests and students for a new scavenger hunt. This time, students would watch (and provide help) as their guests used the student-created field guide to find each of the plants in the guide. It was fun to see how much students knew about their own plants as well as those that had been assigned to classmates. Parents and guests were delighted by the field guide. At the end of the day, students were able to take a copy of the field guide home.

Students' written work was an excellent demonstration of their learning. Developing a rubric with students as they discover what makes a good field guide would also create a useful assessment tool (see Figure 4). The rubric should include criteria for both the science and writing aspects of the project—such as accurate use of vocabulary and using only relevant information. We also asked each child to reflect on his or her experience by completing a short survey. Students said, "People that do a field guide know more about the thing they are studying," and "I never thought I'd learn that much!" Perhaps the best assessment was a story we heard from one student. Stephanie excitedly told one of the teachers on a Monday that she and her family had taken their new field guide out on a hike that weekend. They had found examples of almost every plant!

Extending the Integration

While field guides provide a natural integration of science and writing, they also open other possibilities for integration. Art instruction is a perfect support for children as they attempt to capture what they see in the natural world. Technologies such as digital photography and web publishing also lend themselves to field guide work. Finally, developing a field guide for a local trail, park, or garden makes a perfect service-learning project, so that when students find themselves wondering, "Who takes care of this place anyway?" the answer will be "We do."

Resources

Leslie, C. W., and C. E. Roth. 1998. *Nature journaling: Learning to observe and connect with the world around you*. Pownal, VT: Storey Books.

National Research Council (NRC). 1996. *National science education standards*. Washington, DC: National Academies Press.

Russo, M. 1998. *Watching nature: A beginner's field guide*. New York: Sterling Publishing.

Chapter 27

Nature Detectives
First *Graders Study Yearlong Changes in Nature and Create a School Yard Field Guide*

By Natalie Harr and Richard E. Lee Jr.

With cutbacks on field trips and other school spending, teachers more than ever need practical ways to engage young learners in science at school. Richard Louv's *Last Child in the Woods* (2008) added to a growing consensus to get children outside and experiencing nature. Using ideas from place-based education, we present a simple yearlong project that brings science, nature, and other curriculum standards to life right in your school yard. With a focus on journaling, this project is a novel way to promote nonfiction writing in your classroom. These first graders called themselves nature detectives because they used observation skills and simple tools to investigate a small natural area in their school yard. Students made predictions, recorded data, drew conclusions, and shared their findings about how their study site—including its plants, animals, and environment—transformed with each new season. The project culminated with students creating a school yard field guide, a unique science journal that showcased their ongoing work and discoveries. This investigation provided an ideal way to connect students with science and nature without ever leaving school!

Where in My School Yard

In *Place-Based Education: Connecting Classroom and Communities*, David Sobel (2005) describes place-based education as the process of using one's local environment as a foundation to teach concepts that span the curriculum, using hands on learning and real life experiences.

Whether you teach in an urban or rural area, just look beyond the school building and blacktop and you will find a small natural area nestled in your school yard where you can conduct a nature investigation. If you have difficulty locating a place to study, ask your school maintenance crew to avoid mowing a small section of the school yard. Studying an unmowed area is better because it contains a greater diversity of plant and animal life.

The National Wildlife Federation (NWF) created *Schoolyard Habitats: A How-to Guide for K–12 School Communities* (2001a) and *Schoolyard Habitats Site Planning Guide* (2001b) to help you locate, develop, or enhance existing habitats at your school. Keep in mind that your natural area should be located on school grounds but be a different habitat from the rest of your school yard. Familiarize yourself with the area prior to visiting with students. Check the site for safety hazards such as broken glass, old fencing, harmful plants or animals, and holes or rocks that might cause students to trip. No matter how small or big, the natural area will bring

the science curriculum to life and motivate students to intimately connect and write about nature. As one student said, "Let's miss recess so we can explore the school yard more!"

Meet Your Study Site

"Wow! The green grass is as tall as a first grader!" announced a student during our initial visit to our study site called the bio-swales. The bio-swales are located adjacent to the school's front parking lot and are about a five-minute walk from the classroom. The bio-swales were originally a cornfield until our new elementary school campus was constructed. To meet EPA requirements, a series of retention pools was created to control the runoff and pollution from our school's rooftops and parking lot areas. Therefore, this new, undisturbed wetland

Figure 1. Scavenger Hunt: Our Study Site

Name_____ Date_____

Directions: Use a crayon to circle each item from the list that you find.

Find something that is

bumpy	small
smooth	tall
soft	short
hard	smelly
large	fragrant
prickly	round

habitat was not created for educational purposes, but it has served as an ideal setting for our ongoing nature investigation.

A scavenger hunt is a great way to introduce your students to their new outdoor classroom (see Figure 1). This activity encourages students to focus on and explore their study site by using their senses (excluding taste). Before starting the hunt, be sure to cover safety rules with your students. Define the boundaries of your study site, point out hazards for students to avoid, and reinforce school rules (e.g., no running). The scavenger hunt can be conducted in pairs or small groups or with the whole class. Throughout the activity, be prepared for your students' questions and discoveries by packing a camera and notepad to record their responses. Also, it is important to model for your students how to respectfully interact with nature. This includes working quietly to avoid disturbing the wildlife and gently putting natural objects back where you found them.

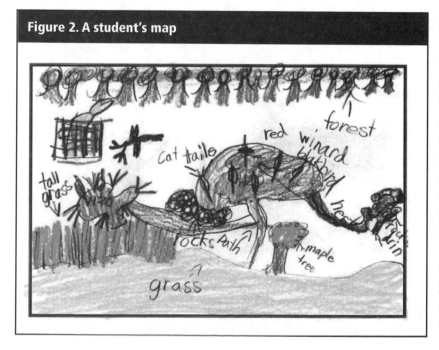

Figure 2. A student's map

Figure 3. Assignments for nature detectives

Group	Task	Scientific tools
Plant detectives	Search for changes in colors, shapes, sizes, and textures of various plants located at your study site. These include grasses, sedges, flowers, shrubs, and trees.	Magnifiers Optional: flower presses, field guides
Animal detectives	Look for evidence of animals in your school yard. These include sightings, tracks, rubbings, fur, feathers, insect galls, etc.	Binoculars Optional: sweep nets, water nets, collection containers, field guides
Weather detectives	Take measurements of current weather conditions in your school yard.	Thermometers Optional: other weather instruments
Soil detectives	Examine soil for changes near the ground at your study site (e.g., leaf litter, mud, snow, ice, burrows, etc.). Measure soil temperature.	Soil thermometer with storage sleeve Optional: Berlese tunnel (North Carolina State University, www.cals.ncsu.edu/course/ent591k/berlese.html)

As suggested in *Take a Tree Walk*, creating a map is an excellent way to familiarize students with nature and their surroundings (Kirkland 2006). At your study site, help your students locate special items and landmarks to include on their maps and discuss where they are in relation to one another. These items include trees, bushes, flowers, bodies of water, rocks, paths, sidewalks, or buildings. Demonstrate how to draw shapes to represent these items and use simple words to label them. When working with younger students, it is helpful to create a class map together first. This activity integrates fundamental writing and social studies standards and will eventually serve as a key component of your school yard field guide. Student made maps can be revisited throughout the year and updated with your students' new insights during the investigation (Figure 2). Signs of animals (e.g., tracks, rubbings, and

Figure 4. Sample data chart completed by the class

November 3, 2009

Fall

The air temperature is 50° cool.
The soil temperature is 40° cold.
The animals are not very active.
We see two birds, but we hear no crickets. We see an empty bird's nest and deer tracks by the water.
The plants are very brown. Some are dry and falling over. Brown, yellow, orange, and red tree leaves are on the ground. Flowers, goldenrod, and cattails have seeds
We see colorful leaves and brown plants
We hear the rustling of leaves in the wind
We smell dry leaves and the crisp air.
We touch squishy mud and prickly seeds

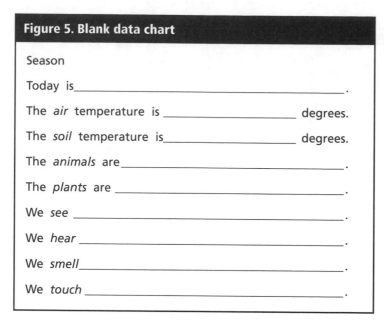

Figure 5. Blank data chart

Season

Today is_____.

The *air* temperature is _____ degrees.

The *soil* temperature is_____ degrees.

The *animals* are_____.

The *plants* are _____.

We *see* _____.

We *hear* _____.

We *smell*_____.

We *touch* _____.

burrows), wildlife sightings, and new plant growth are key items that can be added throughout the year.

Launching the Investigation

The purpose of the project is for students to become nature detectives and investigate a small natural area located at their school. Students make predictions, record data, draw conclusions, and share their findings about how their study site—including its plants, animals, and environment—transforms each season. This project culminates with students creating a school yard field guide, a unique science journal that showcases their ongoing work and discoveries. *No Student Left Indoors: Creating a Field Guide to Your Schoolyard* (Kirkland 2007) is an excellent resource to keep handy throughout the course of the project.

Make Predictions

At least once each season, the nature detectives visit their study site to collect data for their investigation. Prior to each visit, students use their knowledge of the seasons to make thoughtful predictions as to how their site will change over time. Next, students discuss and record their predictions in science journals. These journals are created at school from mostly recycled items. Cardboard from cereal boxes is collected by students and cut to make a durable cover. The school's scrap paper, along with some teacher-made pages, is bound inside. Before our winter investigation, a student wrote in his journal, "I think the dying plants in the fall are now crushed under the snow. I bet they're turning into soil."

Establish Detective Groups

Assigning detective groups encourages students to work well together, experience different aspects of nature, and meet various math and science standards during the investigation (Figure 3, p. 155). Students in each group use their observation skills and simple tools to collect data for the current season. The plant detectives search for changes among the trees, bushes, grasses, and flowers, using magnifiers to examine them closely. Binoculars, sweep and water nets, and collection containers help the animal detectives search for evidence of wildlife. Any collected animals such as insects and tadpoles are examined and then carefully released back to their habitat. The weather detectives use thermometers to measure the air temperature and note current weather conditions. The soil detectives measure soil temperature using soil thermometers. This group also searches for seasonal changes at ground level, noting evidence of dry, wet, or icy soil. The students rotate to a new detective group each season. The scientific tools are relatively inexpensive and can be purchased through a science distributor. Student learning is tracked by taking photographs and writing down their insights and discoveries.

Record Data

After students investigate the school yard for that season, the data gathered by each detective group are discussed, synthesized, and recorded by the class onto a large chart paper. It is important to keep this seasonal data chart simple and concise for the students to reference (see Figure 4, p. 155) for a student sample; see Figure 5 for a blank copy). Students also check their predictions and record their personal observations and discoveries in their science journals (Figure 6). This journaling is an open-ended activity in which students are encouraged to draw pictures, create diagrams, or write sentences demonstrating what they learned about the current seasonal changes at their study site. While journaling, it is helpful for students to keep the seasonal data chart nearby to help them with spelling and recording information. It is also a good time to share photographs that have been taken at the study site. Reviewing current and past photographs with the students will help them draw accurate conclusions about the seasonal changes they see. Interviewing students about their journal responses is a great way to assess their learning. Because your study site provides a great platform to teach other critical science concepts (e.g., living and nonliving things, life cycles, weather, food webs, plant and animal adaptations), the science journals are a valuable tool to document student learning across the entire science curriculum (Figure 7).

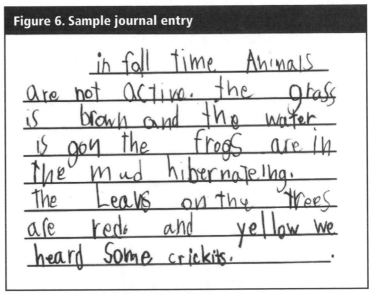

Figure 6. Sample journal entry

> in fall time Animals are not active. the grass is brown and the water is gon the frogs are in the mud hibernateing. the Leaves on the trees are red. and yellow we heard some crickits.

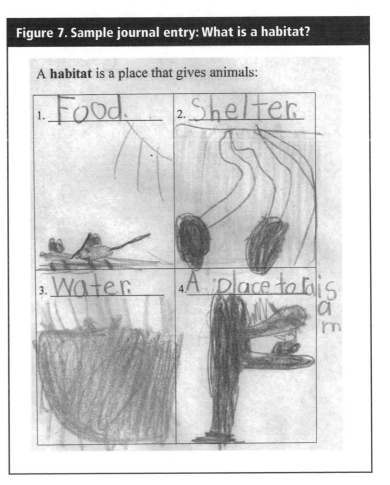

Figure 7. Sample journal entry: What is a habitat?

A **habitat** is a place that gives animals:

1. Food.
2. Shelter.
3. Water.
4. A place to his am

Share Discoveries

The charts and photographs are hung in the hallway throughout the school year to communicate students' discoveries with others. As each season is completed, these items eventually form a large circular shape that simulates the cyclical nature of the seasons. Adding student quotes and descriptions of their findings makes this diagram even more meaningful for the students. By displaying a visual seasonal cycle (summer, fall, winter, and spring), students internalize this natural phenomenon and make astounding connections with nature, such as "I think the school yard makes a cycle. Just like in our story about tadpoles turning into frogs. The circle never ends and will start all over again."

Figure 8. Sample field guide page

Wild Turkeys

Turkeys live at the Bio-swales
I know that turkeys say gobble gobble. and they like to run around. By researching turkeys, I learned they eat acorns, nuts, berries, seeds, and roots. turkeys strut by puffing their feathers and dragging their wings. studing turkeys is fun!

Creating a Field Guide

Students collaborate to create a school yard field guide to showcase their work and discoveries. This final step of the project integrates several reading and writing standards and communicates learning. Provide a field guide from the library as a model for students as they work on their project. To begin, it is easiest to divide your field guide into three distinct sections:

■   Part I—an overview of the study site and a description of the project. Be sure to showcase your students' updated maps as well as photographs, drawings, or descriptive writing about your site's key features. These samples can be collected from your students' journal entries.

■ Part II—your study site through the seasons. Include seasonal data charts and the seasonal cycle diagram. Arranged by season, students create a collage of photographs, drawings, revised journal entries, flower pressings, and personal reflections about their discoveries.

■ Part III—description of the flora and fauna of the study site.

Students create their own pages for the field guide by researching a school yard plant or animal of particular interest to them (Figure 8). To start, your class can review the science journals and seasonal data charts to compile a list of all the plants and animals living at your study site. Once students make their selection, they can then use a K-W-L chart (Figure 9) to organize their writing. Using the chart, students write facts they already know and questions they wonder about their topic. Using these "wonder questions" as a guide, students conduct research and write what they learned in the final column. Once the research is complete, students use the information from their chart to write their paragraph and perfect it using the writing process. Both students and teachers evaluate this page using a rubric (Figure 10). Our first graders took great ownership of the project and were highly motivated to write about their nature experiences (Figure 11). Be sure to share the field guide with your school, families, and the community. We keep a copy in our school library.

School Yard Plans

One of the most significant outcomes of this project is the teachable moments that arise throughout the investigation. When students are immersed in nature, they naturally ask "why" questions that lead to meaningful inquiry. For example, when students were conducting the fall investigation, they became fascinated with insect galls forming on the golden-rod plants. The students were particularly curious as to how these ball-like structures came to be on these plants. These questions led the students to research insects and their winter adaptations (Sandro and Lee 2006). Because the small larvae within the gall survive freezing, this led to more investigations on states of matter as well as insect growth stages.

The implications of this project are endless, and there are future plans to create a school yard science program at our school campus that spans the K–3 grade levels. As students progress through the primary grades, this science program will expand from studying a small section of our school yard to comparing other habitats on school grounds to exploring local watersheds in the community.

Figure 9. K-W-L chart

My Bio-Swale Research Project
K-W-L Chart

deer

K- (What I already Know)	W- (What I Wonder)	L-(What I Learned)
① I know that deer lose their antlers.	① Are they camouflage? ① Are there diffrent kinds? ② Are they big?	① There are 30 kinds of white tailed deer.
② They are awesome.		② Deers fight with other deer in the rutting season.
③ They are easy to shoot.		③ A deer's coat is the same color as their habitat to protect from other animals.

Figure 10. Rubric

My Plant or Animal

Did I ...   Self   Teacher

Write two facts I already knew about it?
Write two facts that I learned about it?
Include a picture of it?
Write in my best handwriting?

Teacher comments:

Figure 11. Sample student reflection

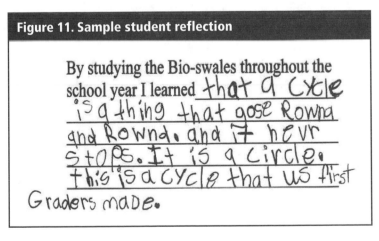

By studying the Bio-swales throughout the school year I learned that a cycle is a thing that gose Rowna and Rownd. and it nevr stops. It is a circle. this is a cycle that us first Graders made.

Just imagine the cohesiveness of science instruction within your school as students build on this investigation year after year.

You will find that by extending your classroom investigations beyond school doors, children develop a strong connection with the natural world and their community. Though there can be unexpected outcomes, such as poor weather or everyday curriculum demands, you'll find that an outdoor investigation promotes meaningful learning that enriches elementary students' school experiences. The creation of a field guide encourages students to write, document, and reflect on their learning and discoveries. By being a nature detective, students learn to work together as real scientists for a common purpose. It also gives you an innovative way to bring the entire curriculum together right in your school yard!

Acknowledgments

This work was supported, in part, by NSF grants #IOS-0840772 and ANT-0837559 and the Ohio Board of Regents. The authors thank Ed Soldo, Pat Betteley, and Matt Sorrick for their contributions to the project.

References

Kirkland, J. 2006. *Take a tree walk.* Lionville, PA: Stillwater Publishing.

Kirkland, J. 2007. *No student left indoors: Creating a field guide to your schoolyard.* Lionville, PA: Stillwater Publishing.

Louv, R. 2008. *Last child in the woods: Saving our children from nature-deficit disorder.* Chapel Hill, NC: Algonquin Books.

National Research Council (NRC). 1996. *National science education standards.* Washington, DC: National Academies Press.

National Wildlife Federation (NWF). 2001a. *Schoolyard habitats: A how-to guide for K–12 school communities.* Reston, VA: NWF.

National Wildlife Federation (NWF). 2001b. *Schoolyard habitats site planning guide.* Reston, VA: NWF.

Sandro, L. H., and R. E. Lee. 2006. Winter biology and freeze tolerance in the goldenrod gall fly. *The American Biology Teacher* 68 (1): 29–35.

Sobel, D. 2005. *Place-based education: Connecting classrooms and communities.* Great Barrington, MA: The Orion Society.

Chapter 28

Students as Authors
Illustrated Science Information Books Created During Integrated Units Are Windows Into Student Understanding

By Maria Varelas, Christine C. Pappas, Sofia Kokkino, and Ibett Ortiz

Are you looking for ways to effectively integrate—and assess—science and literacy learning? Try having your students create their own books! The Integrated Science Literacy Enactments (ISLE) approach to teaching and learning science is one way to develop students' science understandings while simultaneously enhancing their communication skills. We have implemented this approach extensively and studied it in two science units—one on matter and another on a forest ecosystem—with classes of first- through third-grade students in Chicago Public Schools. The ISLE approach engages young children in science through hands-on explorations and numerous literacy-oriented learning experiences, including read alouds of children's literature information books; keeping science journals; creating a class semantic map; dramatic role plays; home projects that include literacy and hands-on components; reading other information books in small-group literature circles and presenting new, interesting ideas to the class as a panel; and more. Each unit culminates in the writing and illustrating of an information book on a topic of students' own choice. The book serves as a tool to assess student understandings developed throughout the unit and is the focus of this article. While the experiences discussed here took place in curricular and instructional units using the ISLE approach, the discussion is relevant to any science learning experience that culminates in the creation of a nonfiction science book written and illustrated by students.

Illustrated Information Books

When students created their end-of-unit books, they had already spent around eight weeks learning about various aspects of the unit theme in a wide range of ways. In the matter unit, children studied solids, liquids, and gases; their properties; similarities and differences among the three states of matter (both at the macro and micro levels—namely, how molecules behave); examples of each state in everyday life; changes of states of matter, such as freezing, melting, boiling, evaporation, and condensation; and how rain is formed (i.e., the water cycle). In the forest unit, children studied a temperate forest community; animals that live under and above the ground; seeds, plants, and food chains and webs; and interactions among living and nonliving entities.

After completing each unit's activities, the students were given the following directions regarding the construction of their own illustrated information book on a topic of their choice:

- Write about a part of what we have studied in the unit—something that other students who haven't studied this unit would like to read.

- Your book should include both writing and drawing, like the books we read.

- You can look at the class semantic map, your journals, and other things we created during the unit, but this book should be your own book on a topic that you are interested in, not something that you have copied from other books.

- You won't be able to write about/draw everything we studied, so you will decide what to include. In making your book, you should think about what ideas you want to explain in writing and what ideas you want to explain in pictures.

Teachers can use any of their favorite ways to make a blank booklet for this activity. We folded four 8.5 × 11 in. sheets of white paper along the longest side and stapled them along the fold. We spent about one week creating the books. First, we reviewed as a class all the activities we had done in the unit and put out all the information books that we had used for read alouds or literature circles. Children had the freedom to work first on their pictures or on their text, depending on what made the most sense to them. If children were stuck, we asked them to tell us about some of the ideas we talked about in the unit, and as they were talking, we pointed out to them that any of their ideas could be good for their books. Usually, children did not have trouble coming up with more ideas after they started on their first page. We avoided providing specific feedback or help on their book content, writing, or illustrating because we wanted to use the books as a major summative assessment tool.

Books as Assessment Tools

After students create their books, we have conversations with individual students about them. An alternative is to have children read their books to the whole class or in small groups and talk about the text and pictures. These books—and the conversations around them—offer teachers an opportunity to explore what children think and have learned about particular ideas of the unit (Varelas, Pappas, and the ISLE Team 2006).

In our individual conversations, we ask students to share the book with us, reading it page by page and explaining their pictures (what the different elements of their pictures are, why they decided to draw these pictures, why they used particular sizes, colors, shapes, etc.). The pictures communicate scientific understandings that students may not be able to express in words, so we treat the illustrations as elements of meaning rather than "embellishments" of the text. In this way, we get a richer sense of children's ideas while also demonstrating for students the idea that pictures in scientific texts are significant and important (Pappas et al. 2008).

There are various dimensions that can be assessed in the children's information books. To accurately assess scientific knowledge presented in such books, it is necessary to examine and interpret both text and pictures and to consider and assess a book not on a page-by-page basis but rather as a whole, related artifact. Here, we focus on how to assess children's scientific ideas developed during instructional units.

The following examples are from children's books from the forest and matter units created in Ibett Ortiz's bilingual second-grade class. As the students were speakers of Spanish who were learning English, she allowed them to express their ideas in Spanish. In the examples, Spanish text has been translated into English. All students' names are pseudonyms.

Figure 1. A page from the book *Ranas/Frogs*

Nacen en wJevo.
They are born in eggs.

Lazaro wrote a book titled *Ranas/Frogs*, in which he portrayed his ideas of metamorphosis and characteristics of frogs. His book began with the text "They are born in eggs" (Figure 1). His picture featured a dark, filled-in circle surrounded by a red membrane. During our conversation about the book, Lazaro specified that around the red membrane there was a "magnifying glass" allowing an up-close view. He added that the frogs were "in the egg with the jelly … and they are not mammals … [because] they are born in eggs."

From this page and the conversation about it, we know that Lazaro has learned that frogs start off as eggs and that frogs' eggs have a certain characteristic—jelly that surrounds the frogspawn. We also know that he understood that frogs are different from mammals, which are not born in eggs.

In another example, Flor wrote about *La Materia/Matter* and expressed some ideas in both text and pictures and some ideas exclusively in pictures. For some concepts she revealed emergent, or developing, understandings, and for other concepts she showed correct understandings. For example, on one page of her book (Figure 2), she wrote about molecules being very tight in solids, so tight that they cannot move, an idea she reiterated during her conversation with us. This molecular

Figure 2. A page from the book *La Materia/Matter*

En solido, estan
pien pegadita que no
se pueden mover
los moléculas.
In solids the molecules are very tight that they cannot move.

closeness was also depicted in her illustration with the small dots all positioned right next to one another. Flor's idea that molecules in solids are not moving at all is not accurate—molecules in solids actually move very slowly. However, relative to liquids and gases, which Flor presented in the rest of her book, a solid's molecules are practically stationary, so this idea should be considered emergent.

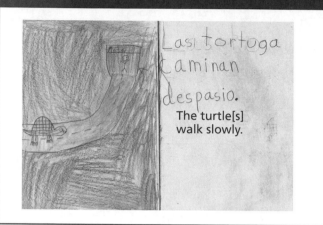

Figure 3. The opening spread from the book *Tortugas/Turtle*

Lasi tortuga
Caminan
despasio.

The turtle[s] walk slowly.

In contrast, Flor revealed her correct understanding that a solid's molecules are very close. In addition, what Flor's picture communicates that her text does not is her understanding that solids have distinct shape. In the illustration, she has drawn a distinct boundary around the solid that she called a rock during the conversation.

A third example is from Cesar's book *Tortugas/Turtles*. Cesar communicated many of his understandings about turtles in both text and pictures. He also introduced some of his understandings and then reinforced them in pictures only throughout his book. For example, on one page (Figure 3), Cesar wrote correctly about turtles walking slowly, and in his picture he depicted a turtle participating in a race versus a person who clearly won. Cesar also depicted the turtle's body parts correctly, including its flippers, shell (upper carapace), head (including eyes and the mouth), and tail. On a later page (Figure 4), he revealed more of his understanding of turtles' shell functions as protecting the turtle and providing camouflage because the shell blends in with the green background.

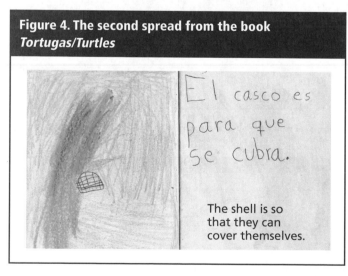

Figure 4. The second spread from the book *Tortugas/Turtles*

El casco es
para que
se cubra.

The shell is so that they can cover themselves.

A final example from this class is Leonara, who wrote a book titled *Todo Sobre Moléculas/Everything About Molecules*. On her final page (Figure 5), she wrote, "In the clouds, when it rains and the molecules fall, the droplets sometimes return again to the droplets." In the picture, Leonara represented droplets as small blue dots in the clouds as well as floating freely in the air. In our conversation about the book, she stated, "When it's raining … the cloud fills up and when the Sun comes … the same little drops go up to the clouds." Using Leonara's text, pictures, and conversation, we know that she understood the idea of the water cycle (even though she did not use this term) as the same substance (water) being in the clouds and evaporating from the ground. However, she did not indicate an understanding of any changes of states associated with the water cycle—liquid to gas (vapor) and vice versa, indicating emergent understanding of the water cycle.

Reflections

These children composed interesting and detailed books that showed what was salient for them and how they made sense of ideas explored and developed in the units. As a culminating activity and an assessment tool, the books enable teachers to see what ideas students chose to communicate and how they do so in words and pictures. Such student-created books can serve as a summative or formative assessment tool. If used as a formative assessment, teachers could revisit with the class the ideas that the students' books revealed to be less well formed than others.

Teachers can easily score such books by creating a list of the main ideas explored in a unit and assigning one of three scores (0, 1, 2) to each idea addressed in a student's book. A 0 can be assigned for a totally incorrect idea; a 1 for an emergent, developing idea; or a 2 for a completely correct idea. Of course, students may not address all ideas in their books, and for those not addressed they will not get any score. A total score for their books may be calculated by averaging the scores they receive on the ideas they addressed.

As these books revealed, children may own scientific ideas without naming them in scientific terms. This is important to remember and consider for all students—including those in bilingual classrooms, like those whose books we described in this article, who made sense of English read-alouds, coordinated them with hands-on and other experiences predominately in Spanish, and wrote and discussed their own books in Spanish. The creation of such books—and their assessment—should focus on authentic understanding of scientific concepts rather than translation and memorization of vocabulary terms and should focus on both words and pictures. Meeting this goal and seeing the pride in students' ownership of their books was worthwhile in many ways.

Figure 5. The last page of the book *Todo Sobre Moléculas/Everything About Molecules*

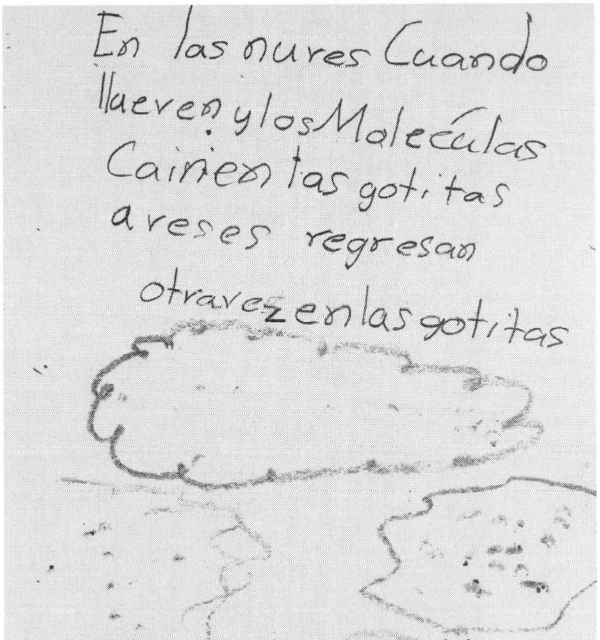

En las nures Cuando llueven y los Moléculas Caimem tas gotitas a reses regresan otravez en las gotitas

In the clouds, when it rains and the molecules fall, the droplets sometimes return again to the droplets.

Acknowledgment

The ISLE program development and research has been funded by a four-year (2004–2008) U.S. National Science Foundation (NSF) ROLE (Research On Learning and Education) grant (REC-0411593). The data presented, statements made, and views expressed in this article are solely the responsibilities of the authors and do not necessarily reflect the views of the National Science Foundation.

References

National Research Council (NRC). 1996. *National science education standards.* Washington, DC: National Academies Press.

Pappas, C. C., M. Varelas, T. Ciesla, and E. Tucker-Raymond. 2008. Journal and book writing in integrated science-literacy units: Insights from urban primary-grade classrooms. In *Talking science, writing science: The work of language in multicultural classrooms,* ed. K. Richardson Bruna and K. Gomez, pp. 19–82. Mahwah, NJ: Lawrence Erlbaum.

Varelas, M., C. C Pappas, and the ISLE team. 2006. Young children's own illustrated information books: Making sense in science through words and pictures. In *Linking science and literacy in the K–8 classroom,* ed. R. Douglas, M. Klentschy, and K. Worth, pp. 95–116. Arlington, VA: NSTA Press.

Chapter 29

Mystery Box Writing

By William Straits

My search for integrated writing and science connections began years ago when I was teaching seventh- and eighth-grade science at a school for dyslexic students. Like any class, the interests and abilities of my students were across the spectrum. However, one characteristic all the students had in common was a reluctance to write.

Although I was the science teacher, it was critically important that I help students develop writing skills along with content, so I made a point that our hands-on science experiences would be accompanied by a related writing lesson. Science, I happily discovered, provided students with a purpose for writing, made writing meaningful, and motivated these normally reluctant writers to pick up their pens.

One of my favorite science writing activities that grew out of this experience is what I've come to call the Mystery Box activity. It can be adapted successfully for use in myriad ways—as part of individual, small-group, or whole-class instruction—and at various grade levels from elementary through middle school. (I know, I've almost tried them all!) I encourage you to try it with your students too.

What's in the Box?

The activity begins when I bring a mystery object or organism into the classroom, hidden in a box. Typically, I select items that will introduce a new unit of study or that relate to the unit we're currently studying. I also sometimes use this as a means for revisiting topics covered earlier in the year. (I notify students when it's a review organism or object; they are otherwise safe to assume that it relates to the day's topic.)

I have used beetles, spiders, screws, and various plants for this activity (see Figure 1, p. 168, for additional suggestions). I also use models by answering questions as if they were the real thing, but I include a discussion of the use of models in science. For example, after revealing a toy airplane, I will ask, "How is this like a real airplane?" and "How is it different from a real airplane?" and then we will discuss why scientists often use models to represent objects and processes in science (e.g., "Why did I use a model airplane instead of a real one?").

Figure 1. Ten "get-you-started," never-fail mystery organisms and objects	
Organism/Object	Notes
Mealworm	These are readily available, yet often completely unfamiliar. They are useful for introducing life cycles.
Goldfish	Students often will focus on terrestrial animals. This activity is great for introducing young children to aquatic organisms.
Tree seedling	The idea that a tree can fit in the box often doesn't occur to students. This mystery organism segues nicely into lessons on (plant) growth.
Magnet	The classic U-shaped magnets seem to work best initially; you can challenge students by using different shapes.
Model of a volcano	In my experience, students sometimes need a little more direction with Earth and space science topics—be ready to give some hints.
Thermometer	This is more appropriate with older children, although primary grades can be successful if they know the mystery object is something you use to learn about weather.
Rock	This is a fun one. Because there are so many different types of rocks, responses sometimes lead students away from the answer. For example, you could say, "Yes, it is magnetic" (magnetite); "It is pink" (rose quartz); or "No, it's not heavy for its size" (pumice).
Globe	This is a readily available mystery space science object. A relief globe, rather than a political one, works best at the science writing center.
Any body part (or model thereof)	This model helps students think of body parts, locations, and functions. This works great as a review—students will identify the mystery organ, bone, facial feature, body part, and other features fairly quickly.
Water	Like rocks, this object can be tricky: It moves—"It must be an animal." It conducts electricity—"It must be made of metal." Finally, it connects to many topics within the science curriculum.

The activity occurs in two phases. The first phase introduces the organism or object to the students and focuses on science-process skill development. Specific skills applied during the mystery organism or object activity include questioning, predicting, interpreting information, observing and recording observations, and thinking critically.

In the second phase, students complete language arts tasks that relate to the mystery organism or object at a writing center. Specific language arts knowledge and skills can include comparing and contrasting, identifying parts of speech, and developing concepts through concept map(s) and/or definition diagram(s).

Start With Questions

When the activity begins, students will want to ask specific questions (e.g., "Is it a soccer ball?" "Is it a kitten?"). In challenging students to determine the contents of the mystery box, I tell students they may ask me three types of questions:

- Does it _____? / Can it _____? (verbs)

- Does it have _____? / Is it a _____? (nouns)

- Is it _____? (adjectives)

These yes-or-no questions help students gather information that will inform their inferences of what is in the mystery box. A typical exchange might be something like this:

- Student 1: Is it alive?

- Teacher: Yes, it is alive.

- Student 2: Can it move?

- Teacher: Yes, it can move.

- Student 3: Does it have six or more legs?

- Teacher: No, it doesn't have six or more legs.

- Student 4: Does it have four legs?

- Teacher: No, it doesn't have four legs.

- Student 5: Wait a minute, does it even have legs?

- Teacher: No, it doesn't have legs.

- Students: (groan)

- Student 6: It's a snake! Is it a snake?

- eacher: No, it's not a snake.

- Students: (more groans)

- Teacher: Okay, write (draw) what you think the mystery organism is.

Throughout this exchange, students (or I) write the information (e.g., "alive," "can move," "does not have six or more legs," etc.) on one of three pieces of chart paper, listing verbs, nouns, and adjectives on separate pieces of paper. After students record their guesses, I call on students for more questions, periodically stopping to record new guesses. The number of questions between guesses depends on the accuracy of the guesses. If the class seems far from finding the answer, I'll answer several questions before asking for guesses; if they are narrowing the possibilities, I'll provide less information between guesses. Used at the beginning of a unit, this exercise helps students activate relevant prior knowledge and gives me a great idea about what students know about the topic before instruction.

When conducting this activity early in the school year, I usually have to answer between 10 and 15 questions before students begin making inferences as to what object is in the box. Students usually figure out the object in 45–50 questions total. By the middle of the year, as

students' questioning and critical-thinking skills improve, inferences and drawings are made after the first 5 questions, and the mystery organism or object is found out in just a few minutes, sometimes in as few as 8 or 9 questions. Interestingly, it's been my experience that rather than waning, enthusiasm for this activity grows as students become more adept at using these science process skills.

I Think / I Infer …

As students ask their questions, I periodically ask them to stop and draw or write predictions based on what they know so far:

"I think/infer (I use *think* and *guess* with primary-level students and *infer* with older students) that the mystery organism/object is _____." We learn about inferences using the "Earthlets" chapter of *Picture-Perfect Science Lessons: Using Children's Books to Guide Inquiry* (Ansberry and Morgan 2005).

I also ask, "Are we 100% certain?" Although many students, especially younger ones, will be extremely confident in their responses, none will be absolutely certain. I then point out that scientists can never be 100% certain either—that's why they keep doing science, asking questions, and getting more information. I then ask, "If we want to get a better idea of what the mystery object is, what should we do?" It delights me to hear a class of young scientists reply, "Ask more questions!"

At the end of the questioning phase, the object in the box is revealed, and the list of verbs, nouns, and adjectives collected in the questioning phase is gathered for use in the next phase of the activity—the writing center.

After a bit of practice, students become adept at asking illuminating questions and honing in on the mystery organism or object. If the class is about to identify the organism or object too quickly (i.e., the word lists are insufficiently developed), I will outlaw noun questions, forcing the class to, in effect, expand their description of the organism or object. Students, particularly students in upper elementary grades, come to see this outlawing as something to be proud of ("Yeah, we got you, Mr. Straits!") and strive to solve the mystery.

Figure 2. Suggested writing center activities

- Create a fictional story using vocabulary lists.
- Write haiku or other poems using vocabulary lists.
- Write "I am a (mystery organism or object)" riddles.
- List as many observations of the organism or object as possible.
- Draw a picture of the organism or object.
- Research the organism or object and list 10 facts about it.
- Make a Venn diagram for characteristics of the organisms or objects from the past two weeks.
- Make a concept map(s) for the anatomy or composition and/or behavior or uses of the organism or object.
- Make a definition diagram for the organism object:

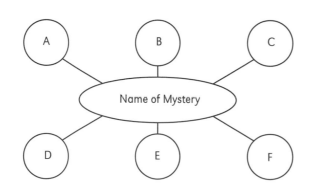

A. Dictionary definition
B. Important facts from vocabulary lists
C. Examples of the organism or object
D. Your personal definition of the organism or object
E. Important facts you discover on your own
F. Negative definition

When a class is unable to identify the organism or object within the allotted time, students often analyze questions and answers, looking for the information that led them astray. Occasionally, this leads to some great debates. "Do chrysalises move?" "Does water move?" "What color is a chameleon?" Sometimes after revealing an organism or object that had stumped the class, we will brainstorm questions that the class should have asked. I value this analytical thinking.

The reveal brings up an important misconception about the nature of science to address: Scientists are not able to "look into the box" and find an absolute answer; they must always keep asking questions. Cutting the activity short and not revealing the mystery organism or object is a good way to initiate this discussion.

Inspired to Write

In the second phase of the activity, small groups of students work independently at a writing center. Like all learning centers, the writing center is a designated area of the classroom where students are provided the needed materials as well as time and prompts to explore a particular topic. Each week we spend 30–45 minutes in "centers." Over the course of the week, students complete five centers, of which a student favorite is the writing center. This arrangement allows me to work with a small group of students each day—addressing specific student needs and allowing students opportunities to work independently as well as collaboratively. These opportunities are valuable not only in terms of learning the subject matter but also in developing decision-making, social, and investigative skills.

Figurere 3. Student examples

In the writing center, which has chairs and table space for three to five students to work, I typically post the vocabulary lists and place the mystery organism or object. I also provide various materials (e.g., paper, pencils, rulers, crayons, colored pencils, magnifying glasses, diagram templates [Venn, concept map, definition map], and students' previous work [examples of haiku, riddles, etc.]). This center becomes a place where students can purposefully apply the various techniques and writing genres we are studying in language arts.

Typically, rather than assigning a specific writing task, I offer students a choice from three or four tasks, including story writing, creating a concept map, and others (see Figure 2, p. 170). I keep a record of the types of work each student selects and encourage them to try others, either through discussion with the student or by only offering the avoided options.

The student work examples, shown in Figure 3 (p. 171), demonstrate the flexibility of the assignment. Some students embrace the assignment as an opportunity to write creatively, others as a chance to display their understanding of science vocabulary and concepts. Some choose to do both, writing creatively and incorporating science concepts. Subsequently, my assessment of these assignments includes a combination of language arts and science goals. Is the drawing accurate? Are the observations detailed? Does the haiku follow five-seven-five convention? Do the fictional stories demonstrate creativity? These questions are all equally important as I evaluate student work.

It's No Mystery

I bet many teachers use some kind of Mystery Box activity as a science lesson at some point in the school year. By using it routinely as part of my science lessons and by adding the dimension of incorporating a writing assignment into the experience, I've discovered these activities can greatly develop students' abilities to ask questions, make inferences, and think critically—and to motivate even the most reluctant students to get writing. What a terrific combination!

References

Ansberry, K. R., and E. Morgan. 2005. *Picture-perfect science lessons: Using children's books to guide inquiry.* Arlington, VA: NSTA Press.

National Research Council (NRC). 1996. *National science education standards.* Washington, DC: National Academies Press.

Resources

Di Biase, W. J. 1998. Writing a letter to a scientist. *Science and Children* 35 (6): 14–17, 66.

Reinemann, D., and J. Thomas. 2003. New species found! *Science and Children* 40 (8): 28–33.

Rillero, P., J. V. Cleland, and K. A. Conzelman. 1999. The nature of haiku. *Science and Children* 37 (2): 16–20.

Zertuche, A. A. 2002. Travel without leaving the classroom. *Science Scope* 26 (3): 28–31.

Chapter 30

Nature's Advice Book

Third-Grade Students Examine Their Knowledge of Life Science by Considering the Lessons Learned From Nature

By Kathryn Mahlin and Amy Robertson

What do we learn from the world around us? Can a tree really teach us something about life? Many times teachers provide students with facts about nature but fail to consider what we can learn from the natural world around us.

After many months of exploring various ecosystems such as the prairie, rain forest, and desert, I was anxious to assess what my third-grade students had learned and gain insight into their ideas about nature in a creative way. So, to learn more about my students' science understanding and help them refine their writing skills, we created *Nature's Advice Book* as part of an integrated science and language arts lesson.

Book Brainstorming

We began the one-and-a-half hour lesson with a discussion about advice. We talked about what students' parents tell them about life and what advice they offer. Many chimed in with "always do your best" and "be respectful." Next, I asked students what advice they might have for second-grade students who are going to be in third grade next year. I encouraged students to think about receiving and offering advice and to consider all the people and places from which they receive advice. Finally, I posed the question, "What does nature teach us about life?" I told students to think about this question because it would be our guiding question for the day's writing lesson.

Whenever I do a writing activity in class, I find that students are more willing to write if I write along with them. I set the timer for one minute and instructed students to list everything in nature that they thought of while I created my own list on chart paper at the front of the room. At first, the list was very short, with only nonspecific items such as grass, trees, and flowers. Then, for about 15 minutes, I asked a few students to share their lists, and I recorded their additions to my list and invited them to do the same. I reminded students to think about all the different ecosystems we had studied this year and to recall what was unique to each. Soon we were adding specific types of insects, flowers, and bodies of water to our lists.

Choice Topics

After our group brainstorming session, I asked students to circle five items on their list they either especially liked or knew a lot about. Some students grumbled because they said it was too hard to choose, but I encouraged them to do so anyway.

After all of the students made their selections, I had them write on the back of their paper the five choices they circled, skipping lines in between. I set the timer for three minutes and had students record the characteristics and behaviors of each item on their shortened list.

I explained that this part of the writing assignment was like taking notes, and, because time was limited, I asked students to just write words or phrases that described each item. As I had done before, I wrote along with students on my chart paper, which provided an immediate model of my expectations.

A few students wanted to write about their dog or cat. I encouraged them instead to think of an organism from the rain forest or desert they could write about. Some students chose topics that were more appropriate to what we had studied throughout the year. One student wrote that orangutans "swing and move around, have the colors brown and black, and like to scratch."

Also, many students chose broad topics, such as birds or insects. In these cases, I asked students if they could think of a specific type of bird or insect they could write about, such as a hummingbird or an ant. I think one problem area was that the initial nature list was too broad. Perhaps listing the different ecosystems at the top of chart paper and then having students brainstorm the different organisms within each category would have prevented students from choosing broad topics or topics that didn't relate.

When the timer went off, I gave students a minute or two to wrap up their ideas and come to a good stopping point in their writing. Students love to share their writing because it validates their work and effort, so I asked a few to share some of their notes and thoughts. One student shared her list of five items, which included wildflowers (petals, colorful, leaves, stem, grows); ladybugs (spots, red, black, flies, six legs, wings, moves); deer (antlers, fur, legs, brown, white); lions (eat meat, big); and cacti (desert, spikes, green, tall).

Guiding Question Revisited

Afterward, I reminded my students of the initial inquiry, "What does nature teach us about life?" I asked them to read over their list of descriptions of the five items and choose one item they felt could teach them a lesson about life. I then asked students to put the one item they had chosen at the top of a new piece of paper and think for a minute about all it can teach them about life.

Some students needed further prompting, so I suggested they pretend they were having a conversation with the organism or item they had chosen. Because this lesson came after a unit on myths and fables, I reminded students that sometimes writing involves mixing truths with our own creativity, just like in the myths and fables we had read. We talked about the fact that although animals can't actually talk to humans, we can still learn from them, and that we were just imagining what they might say based on what we know to be true about them, as we had talked about with the fables.

I asked one student what kind of advice the organism would give if it could talk. This turned out to be a popular alternative prompt and an easier way for my students to present a creative take on the factual information they had learned in the ecosystem units. Next, students wrote for about 10 minutes on the specific topic they chose. They were asked to write at least one-half page about the animal or item they chose and what they could learn from it. For example, one student chose to write about ants—how even if you're small, you can still work together and do big things.

Amazing Essays

After students had written, they shared their ideas. I assessed students by looking for facts in their creative writing and also at their ability to personify different organisms. For them to be creative, students had to first use their knowledge about the different organisms they were writing about.

As they usually do, my students amazed me with some of their pieces. One of my students wrote about a butterfly telling him that "sometimes you have to change directions and migrate" and "that is how life is sometimes, but whatever happens you will be okay."

Another student shared her essay about how it is important for a camel to store water because there is not a lot of water in the desert. She went on to say that it is important for people to save as well. The class discussion that followed her sharing was beneficial for the whole class to make any other links verbally. Another student added during the sharing time that we have to save water, so we do not run out. Providing time for students to share their work allowed the students and me to ask questions and get a further glimpse into their knowledge.

Finally, we compiled the essays into a class book called *Nature's Advice Book,* which was read over and over again by many of the students. If we had had more time, I probably would have had my students take their pieces through the complete writing process—revising, editing, and publishing—before compiling our book. However, I was very happy with what we ended up with: between a half and full page of writing from each student that incorporated previous learning about a specific organism with each student's own creativity.

At the end of the project, I think we were on the brink of an even greater creative science writing experience. When I do this science writing exercise again next year, I plan to allot a week to give my students time to deepen their writing and the opportunity to continue their conversations with nature. My students enjoyed the creative writing weaved into science, and I believe they would be very interested in continuing to display their science knowledge in a creative format in the future.

Resource

National Research Council (NRC). 1996. *National science education standards.* Washington, DC: National Academies Press.

Chapter 31

Ecosystem Journalism

Allow Your Students to Display Their Understanding of Life Science Concepts by Creating an Imaginative Newspaper

By Amy Robertson and Kathryn Mahlin

I f the organisms in a prairie ecosystem created a newspaper, what would it look like? What important news topics of the ecosystem would the organisms want to discuss? Imaginative and enthusiastic third-grade students were busy pondering these questions as they tried their hands at "ecosystem journalism." The class had recently completed a study of prairies; now they were deeply involved in sharing what they learned in a student-written newspaper about this ecosystem. This newspaper project thoroughly engaged students and was a perfect way to encourage students to write creatively about science concepts.

It's Where We Live

The activity was used as an assessment tool at the end of an extensive unit on prairie ecosystems. We studied the prairie ecosystem because much of the surrounding area around the school used to be blackland prairie, named for its characteristic black soil. The class had also previously taken a field trip to learn about prairies. "Because the child's world at grades K–4 is closely associated with the home, school, and immediate environment," the *National Science Education Standards* state, "the study of organisms should include observations and interactions within the natural world of the child" (NRC 1996, p. 128). Our newspaper focused on prairie ecosystems because that was what these students were familiar with, but the activity could be done with any ecosystem.

The articles written in the ecosystem newspaper were intended to be an assessment of the students' depth of understanding of several life science concepts. As suggested in the *National Science Education Standards,* this activity focused on "establishing the primary association of organisms with their environments and the secondary ideas of dependence on various aspects of the environment and of behaviors that help various animals survive" (NRC 1996, p. 128–129). It allowed the students to demonstrate what they learned through application and synthesis by producing a piece of creative literature. The project took the class approximately six 45-minute periods to complete.

Day 1: Brainstorming

To introduce the activity, the class discussed the different parts of a newspaper. A copy of the city newspaper helped jog the students' memories of the different sections. As students named different sections, the teacher listed them on the board. Groups of about four students each chose a section to write. The sections chosen included the classified ads, travel, sports, general news, and weather. Sections such as the comics and crossword puzzles were saved for extra credit if the groups finished early.

The class then brainstormed types of information that would be included in each section of the newspaper. For example, for the main news headlines, the class came up with ideas about newsworthy events that might happen on the prairie, such as a fire or tornado. For the travel section, the class discussed where the prairie animals might visit and how that location and ecosystem would be different from the prairie and how the animals might react. As the students gave suggestions for possible topics for each section, the teacher guided them to think about what types of questions each article would answer, while encouraging them to keep their topics mostly fact based. When discussing the sports section, the teacher explained how the students should use what they know about the characteristics of animals when they are choosing the sports events to cover and in creating the section in general.

Broad questions for each section were then written on the board:

- Weather: What would the weather be like on a typical day on the prairie? (The group writing this section was also responsible for choosing the date of the newspaper and wrote the weather according to the appropriate season.)

- Classifieds: What resources might an organism have that other organisms might want?

- Travel: If some of the animals traveled outside of the prairie ecosystem, what would the experience be like for them?

- Sports: What adaptations do certain animals have that help them with certain sports events?

- General News: What exciting event could happen on the prairie?

The class as a whole created an assessment rubric that was used to guide them through their assignment (Figure 1). After talking about what the end product should contain, the class made a list of all the requirements, and this became the criteria for earning a "4." The teacher then took the criteria chart generated in class and created a tiered rubric for students to use to judge their work throughout the process and check to make sure they included all the needed elements.

Day 2: Research

The second day was dedicated to researching information for each group's section (Figure 2, p. 180). The students were familiar with most of the resources and had used them in other activities during the prairie unit. The students used this time to look up any additional information that they needed for their section and to fact check what they had already learned. Had there been more time in the curriculum, the students would have searched for more of their own books and websites.

The students worked on note taking from the resources so the information could be used during the writing phase. This prewriting technique helped students list the key ideas they wanted to incorporate in their articles. The notes from each group were collected at the end of the day so the teacher could provide feedback on whether or not the groups were working in the right direction. Reviewing the notes also allowed the teacher to pinpoint groups that needed more guidance. At times, the teacher needed to remind students to include more factual information or to check their assessment rubric to make sure they were working on all aspects of the project.

The notes that the students took were handed in with their final product, along with a list of the resources they used for gathering information.

Figure 1. Assessment rubric

	4	3	2	1
Content and creativity	Key facts are included and the information is accurate and written in a creative way.	Key facts are included and most of the information is accurate and written in a creative way.	Some key facts are included and most of the information is accurate and written in a creative way.	Missing key facts and/or most information is inaccurate and may or may not be written in a creative way.
Spelling and grammar	No spelling or grammar errors.	No more than two spelling or grammar errors.	No more than three spelling or grammar errors.	Several spelling or grammar errors.
Notes and references	Each person in the group has turned in completed notes and references.	Each person in the group has turned in notes and references but some are incomplete.	One missing set of notes and/or references with some incomplete notes and/or references.	Several sets of missing notes or references within the group.
Knowledge gained	All students in the group can accurately answer all questions related to the article they worked on and the process.	All students in the group can accurately answer most questions related to the article they worked on and the process.	Most students in the group can accurately answer most questions related to the article and the process.	Several students in the group appear to have little knowledge about the facts and the process.
Teamwork	Each person in the group has contributed without prompting from teachers or peers. No major conflicts.	Each person in the group has contributed with a few reminders from peers. No major conflicts.	One or more students in the group required quite a lot of assistance from peers before contributing. A few conflicts.	One or more students in the group did not contribute. Many conflicts.

Days 3–4: Writing and Editing

The students spent two class periods on writing and editing their sections. Their articles became more polished through the revision of several drafts. This was possible because these were relatively short articles, not long compositions. Students from other groups edited each other's first draft for coherence.

Once this draft was revised, the group had a teacher conference to check the article for spelling, punctuation, and grammar errors. The group then revised the article until all of the students in the group were satisfied with the final product. When some groups finished their sections earlier than the rest of the class, they were allowed to find pictures that supported their article or create another section, such as a comic, a crossword puzzle, or a word find related to prairies.

Days 5–6: Presenting and Publishing

Each group presented its section to the class. The class as a whole discussed which parts of each article were fiction and which parts were based on fact. For example, the class pointed out how hawks really are fast flyers because of adaptations such as strong wings and an aerodynamic shape, but that they do not really compete in races across the prairie with other animals.

Comments from other groups during the presentations provided feedback about the articles. The groups could then make any last-minute changes or additions to their article based on suggestions from the other groups before final publication. In one case, when discussing an article about a tornado in a nearby area, a student pointed out that information about what to do when a tornado comes would be important to those animals reading the newspaper. Based on this suggestion, the group decided to add the information into its article.

The students typed their articles on the computer, and the teacher put the different sections together to complete the newspaper. (Any word-processing program can easily create a newspaperlike format, and some programs may even have templates that can be used.) The completed newspaper displayed what the students learned in a creative and meaningful way.

Outcomes

Creating a newspaper proved to be an effective way for the students to demonstrate not

Figure 2. Selected prairie resources

Nonfiction books:
Johnson, R. L. 2001. *A walk in the prairie.* Minneapolis, MN: Lerner.
Patent, D. H. 1999. *Prairie dogs.* New York: Clarion Books.
Patent, D. H. 1996. *Prairies.* New York: Holiday House.
Wallace, M. D. 2001. *America's prairies and grasslands: Guide to plants and animals.* Golden, CO: Fulcrum.

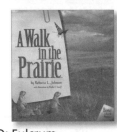

Fiction books:
Bouchard, D. 1998. *If you're not from the prairie.* New York: Aladdin Library.
George, J. C. 1996. *One day in the prairie.* New York: HarperCollins Children's Books.
Lee, E. 1998. *Bluestem horizon: The story of a tallgrass prairie.* Norwalk, CT: Soundprints.
Saunders, S., and J. E. Bosson. 1995. *Jackrabbit and the prairie fire: The story of a black-tailed jackrabbit.* Norwalk, CT: Soundprints.

Websites:
Grasslands
http://mbgnet.mobot.org/sets/grasslnd/index.htm

On the Prairie
www.bellmuseum.org/distancelearning/prairie

only the facts that were learned but also the depth of their understanding of many life science concepts. The ecological concepts of interdependence, adaptation, climate, and competition were all evident throughout the newspaper.

The students wrote about a prairie dog that had extra space in his burrow for rent, demonstrating their understanding that animals have to share resources such as living space. Another group wrote about an uncomfortably hot buffalo that visited Hawaii. In this article, the buffalo wished he could shed his winter coat because the climate in the winter in Hawaii was much warmer than on the prairie. The articles also describe two natural events that occur on the prairie, a fire and a tornado. Within the descriptions of these events, the students talked about the prairie organisms' responses to and adaptations for these types of occurrences.

During this activity, all of the students were enthusiastic about putting a creative spin on what they learned about ecosystems. The teacher periodically reminded the groups to incorporate what they know about prairies and the characteristics of the animals, and this seemed to keep the students on track. Their writing proved to be at a high level because of this enthusiasm for the topic. Furthermore, the students spent more time writing and editing than usual because the final draft was going to be "published" in the form of a newspaper.

Although this activity was successfully implemented at the third-grade level, it could be easily adapted to many different grade levels. This class did the activity at the end of the unit, but with a little added time for research, this activity could also be done in the middle of an ecosystem unit during the learning process. If there is even more time in your curriculum, as a variation of this activity, you can allow each group of students to create an entire newspaper, each with a different ecosystem. The groups can then come together as a class and compare ecosystems and their organisms. The possibilities are endless; so is your students' creativity!

Reference

National Research Council (NRC). 1996. *National science education standards*. Washington, DC: National Academies Press.

Chapter 32

Linking Science and Writing With *Two Bad Ants*

A Trade Book Inspires Two Teachers to Connect Their Curricula in a Creative Way

By Ingrid Hekman Fournier and Leslie Dryer Edison

A few years ago, a fellow teacher and I began working together to develop connections between our third-grade English language arts program and science curriculum. My colleague, a writing teacher, was researching how to include local authors in our reading and writing curriculum. I, a science teacher, wanted to help students develop their science investigation skills while making connections to the writing process. When my colleague discovered Chris Van Allsburg's work, things started to gel. Chris Van Allsburg's adventures and fantasies are entertaining to students, but the books also have real-world connections. He includes just enough scientific information in his fiction to make it easy to springboard into researching the scientific facts.

The following lessons were inspired by the book *Two Bad Ants* (Van Allsburg 1988), a fictional story detailing the journey of two "bad" ants that stray from their colony and choose to stay in a container full of large, white, sweet-tasting crystals (sugar). Through artwork and text, students observe human life from the perspective of two small insects.

The book was the catalyst for an engaging five-day study with third-grade students—in science, the story led to a hands-on investigation with live ants that introduced students to the processes of investigation; in language arts, the story ushered in lessons about understanding point of view, using sensory details, and developing the writing process. We share our experience connecting our two curricula here.

Description and Prediction

Our study began in language arts class, with lessons modified from online lessons based on *Two Bad Ants* (see Internet Resource for an example). The writing teacher reviewed a few Chris Van Allsburg books that students were familiar with (*Polar Express* and *Jumanji*) and shared that Chris Van Allsburg had grown up in our hometown of Grand Rapids, Michigan. She told the students that they were going to begin studying ants in science and learning about

point-of-view writing in language arts. As she read *Two Bad Ants* aloud, she asked students to listen to the descriptions on each page and to predict what the ants were seeing or experiencing (e.g., sugar crystals, cup of coffee, the view of a teaspoon coming down into their "hot brown lake" of coffee, being spun around in a garbage disposal, the inside of an electric socket). Students enjoyed discovering these places from the ants' perspective. Afterward, students made charts comparing human and ant points of view from various situations not described in the book.

Later that day, in science class, students began researching ants in preparation for a guided hands-on investigation planned for the next day. Students worked in small groups using nonfiction texts about ants from our school and local libraries. I also presented an ant farm that we would be keeping in the classroom so students could make observations of live ants. (Ant farms can be purchased from science suppliers.)

Students observed the ants and recorded their observations in their science journals. Before beginning observations, I prompted them with questions: "What are the ants doing?" "Does it seem like they are communicating? If so, how?" "Do they appear to be working or resting?" The students were amazed at how the ants dug tunnels. They observed that some of the ants were physically moving the sand, while others were carrying it away. They were definitely working as a team. The students also noted that when we turned on the light over the ant colony, the ants seemed to slow down in their work. This prompted some students to wonder whether ants work better in daylight or at night.

Ten Hungry Ants

The next day, we built upon the previous day's experiences. In language arts class, students chose one of the numerous situations from the prior day and wrote a more extensive description of the two points of view (human and ant). This took the students' writing from one-line observations—such as a person viewing a swimming pool from a high diving board as a "cool blue pool" and the ant viewing it as a "large ocean"—to multiline descriptions:

"My legs begin to quiver. I am scared. I do not want to dive. The blue water below looks so far away. Can I jump?" (human's perspective)

"Where am I? I'm really tired. That was a long hike straight up. What's that blue rug down there? Why is it so shiny? Is that water? Yikes! How do I get down from here?" (ant's perspective).

Later that day, in science class, students observed the ants in the ant farm again, recording their observations in their science journals, and we started talking about the kinds of food ants might prefer. The students mentioned that the ants in *Two Bad Ants* really seemed to like the sugar crystals. They also made connections to seeing ants swarm around watermelon and spilled soda on their porches during the summer. We discussed what was in these foods that may have attracted the ants. Sugar, salt? Then, I introduced our class investigation. Because my students hadn't yet had a lot of experience with inquiry-oriented science investigations, I planned this guided investigation so that students could gain practice in investigation skills (e.g., making predictions, following procedures, recording data, graphing results, writing conclusions). To simplify matters, I created a worksheet listing four possible food preferences and a procedure for testing the ants' preferences (see Figure 1).

Figure 1. Ant investigation worksheet

Purpose
The purpose of this investigation is to determine which food (chips, an orange, bread, or strawberry jam) ants prefer to eat.

Prediction
I predict the ants will eat the _____ because _____
_____.

Materials
1 shoebox, divided into four equal sections
10 ants
1 tsp. of each of chips, an orange, bread, and strawberry jam

Procedure
1. Gather all materials.

2. Place one teaspoon of each of the foods in a far corner of the shoe box. Place chips in one corner, jam in another, and so forth.

3. Place 10 ants directly in the center of the shoe box.

4. Record on the data sheet which foods the ants go toward and touch.

5. Repeat the procedure two more times.

6. Record all results.

7. Conduct error analysis.

Problems I encountered with this investigation were _____
_____.

Results
Food	Number of Ants
Chips	_____
Orange	_____
Bread	_____
Strawberry jam	_____

Conclusion
In conclusion, my prediction was _____ (supported/not supported).
I predicted that the ants would prefer _____.
I learned that they prefer to eat _____.
This project will help me in my daily life because _____
_____
_____.

After reviewing the worksheet together, students recorded their predictions based on their own personal experiences with ants. Since students had seen ants outside in their yards around their own foods, their predictions included such ideas as, "I think the ants will eat the potato chips because the chips have a lot of grease" and "I think the ants will eat the strawberry jelly because it has a lot of sugar."

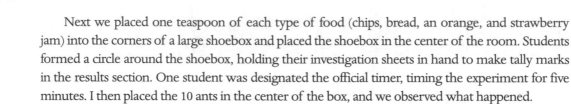

Next we placed one teaspoon of each type of food (chips, bread, an orange, and strawberry jam) into the corners of a large shoebox and placed the shoebox in the center of the room. Students formed a circle around the shoebox, holding their investigation sheets in hand to make tally marks in the results section. One student was designated the official timer, timing the experiment for five minutes. I then placed the 10 ants in the center of the box, and we observed what happened.

We quickly realized that we needed to determine what constituted "ants preferring a food." Did they prefer it if they wandered into the square? Or did the ants have to be touching the food directly? Together we concluded that the ants had to be touching the food directly to mark it on our data table.

After five minutes, students returned to their seats to graph the results. I gave each student a section of graph paper titled "What Food Do Ants Prefer?" and together we created a graph. I drew a sample graph on an overhead projector and students added the appropriate information to their graphs on paper. I asked the students how to determine what goes on the *x*-axis and what should go on the *y*-axis. Students decided that the types of food should go along the bottom based on their past experiences of working with bar graphs in math and science; they felt it was important to have the numbers on the *y*-axis show the patterns of numbers. We titled the *x*-axis, "Foods," and wrote the four types of food on that line. Next we looked at the data table to the highest number of ants that preferred a food—it was seven. I asked the students what could be done with that information. Students commented that we needed to determine what numbers would go on the *y*-axis. Some students suggested writing the scale in increments of 5, others suggested 10. A few students argued the case to write the scale as numbers 1 through 10. When I asked why, one student explained that it would be easier to see the results, and the graph had more than 10 blocks so we could do it by ones. The class agreed that this would be best.

Then I asked students what the title of the *y*-axis should be, and students said, "Number of Ants." Next, I asked two student volunteers to come to the overhead to complete the bar graph, with the rest of their classmates following along on the graphs at their desks. When all the graphs were complete, I asked the students to determine which food the ants most preferred. Students noted that the ants preferred the strawberry jam. Students commented that the graph helped them see the main idea better, which I pointed out was one of the reasons that graphs are helpful.

Mystery Places and Results

On the third day in language arts, students were asked to describe a mystery place using the five senses, from both the point of view of a person and an ant. This helped the students further develop their ideas as well as include sensory details (we had studied the senses earlier in the year in science class).

Meanwhile, that day in science class, we discussed our "error analysis," or how we could have made the project better. Most students commented that they would have changed the container in which we conducted the experiment because some of the ants escaped by climbing over the wall of the shoebox and abandoning the project.

Students then created science boards using the data from their worksheets. I gave each student a large piece of construction paper, which they folded into three sections, two equal-size pieces on the sides with a larger area in the middle. In the center they each displayed the title of our project, a drawing of an ant, and their graphs. Students pasted their predictions and procedures on the left side of the boards and results (data tables) and conclusions on the right side.

For their conclusions, students restated whether their predictions were supported and what they learned from the project. For example, one student wrote, "I predicted that the ants would prefer the chips, but I learned that the ants preferred the strawberry jelly."

Writings and Assessments

In writing class, for the final two days, the students finished their points-of-view writings from a mystery location by revising and peer editing their papers. Students worked in pairs to determine whether or not the writing presented an original point of view (not one used by Chris Van Allsburg or the teacher). Students also helped one another make sure at least four of the senses were represented in the writings. At the end of class, students shared their final draft pieces with the class.

In science class, students spent the final days making additional observations of the ant farm and writing a summary paragraph of the experience. Some comments included, "This experiment was cool because we got to see what some ants' favorite foods are. This was probably my favorite project in third grade so far. If you ever do this project, beware the ant will climb out."

In addition to the ongoing teacher observation assessment that occurred during class, we evaluated students' work samples. In science, the summary paragraphs were to cover the main points of the experience, and the science boards needed to be complete with a clearly written prediction, the collected data from the experiment, a clearly labeled graph, and a conclusion.

Success

All of us—students and their two teachers—had a great time with these lessons. Upon reflection, the next time we conduct these lessons, we plan to let students drive the content more. What do students want to discover about ants? What is a driving question we could work together to answer? How can students design their own experiments to study ant behavior? With this successful experience under our belts, we are ready to take on bigger challenges and continue to get students excited while participating in our science and writing classes.

References

Van Allsburg, C. 1981. *Jumanji*. Boston: Houghton Mifflin.
Van Allsburg, C. 1984. *The polar express*. Boston: Houghton Mifflin.
Van Allsburg, C. 1998. *Two bad ants*. Boston: Houghton Mifflin.

Internet Resource

Teaching Point of View With Two Bad Ants
   www.readwritethink.org/lessons/lesson_view.asp?id=789

Chapter 33

Partners in Crime
Integrating Forensic Science and Writing

By Erik Hein

Writing across the curriculum has become an ever-present theme in schools around the nation. The push comes at a time when test scores drive curriculum and standards are the holy grail of education. How, then, can teachers keep education interesting while closing the achievement gap? It can be done by thinking outside the box and collaborating with other teachers and community members. For example, forensic science lends itself to many academic areas. Aside from the science itself, writing plays a major role in the investigation process as well as the courtroom. It is paramount that students learn how to write proficiently when recording results or writing evaluations and reports, just as forensic scientists must do. This skill can also be developed through narrative, persuasive, and expository writing.

Our project, Partners in Crime, has been running for eight years. Its success is due in part to our partnerships with the community and a Toyota Tapestry Grant. The money has been used to purchase crime scene supplies, science consumables, and forensic books for the library. Our partnerships in the community range from various areas of the police department to the assistant district attorney. On a large scale, this project takes a great deal of planning, but it can be successfully modified to a much smaller scale that still combines science and writing.

The project's scale determines the amount of preparation required. Curriculum also dictates when areas of forensic science can be integrated. A small-scale project might be one case involving two pieces of forensic evidence and span three to four days. For example, the student government cash box has been stolen from the office. Upon investigation, fingerprints and a torn piece of cloth surface as evidence. Students need one class period to learn about fingerprints—where they come from biologically; how they appear on certain surfaces; and how to dust for, lift, and identify them. The teacher should call the local police department detective unit and invite them to give a lecture about fingerprints. After the lecture, and if the necessary materials are available, the detective may run a short lab with stations. Students can rotate to stations that deal with dusting, lifting, and identifying prints. If a detective is not available, the teacher can do some quick research on websites such TruTV (formerly CourtTV), the FBI, or the National Institute of Justice (see Internet Resources). These websites also have reproducible handouts showing different fingerprint patterns and details for identification.

Use another class period for discussing hair and fiber analysis. A simple identification for fibers includes using a compound microscope and the burn test. (The burn test should only be done by the teacher using proper ventilation.) All fibers will have different appearances under the microscope. They will also burn differently, which students can record in their lab books. Now students are incorporating sensory details into their writing. Again, this information can be found on the internet or in forensic books for teacher use.

The next class can be the actual scenario of what was stolen and what was found. The teacher can prepare lifted prints beforehand, and have a fiber sample of the cloth found at the crime scene. Students should record their information in lab books using descriptions and drawings. The class can work in two stations, one for fingerprints and the other for fibers.

After the crime is solved, students write an expository essay explaining the steps involved in testing the evidence. Students should be able to list each step in sequential order from beginning to end. They should write in complete sentences and paragraph form. The teacher should be looking for content and sequential order. Do not worry about comma splices and bad subject-verb agreement. The English teacher can cover that in his or her class. The objective is to encourage students to write about science and the process involved. Yes, if the teacher feels comfortable correcting grammatical errors, then by all means, go for it, but the focus should be on whether the students understand the scientific process and its relationship to the case.

Community Involvement

Before setting up a mock crime scene, invite several community members into the classroom to discuss how writing and science are linked. A detective, a forensic scientist, and a lawyer are good choices.

Bringing a detective into the classroom provides an opportunity to discuss crime scene integrity and protocol. They are usually more than willing to work with students and even run labs with their equipment. Forensic reports must be written with prudence, for they are used in court. Students should learn how to approach a crime scene, document it, collect evidence, label it, and prevent contamination. The detective should also have some samples of official documents that are used at crime scenes. If you do not have detectives or specialists available, use the websites listed under Internet Resources. Fill out a few of these documents and have students proofread for errors in grammar and sentence structure. Students should also be looking for details, sequential order, and organization. Remind students that these papers are official court documents and should be very explicit in nature. The teacher can give an example and exaggerate the absurdity by explaining every single detail down to the half-eaten piece of pepperoni pizza that was found underneath the right side of the green plush couch next to the white marble table with the red rose floral arrangement in the clear crystal vase (they should get the point). Does the writing clearly explain the item discussed? Does it ramble on? Can certain words be deleted or added for better coherency? Make a list of these on the board for students to use as reference.

Another valuable person to have in the classroom is a forensic scientist who works for a state or independent crime lab. If one is not available, go to the internet and set up a video conference. There are many accredited associations who will list experts and contact information, such as the American Academy of Forensic Science or the Virginia Institute of Forensic Science and Medicine. The FBI and TruTV might also be worth a request (see Internet Resources). If you're working with someone from the police department, he or she might have contacts at local crime labs or other organizations. Your forensic expert should discuss responsibilities as a scientist and the role writing plays in the job. A forensic scientist's results play a major part in an investigation and could end up in the courtroom as well.

Another possible community member to include is a lawyer, preferably a criminal lawyer. He or she should discuss the importance of persuasive language in the courtroom as well as in writing. Clarity and accuracy of diction are vital. As an extension to this visit, students could choose to argue for the prosecution or defense in a case. They should write in the first person and state their points with confidence and authority. If at all possible, share some ideas with the lawyer beforehand to tailor a lesson plan for the day. A relevant and efficient lesson focuses on specific, existing problems in some of the writing pieces.

A very effective method to use is K-W-L. Have students write a short piece on what they already know about the subject and how writing might be involved, then list what they want to know and generate meaningful questions. Students should stay away from what-if questions, because they rarely offer academic answers. They usually elicit a story from the speaker, which is fine the first time, but it often spurs a barrage of other what-if situations, and important information is missed. After the lawyer's lecture, students should go back and write down what they have learned from the presentation, as well as any unanswered questions.

A Mock Case on a Larger Scale

After the visits are completed, the teacher might construct a mock crime scene and give students a chance to peruse it. The science teacher should begin with a scenario of an investigation. For example, a person is reported missing, and the only clues in the ransacked apartment are a piece of rope, fingerprints, cigarette butts in the sink, and lipstick prints on a wine glass. These items all fall into different categories—fingerprint identification, hair and fiber analysis, DNA, and chromatography.

The teacher can actually set up a crime scene that is similar to the one in the scenario. Be careful what kind of scenario is used and stay away from blood, guts, and gore; students have enough of that on television, in the movies, and in their video games. As students view the scene, they should take copious notes of the surrounding area and identify pieces of evidence in reference to the room. Were the cigarette butts found in the sink smoked? What color is the lipstick on the glass? Are there visible fingerprints on it? Is the rope tied in a knot? How long is the rope? These are all essential questions students should be asking themselves as they document the scene. As students begin writing, they should consider parts of speech other than adjectives, such as prepositions. Prepositional phrases are used to show where pieces of evidence lay in reference to the room. Above the table or below it? Near the corner or far away from the bedroom? Adverbs are also important because they tell where, when, how, and to what extent.

Once students have their notes, and evidence is documented and collected, they may begin to test evidence and record findings in their lab books. For example, a lab using chromatography can be set up with the lipstick. Fingerprints can be lifted from the wine glass and identified using a magnifying glass and a chart of common fingerprint patterns. As more evidence is tested, the perpetrator's profile should come together. The teacher can also consider listing information about suspects to promote deductive reasoning. For example, there is a man missing in the scenario and it turns out he had a few enemies. Which one wore lipstick and liked to drink wine? Did any of them smoke? These pieces of information give students something to consider while they are testing evidence and putting together a hypothesis about the guilty party. Students can work in groups while testing evidence, but they should be writing in their own lab books.

To incorporate more formal writing, have students use official forms to document the scene. They can also attach a one-page narrative documenting their steps throughout the processing of the scene. This can later be turned into a short narrative piece to be submitted to court as their deposition.

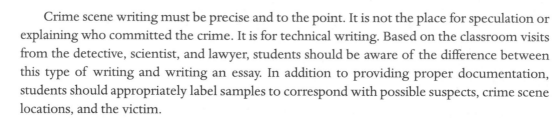

Crime scene writing must be precise and to the point. It is not the place for speculation or explaining who committed the crime. It is for technical writing. Based on the classroom visits from the detective, scientist, and lawyer, students should be aware of the difference between this type of writing and writing an essay. In addition to providing proper documentation, students should appropriately label samples to correspond with possible suspects, crime scene locations, and the victim.

Now is the time for the English teacher to enter the picture. He or she should be made aware of the scenario, evidence collected, and labs completed. The job of the English teacher is to have students write a narrative piece explaining what happened in the crime. Through the results of their tests, a hypothesis about the guilty party should emerge, and eventually the crime can be solved. The assignment is for students to retell the crime from one of the following points of view: the perpetrator, victim, detective, forensic scientist, prosecution, or defense. Creativity is necessary here to fill in gaps of the story. Students may even wish to change results or pretend the evidence was contaminated to help their case. This requires students to evaluate information and make educated decisions about the outcome of their papers. Writing with fluency is also important because chronological order must be followed to keep the paper focused. The English teacher might grade the essay on the elements of literature (plot, character, setting, and theme), use of scientific terms, and lab results. Other elements incorporated and graded might include parts of speech, clauses, use of dialogue, and proper punctuation of quotes. These items should be incorporated throughout the entire paper to achieve coherency and precision.

Conclusion

The results are amazing. Students are actively engaged in learning while improving and honing their skills as writers. They talk about the case outside of class and exchange ideas during lunch. They are not only writing the scientific process, but they are also using higher level thinking skills to evaluate and weigh evidence in correlation to the case. New relationships are developed with the community, and students embark on a real-life journey of a crime scene investigator. The more they delve into forensic science, the more students will be running up to you to explain how television shows are incorrect and improper evidence collection ruled throughout the show. Now that's real detective work!

Internet Resources

American Academy of Forensic Science
   www.aafs.org
CourtTV
   www.trutv.com
FBI
   www.fbi.gov
National Institute of Justice
   www.ojp.usdoj.gov/nij

Chapter 34

A Reason to Write

By Peggy Ashbrook

Children love seeing their work and photos of themselves at work. Make this an opportunity for an early literacy experience by creating a book about a classroom investigation. Document each step of a process with photographs and student drawings. With help, young children can add further explanation, describing their actions or thoughts. A National Institute for Early Education Research Preschool Policy Brief states that "young children build vocabulary when they engage in activities that are cognitively and linguistically stimulating by encouraging them to describe events and build background knowledge."

Lessons on buoyancy work well as explorations to document and are part of the National Science Education Content Standards A, science as inquiry, and B, physical science, properties of objects and materials. Children know that some objects sink in water and others float. The relationship between volume and density and floating can be explored—if not measured—in the early years with the following materials (some of which challenge assumptions): sponges, pumice, fruit, small-lidded containers (some filled with water, some with air), soap, dense plastic models of animals that swim, various balls, jar-and-bottle lids, keys, coins, plasticine, and sea shells.

Teachers may find it helpful to review resources before doing a "sink or float" activity with students (Robertson 2007). When talking about testing for sinking or floating, use the complete phrase "sink in water" to invite trying this activity with other liquids such as milk, vegetable oil, or corn syrup. Discovery bottles filled with liquids such as corn syrup offer additional nonmessy experiences (Watson 2008).

Before putting anything in the water, children can draw objects they think will float and label them as such. Children often reveal their incomplete understanding when telling why they think something will sink. Challenging incomplete understanding with heavy objects that float presents additional experiences on which to base their ideas. If they say "All rocks sink," give them a piece of pumice (often sold at hardware stores) among a varied set of rocks to test this hypothesis.

After the classroom investigation is complete and the book documenting the activity is assembled (see Figure 1, p. 195), students may at first peruse the book looking only for evidence of their participation, shouting, "I drew that!" At later readings, however, they become more interested in discussing the meaning of the work. Help the children refine their vocabulary and thinking by asking, "Do all hard things sink?" "What is the difference between hard and heavy?" "Can heavy things float?" Plans can be made to revisit the activity to test new predictions. The book can be amended. Buoyancy is a complicated topic that requires repeated experiences for understanding. However, by documenting their scientific investigation, students not only gain understanding of a difficult concept but also have opportunity to revise their thinking.

Sink or Float

Objective:
To gain experience with the nature of density for the creation of a book

Materials:

- Water table or large tub (clear plastic is best for easy viewing)
- Water
- Towels
- Some objects that will sink and some that will float in water: plastic and metal bottle lids, small pieces of wood (sticks or slices), old keys, stones (including pumice), small pieces of cloth, shells, sponges, fruit, small-lidded containers (some filled with water, some with air), soap, plastic toys (including dense plastic models of animals that swim), coins, Plasticine, golf balls, and balls that do and do not float
- Writing and drawing materials
- Camera (optional)
- Page protectors and notebook

Procedure:

1. Propose that the class make a book about a science activity for others to read and repeat the activity. Examine a published book of science activities as an example of what might be useful to other student scientists (see Resource). The class's book can contain drawings, writings, and photographs. Choose an activity to document; here we describe a sink/float activity.

2. If students are new to journaling their work, explain the idea of recording their thoughts and observations to refer to later.

3. Prepare materials for documenting work (e.g., writing and drawing materials, a camera).

4. Demonstrate *float* and *sink* with two objects in a tub of water.

5. Explain what it means to make a prediction. Ask, "Which object do you predict will float in water? Which objects do you predict will sink in water? Why do you think so?"

6. Have the children choose objects they think will sink and objects they think will float. Then have them draw the items ("floaters" on one page and "sinkers" on another). Older children can write a label or sentence. All children can take photographs to document the experience.

7. Let the children discover whether their predictions are true through experience, supporting their explorations with open-ended questions such as "What happens when you put [the object] in the water?" and "Does it always do that?"

8. Have the children view objects through the side of the tub and check to see if the object actually touches the bottom or if it floats above it. (They can also feel gently with their fingers). Ask, "Is [the object] touching the bottom of the container? Is it near the top of the water?"

9. Have the children record the results they observe, drawing the objects on a teacher-created cross-section or outline of the container with the water level drawn with a symbolic wavy line. Children's understanding of representation, and of sinking and floating, can be assessed by their placement of the object in the picture relative to the waterline.

10. Assemble the children's documentation into a book. Page protectors cover the documentation during reading. Read it aloud, and refer back to it later.

This activity requires some teacher follow-up time to format the documentation for book form. Much of the work can be done with students—a few pages at a time or in small discussion groups to allow for varying attention spans—over several sessions. To switch things up, have students create an audio book, voice recording their initial predictions, data, and observations. You can even revisit this activity with seasonal natural objects such as pumpkins, seeds, snowballs, or leaves to renew interest in buoyancy. By repeating their play, children learn that objects act in predictable ways. Each time students read the book about their work, they discuss their ideas again.

Figure 1. Sample pages from a class-made science activity book

Water is an interesting material.

Water You can play in water, water feels soft and wet and is very light. Water can move.

In water, some things sink and some things float.

Floating is when it staysabove the water.

Sinking is when staysunder water.

The block is floating and the rock sank to the bottom.

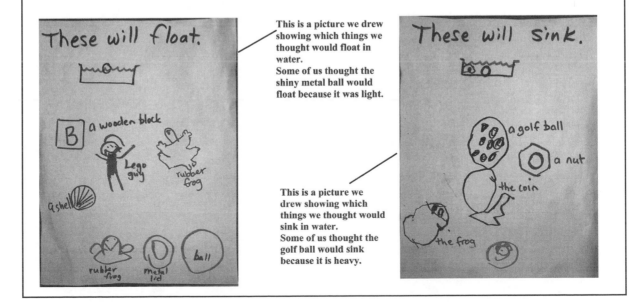

These will float.

a wooden block

B

Lego guy

rubber frog

a shell

rubber frog   metal lid   ball

This is a picture we drew showing which things we thought would float in water.
Some of us thought the shiny metal ball would float because it was light.

This is a picture we drew showing which things we thought would sink in water.
Some of us thought the golf ball would sink because it is heavy.

These will sink.

a golf ball

a nut

the coin

the frog

References

National Research Council (NRC). 1996. *National science education standards.* Washington, DC: National Academy Press.

Robertson, W. C. 2007. How can an ocean liner made of steel float on water? *Science and Children* 44 (9): 56–59.

Strickland, D. S., and S. Riley-Ayers. 2006. Early literacy: Policy and practice in the preschool years. Issue 10 of *Preschool policy brief,* ed. E. Frede and W. S. Barnett. New Brunswick, NJ: National Institute for Early Education Research. *http://nieer.org/resources/policybriefs/10.pdf.*

Watson, S. 2008. Discovery bottles. *Science and Children* 45 (9): 20–24.

Resource

Ardley, N. 2006. *101 great science experiments.* New York: Dorling Kindersley Children.

Chapter 35

A Key to Science
A Simple Writing Technique Helps Students Communicate Understanding of Important Science Concepts

By Jo Ann Yockey

We're always finding new ways to communicate the wonders of science to our students—hands-on discoveries, observations, and experiments. But perhaps we should spend more time helping our students communicate what they have learned.

Think about it. This is the age of information technology, which means not only gathering information but also sharing it with others. Even primary-age students are chatting over the internet, sharing their knowledge with one another. "Did you see that story on the news last night … ?" "Let me tell you what we did in school today … " When it is retold, or shared, the information often becomes theirs.

Over the past 14 years, I have used many useful hands-on activities for science curriculums, yet it has always been a challenge to find a way for students to communicate to me those fundamental principles they learned. When I began teaching at my current school, however, a solution presented itself in a surprisingly simple way.

My school is composed of an early school, which starts at age two and continues through transitional kindergarten, and an elementary school, which picks up at kindergarten and goes through eighth grade. Beginning as early as kindergarten, the curriculum integrates skills across content areas. At the heart of this integration is our writing program. One way we help students develop their writing skills is through the "key-word process."

The Process

In this method, students select key words about a topic and use those words to build their own sentences and paragraphs. The key-word process can be expanded from paragraphs to create outlines, stories, essays, and research papers. The key-word process helps children learn not only how to write but also what they are writing *about*. This model produces extraordinary results when applied to the science classroom. My students no longer have trouble communicating the content of what they have learned.

The National Science Education Standards Content Standard B for grades 5–8 states that all students should develop an understanding of properties and changes of properties in matter. To inspire students' curiosity, we began with a simple version of the game "I Spy." My students described objects in the room, giving exact details. This led to a discussion of the physical properties of these "things." How could we group the objects according to their properties? We could make a group of red things and not-red things. We could make a group of soft things and not-soft things. As students tried to be exact in their descriptions, they were inspired to look at the actual space that the object took up. It seemed that all the objects in the room could be put in one group—matter that takes up space.

The children then selected objects—pencils, blocks, paper polygons, erasers—and traced on paper their outlines, which they could measure. For irregular objects, they used lengths of yarn to place around the shapes, then measured the yarn with a ruler. Integrating mathematics, we reviewed that the distance around the traced drawing was the object's perimeter. The children then recorded the perimeters next to their drawings and drew a conclusion: All the objects took up a definite space.

Students wondered, "How could you change that space?" To find out, they traced their hands with fingers outspread. Then they were instructed to change the shape of the hand and trace it again. They crumbled or cut paper and yarn. Again they observed that even if the malleable objects were cut or torn, they still occupied a definite space. The objects changed their space or shape ONLY when a force acted on them.

However, when the class began to examine water in this context, students quickly observed that while it occupied space, the size and shape of that space depended on the size and shape of the water's container. They recognized on their own that we were dealing with two distinct types of objects. They even came up with the group names: *solids* and *nonsolids*.

Using water, eyedroppers, and wax paper, the students moved drops of water, observing that when one drop bumped into another drop, the two joined easily. Unlike the solids, however, the drops could not be torn or cut to change their shape. Thus we observed the properties of the nonsolid group as it related to space. This group could be classified as matter, because it too occupied space, but not as solid, because its space was not definite.

What else could students learn that was common to these objects—both solids and nonsolids? The students observed that even though two objects might seem to occupy the same amount of space, they were not necessarily alike. One student put a ball in a glass and filled a similar glass with water. When she held one glass in each hand, she exclaimed, "They feel different!" The glasses held different amounts of matter. One was light and one was heavy.

This led students to a balance, where they explored the weight of various objects. Using gram weights, they estimated the weight of common classroom items, then put them on the scale to check their estimates. The data they collected was used to make a graph.

Because this was a new concept, we did not deal with the difference between mass and weight. Gram weights were used for simplicity. However to introduce the concept that weight is a function of gravity, the students also used spring scales. The stretching of the springs by the "weight" of the object helped the students visualize the concept of gravity's pull. If two objects looked the same, and they seemed to take up the same space, why was one object heavier than the other? What made the lead ball heavier than the rubber ball? Could students' exploration of solids and nonsolids lead to an introductory understanding of the mass of objects?

Learning About Volume

Our consideration of mass began with an exploration of volume. To visualize the inability of two objects to occupy the same space, students partially filled a beaker with water and recorded the water level. Then students placed a solid object, a rock, into the beaker and observed the water level rise. We discussed that the liquid was being *displaced*, or pushed aside, by the solid object. Was the amount—or volume—of water that the object pushed out of its way the same volume as the rock's? If so, a solid object's volume could be determined by the amount of water it displaced.

Volume and mass are two concepts that are difficult to understand. The children were aware of the differences in weight and could easily predict which objects would float or sink. And they knew that, generally, heavier objects would sink. But they found that this concept wasn't as simple as it appeared. I decided that it was time for some background information, so we continued learning by reading a story about Archimedes, the Greek scientist who had a scientific "breakthrough" as he realized that volume could be measured as water was displaced.

The class was ready to do an investigation of its own. This time, groups of students carefully measured 50 ml of water into beakers before placing a rock into each beaker. Like Archimedes, they observed and recorded both the original and the new water levels. By subtracting the old ml levels from the new, they calculated and recorded the volume of the rocks.

After a class discussion and their hands-on experiences, students stated that *volume* is the amount of space occupied by a three-dimensional object. They also verbalized answers to the following questions: What is matter? What is a solid? What is volume? They stated that *matter* is anything that occupies space and has mass; a *solid* is matter that occupies a definite space. All objects have *mass; volume* is the amount of space occupied in three dimensions, that is, the space occupied by matter.

Essential Matter

Once everyone had independently verbalized the definitions of these key vocabulary words, students each wrote a paragraph on the topic of matter using the three key words—*matter, volume,* and *solid*. As they had learned in language arts, students knew the paragraph had to have a topic sentence, at least two detail sentences, and a conclusion. Here were a few examples of students' paragraphs on matter:

■ Matter is very interesting. Matter is anything that takes up space and has mass. Some types of matter are liquids and gases (which are fluids) and solids. A solid is something that takes up a definite space. One example of a solid is ice. Matter is everything!

■ Matter is very interesting because it is anything that takes up space and has mass. Matter can either be a solid or a fluid. All matter takes up volume, even things you can't see. All solids have a definite space. Matter is very exciting.

■ Matter is very interesting. Matter has volume, which is the amount of space matter takes up. There are three different kinds of matter: solids, which have definite space; and liquids and gases, which are called fluids. Everything you see is matter. Matter is a strange thing.

Although the paragraphs showed that students needed to work on having more variety in topic sentences, two things were apparent. First, it was obvious that the children remembered the concepts taught, and not only did they remember, but they also were able to write about them intelligently. Second, it was clear that students were beginning to formulate an elementary understanding of the concepts.

Continued Learning

As students realized that solid objects of the same space might have different volumes, they were ready to explore *density,* the amount of matter within an object (mass) divided by its volume.

We began this time not by looking at solids but by looking at a nonsolid—water. Could they make water hold up or float an object that would ordinarily sink? Could they make water have more "push"? From their personal experiences, it was not hard to hypothesize. After all, one student contributed, "Isn't it easier to float when you are at the beach?" They believed they could change the density of water by mixing a solution of saltwater.

To explore this idea, the students were given a ballpoint pen top and some clay to insert into it, so that the plastic pen top would sink when placed in a jar of ordinary tap water. Next, students gradually added salt to the water. As the salt increased the water's density, the pen top began to float. The students were excited that their hypothesis was proving correct. Their saltwater solution was indeed denser than pure water. Furthermore, they observed that the color of the water had changed. It was not as clear, and one boy could "see" the change in the matter.

I explained to students that the pen top floated because of an upward push, called *buoyancy force,* of water on the cap. This force increased with the density of the saltwater solution. The buoyant force depends on the difference in densities of the object and the solution. The floating cap acted like a *hydrometer,* an instrument used to measure the density of a liquid, and it rose closer to the surface as the density of the salt solution increased.

The students were excited to make the cap bounce up and down. I let their natural curiosity take them on free exploration to see if any of the rocks and seashells in our collection could be made to float. Free "play" continued as salt solutions were mixed in brave attempts to raise even the heaviest of objects to the surface, with varying degrees of success of course.

Students' curiosity extended to exploring the density of other liquids, as groups of students worked with corn syrup and cooking oil. At the end of the activity students knew that not all cups contained liquids of equal density. Like the solids, fluids that occupied the same amount of space did not necessarily have the same density. A cup of salt water did not have the same density as a cup of oil.

Good Vibrations

Through these activities students began to understand that matter is made of particles too small to see. How much matter is in a rock? How much matter is in a cup of water? How much matter is in a cup of salt water? Those small pieces of matter that we could not see are called *atoms* or *molecules*. With even this rudimentary knowledge, I hoped to extend the children's knowledge of solids, liquids, gases, and density. I wanted students to begin to understand that the invisible particles that make up matter are all in constant motion, or *vibrating*, even though their movement is not seen by the naked eye.

Are molecules really "pushing" on one another? I suggested a demonstration that would give students some clue to the answer. Students filled a beaker with 400 ml of water, added two drops of food coloring, waited, and observed. Students saw that the small particles of dye were "pushing and shoving." The food coloring moved. What force was doing the moving? Was anyone stirring or shaking the beaker? No. Given enough time, the colored particles spread evenly throughout the container of vibrating water. One student excitedly commented, "Wow, nature doesn't need a swizzle stick!"

What moved the food coloring? "The molecules!" students concluded. While the students couldn't actually see the molecules, they could see the results of their movement. I told the students that all matter has particles that *vibrate*. However, all molecules want to stay together. That force is called *cohesion*. These were new vocabulary words but not difficult concepts to grasp because the students were able to "see" the effects of both vibration and cohesion as they looked at the colored water.

If the cohesion is strong, as in the solid beaker, the glass is able to keep its shape. While the particles do vibrate in solid matter, the vibration is in place, and solid matter holds its shape because its cohesion is stronger than the vibration. In liquid matter the vibration is greater than in solid matter. Those particles of liquid move about, or vibrate, rapidly. This is why liquids have no shape of their own but are able to hold the shape of their containers. Therefore, the *cohesion* and *vibration* are in balance.

For continued fun and learning, the students made "bubble domes." A simple solution of detergent, glycerin, and water gave them the opportunity to investigate how liquids and gases flow and take up space and, at the same time, to learn more about cohesion and vibration.

After pouring a bit of their detergent-glycerin solution onto a flat tray, each student took a straw and blew slowly into the solution. The result were bubble domes! As they blew more air, the volume of gas inside their domes increased. They discovered that, after wetting their straws, they could pull them in and out of the soapy solution. In this manner they were able to form second bubble domes inside the first ones. The swirling colors on the surface of the bubbles were never still.

What force moved them? Students watched in silent fascination as the most patient children intently blew and their bubbles stretched and stretched. Students began to wonder what force was moving the incandescent colors around the surface of the domes. For every movement there must be a force. There was no wind, no push by a straw, no push by moving water, no push by gravity. The students thought it must be the molecules pushing the colors! The bubbles' thickness changes due to molecular motion and this produces changing colors. We watched the colors curl and spread out as children stretched the soap solution until each bubble dome finally burst.

Communicating Concepts

Yet for all the excitement of the hands-on exploration, this was only one part of students' learning. For me, the real challenge was to get children to communicate these scientific concepts in an intelligent way. Through *writing,* the words and the concepts could become truly theirs. Thus, after their bubble dome exploration, students wrote key-word paragraphs using *cohesion, vibration, gases,* and *liquids* as their key words. Here is one of those paragraphs:

Bubble Dome Fun

On February 18, the class went to the science lab. Mrs. Yockey poured water, dishwasher detergent, and vegetable glycerin into trays. We each chose a straw. Everyone stuck their straws in the liquid and blew gas into the tray. Soon there was a buzz of excitement in the air and cries of competition, yelling, "Who will make the biggest bubble?" But within that excitement and fun there was much to learn. The rainbow swirls in the bubble were caused by vibration on the surface. The bubble domes could expand because the cohesion kept their molecules together.

Even students who were not able to incorporate all of the key words turned in successful paragraphs:

How to Make a Perfect Bubble

In science we made bubble domes. They were all different shapes, sizes, and colors. The color lit up the room. It was so pretty when the light hit it. It made a rainbow. To make the bubble we needed water, detergent, and vegetable glycerin, which made them stronger. Also we needed a straw to blow the bubble. You must wet your straw constantly so you don't break the cohesion. This is how to make a perfect bubble.

Using the Strategy for Longer Projects

The information in the students' key-word paragraphs became information that they knew—it stuck. Students remembered their paragraphs when it was time to provide short answers on tests. They found they could easily communicate their content knowledge.

I also have used the strategy for longer projects. By answering a string of questions using key words as answers, students are able to develop clear and serviceable outlines for their first research papers. My students wrote research papers on matter (Figure 1).

All-Around Benefits

Sharing discoveries is as important in the science classroom as it is in the laboratory. Your students may shuffle computer files rather than papers, but by using key words, they write their discoveries in accurate phrases, clear sentences, and intelligent paragraphs.

At my school, the value of words and the power of communicating are established from the beginning of each content area, not only in language arts but also in social studies, foreign language, mathematics, and science. This means more than having students write down an observation. Science must be integrated into the writing curriculum, and writing must be integrated into the science curriculum. Students can enjoy not only the excitement of discovery, but also the pride that comes from being able to communicate what they know.

Figure 1. A student's research paper, created using the key-word process

thanks to Archimedes.

Archimedes was a Greek scientist. He was asked by king Hieron to determine if the king's crown was gold, or a cheap alloy. Archimedes couldn't figure this out, so he decided to take a nice, long bath.

When he got in the tub, Archimedes noticed the water level rose. He was so excited, he "ran" through the streets yelling "Eureka"! His principle is:

Anything submerged in a fluid is pushed back up by a force equal to the weight of the fluid displaced.

This meant King Hieron's crown really was gold because of buoyancy, or the ability to float.

Resources

Franklin, B. 1996. *The autobiography of Benjamin Franklin*. Mineola, NY: Dover.

Gardner, R. 1995. *Experiments with bubbles*. Hillside, NJ: Enslow.

Glover, D. 1993. *Solids and liquids*. New York: Kingfisher

Hewitt, S. 1998. *Solid, liquid, or gas?* New York: Children's Press.

Hirsch, E. D., Jr. 1988. *Cultural literacy: What every American needs to know*. New York: Vintage Books.

National Research Council (NRC). 1996. *National science education standards*. Washington, DC: National Academies Press.

Pudewa, A. 1998. *Teaching writing: Structure and style*. Moscow, Idaho: Institute For Excellence in Writing.

VanCleave, J. P. 1989. *Janice VanCleave's chemistry for every kid: 101 easy experiments that really work*. New York: John Wiley.

VanCleave, J. P. 1996. *Janice VanCleave's 202 oozing, bubbling, dripping, and bouncing experiments*. New York: John Wiley.

Chapter 36

Taking a Look at the Moon

By Craig R. Leager

The communication skills of reading and writing go hand in hand with science as natural partners for fostering students' understandings of the world. The similarities that exist between reading and writing strategies and science-process skills add depth to instruction when these subject areas are brought together. In this unit of study, students integrate reading, writing, and science to learn more about the Moon.

The Moon has a powerful allure—it is full of beauty, legend, myth, and romance. People have gazed at the Moon in the day and night skies since the dawn of humanity. Our curiosity as humans has led us to observe, speculate, and draw conclusions about this celestial body; it has become intertwined in the culture of humans.

Now You See It, Now You Don't!

The observable changes in the Moon's apparent shape make it an engaging topic for scientific inquiry. One complete cycle through all of the Moon phases takes about 29.9 days—a convenient length of time for student observations.

The lunar cycle is a continuous process and there are eight recognizable shapes that we have named *phases* (Figure 1, p. 206). These phases are caused by the relative positions of the Moon and the Sun in the sky.

In the following unit of study, students use science-process skills as they observe and record changes in the Moon's appearance. Their growing knowledge of the Moon and its phases is strengthened through reading and writing strategies.

Taking a Look at the Moon: Why Does the Moon Seem to Change?

Objective

Use science-process skills (observing, collecting data, inferring, predicting, and communicating) to understand the Moon and its phases.

Grade Level

3–6

Figure 1. Phases of the Moon

New Moon—The Moon is not visible to us on Earth, except during a solar eclipse. This is because the side of the Moon facing Earth is unilluminated. Also, the Moon is very near the Sun and therefore hard to see.

Waxing Crescent—The side of the Moon facing Earth is less than 50% illuminated by direct sunlight. During this phase the illuminated portion is increasing daily.

First Quarter—One-half of the side of the Moon facing Earth is illuminated by direct sunlight. The illuminated portion is still increasing daily.

Waxing Gibbous—The side of the Moon facing Earth is more than 50% but not fully illuminated by direct sunlight. The illuminated portion is still increasing daily.

Full Moon—The side of the Moon facing Earth appears to be completely illuminated by direct sunlight.

Waning Gibbous—The side of the Moon facing Earth is more than 50% but not fully illuminated by direct sunlight. During this phase the illuminated portion is decreasing daily.

Last Quarter—One-half of the side of the Moon facing Earth is illuminated by direct sunlight. The illuminated portion is still decreasing daily.

Waning Crescent—The side of the Moon facing Earth is less than 50% illuminated by direct sunlight. The illuminated portion is still decreasing daily.

Materials Per Class

- Several pictures of the Moon in various phases of the lunar cycle
- 30-day calendar template (desktop size or larger)
- Assortment of books about the Moon at various reading levels
- Art materials (any combination of markers, colored pencils, paint, etc.)

Materials Per Student

- Notebooks (spiral or bound) with a minimum of 50 pages
- Pencils or other writing utensils
- Poster board (any size)

Teacher Preparation

Plan to begin this lesson on the New Moon. (Determine when a New Moon will occur by checking a lunar calendar like the one available at the U.S. Naval Observatory's website: *http://aa.usno.navy.mil/data/docs/MoonPhase.php.*) Discovering that a New Moon is not visible builds students' sense of wonder and spawns questions.

Prepare (or have students help prepare) interactive notebooks. Count out the first 30 pages of each notebook and label that section "Daily Moon Observations." The remaining pages will be designated for interactive notebooking.

Gather accurate books about the Moon (see Resources).

Engage

Show students, in no particular order, pictures of the Moon in different phases of the lunar cycle. Allow 10 minutes for small-group sharing. Gather back together as a whole group. Pose the question, "How and why does the Moon seem to change?" (This is a guiding question, not one to be answered immediately by the students.) Students may reply, "The Moon is always moving and turning, but not exactly the same as the Earth. So, we can't see all of it all of the time and that is why the Moon is always in a different spot in the sky each day." Or, "The Moon is like a mirror. It reflects the light of the Sun, but because it is moving we can't always see the part that is reflecting the Sun's light." Explain that for the next month or more, the class will observe the Moon and record their observations to better understand the Moon and its phases.

Explore

Starting with the New Moon phase, instruct students to observe the Moon daily and record their observations (in text and drawings). Instruct students to try to make their observations in an open field (like a park or soccer field) and, at the beginning of the Waxing Crescent phase, to look west just after sundown, looking east one hour later each night.

Each subsequent school day, students will share their observations (through partner sharing, small-group discourse, or whole-class discussions). After each of these sharing sessions, the class will add their collective daily observations to the class calendar. Throughout

the month, ask students what changes they have noticed in the Moon, and have them predict where the Moon will be that night and what it will look like.

When data is missing as a result of inclement weather or a missed observation, students can access information from reliable scientific sources like the U.S. Naval Observatory's website (see Teacher Preparation). Another method to deal with missing data points is to observe the pattern in the collected data and make predictions that can be verified by checking with other sources, such as the U.S. Naval Observatory.

Explain

After the first week of observations, students will likely have many questions (Where was the Moon at the beginning of the week? Does everyone on Earth see the Moon the same way we do here?). This is the perfect opportunity to integrate reading and writing into their search for answers. In read-aloud, shared reading, or independent reading situations, students can use their notebooks as a tool to help them condense or summarize ideas from one or more texts and compare and contrast information from one text to another. Students can format their notebooks as follows: notes from a mini-lesson, lecture, activity, reading, or class discussion go on the right side. The left half of each page is used solely for students' interactions with the information on the right half of the page (Figure 2).

Figure 2. Interactive notebook strategy

On the left side of the notebook page, students

- paraphrase information;
- add a drawing or photo that illustrates the concept, idea, or fact;
- pose questions;
- form and express an opinion;
- predict outcomes or next steps;
- write a reflection about the information; and
- make connections between the information/text and your own life, another text, and/or the world.

On the right side of the notebook page, students take notes on

- mini-lessons;
- lectures;
- activity/labs;
- readings;
- film/videos; and
- small-group or large-group discussions.

At the end of each week, the class should have an explicit discussion about the observational data that has been collected and compiled on the class calendar. Ask questions such as these: "What do you notice about the data we have entered on our class calendar this week?" (The Moon seems to be getting bigger. We could hardly see it at all last weekend, but now there is a crescent.) "What information have you gathered in your interactive notebooks that support your thinking?" (Well, I read that the Moon is darkened when it is a New Moon. Yeah, I saw in a book where the Moon goes through a cycle every month; that is why it always seems to be changing.) "How can we verify the information you have been reading?" (We could check in other books to see if they have the same information. I think we should keep observing the Moon to see if what really happens matches the book's information.)

As students begin to identify and use terminology from their readings, always stop the class to highlight these terms and emphasize their appropriate use. This will be an ongoing process throughout the unit.

Elaborate

Throughout this unit of study, as students learn more about the Moon, they will undoubtedly develop new questions to pursue. Students should be encouraged to record these questions in their interactive notebooks. Allow approximately 20 minutes or more each week for students to share some of their questions in a whole-group setting and their plans for answering their questions. This time will develop a collaborative scientific community of learners.

After observing the Moon for a month, students should begin to recognize the predictable phases of the lunar cycle. This is the time, now that students have made their own observations, to explicitly teach the phases of the Moon.

Evaluate

Let students know that scientists communicate their understandings in many creative ways (presentations, journal articles, conversations, poster sessions, etc.). Challenge students to work individually to create a poster to communicate their collective understandings of the lunar cycle. The posters should include a graphic representation of the Moon through a full lunar cycle.

Resources

National Research Council (NRC). 1996. *National science education standards*. Washington, DC: National Academies Press.

Olson, G. M. 2007. *Patterns in nature: Phases of the Moon*. Manheto, MN: Capstone Press.

Rau, D. M. 2005. *Amazing science: Night light—A book about the Moon*. Minneapolis, MN: Picture Window Books.

Simon, S. 2003. *The Moon*. New York: Simon and Schuster.

Trundle, K. C., and T. H. Troland. 2005. The Moon in children's literature. *Science and Children,* 43 (2): 40–43.

Chapter 37

Creative Writing and the Water Cycle

By Rich Young, Jyotika Virmani, and Kristen M. Kusek

Albert Einstein once said, "Imagination is more important than knowledge." He might also agree that the ability to combine the two is a powerful asset for any individual. Creative writing provides one strategy for helping students combine their powers of imagination with their arsenal of knowledge. Teachers also can use creative writing exercises to assess student understanding of science content.

Use the story "The Life of a Drop of Water" (pp. 212–213) as a springboard for the following creative writing activity, which draws students in by taking advantage of human fascination with natural disasters. Ask the class to read the story about a water droplet that experiences a host of natural disasters during its adrenaline-pumping journey on land, through air, and underwater. When students have finished reading the story, review the basic steps of the water cycle to familiarize them with related concepts, such as evaporation, condensation, and precipitation.

As a further review of the concepts they'll work with during their assignment, ask them to research the types of natural disasters found in the story. You might want to create a study guide to make sure they cover all the relevant concepts. The guide could ask them to

- identify each type of natural disaster found in the story;
- define tsunami, tornado, typhoon, and the other weather-related events;
- explain what type of conditions create these storms;
- describe the conditions that cause the water cycle to produce a hail storm; and
- answer any other guided questions that would help them with their writing assignment.

As an introduction to the actual assignment, ask students to imagine that they are droplets of water caught up in a natural disaster. Use specific questions to start the creative juices flowing. Which major storm would you want to be a part of? What forces would affect you? How would you be transported from a puddle on the ground to a cloud up in the atmosphere? What factors in the atmosphere cause you to form into a cloud? What causes your cloud to separate into many clouds? If it gets very cold, what happens to a liquid such as water? When water is heated, what state of matter does it change into? Why?

The Life of a Drop of Water

Your body and the Earth's surface have a lot in common. Both are mostly water, and the composition of your blood actually is not that different from seawater. Our Sun is like the Earth's heart: Energy from the Sun pumps water from the tropics to the poles in a vast network of currents. However, occasional "hiccups" in the water world spawn hurricanes, floods, and tsunamis that slosh around mega-buckets of water in a way that disrupts the normal flow of the system, often with disastrous results.

Imagine that you're a droplet of water in the vast, tropical Sargasso Sea in the Atlantic Ocean. It's the end of August 1992; the sea is warm and salty, but not at all calm. A 160 kilometers per hour wind is whipping the waves into a seething cauldron. They'll call this Hurricane Andrew back in Miami, and you're a part of it, feeding it enough energy to make 12,000 meter high clouds spiral into walls around a low-pressure "eye." You are a speck of froth on the water and are swept across the Gulf Stream as you add warm moisture to the hurricane's fury. Driven by 230 kilometers per hour winds, you slam into south Florida as part of a 5 meter high storm surge, destroying hundreds of homes and huge tracts of ecologically important mangroves. You now have the dubious honor of being part of the costliest storm in American history. Had you come ashore only 32 kilometers north and hit Miami squarely, you would probably have been part of the deadliest one too.

A 400 kilometers per hour tornado drops out of the sky and sucks you off the face of the Earth, spraying you 4,500 meters into the clouds. It's so cold that you freeze into ice and plummet thousands of feet until strong updrafts within the thunderstorm below waft you up another 10,000 meters. Along the way you pick up static charges that attract ice crystals. You grow into a pea-size hailstone. After several more wild roller coaster rides through the clouds, you grow to the size of a golf ball. With the added weight of the ice, you break loose from the convection drafts and hurtle down to the Earth in central Florida, the lightning capital of the western hemisphere.

A 27,760°C bolt of lightning, five times hotter than the surface of the Sun, connects with the ground from 10,000 meters and discharges 100,000 amperes of electricity from the cloud. The stroke superheats the air and creates a shockwave that is heard as thunder for miles around. It ignites years' worth of accumulated forest debris and starts a brush fire. Ice doesn't stick around long in central Florida in the summertime, so you melt and mix into the falling rain, dousing the fire. Florida was lucky you were around to help put that fire out because wildfires consume hundreds of square miles of brushland, forests, and homes every year.

Now you are swept up in surging stream water that sends you into a lake already filled to the brim from the torrential rains. The lake doesn't normally receive that much water, so the river draining it floods and forces you to take a leisurely flow through several homes built on the floodplain. Your meandering destroys homes— and the lives of their owners.

Next, you are sucked into a swirling sewer and pushed through an outfall back into the sea. An along-shore current washes you up and down the coast with the tides. You pick up some sand along the way and erode pockets of the beach—one grain at a time.

An offshore breeze jets you into the Gulf Stream current, which carries you to the cold North Atlantic. After weeks of evaporation, you have become saltier and denser. You sink into the dark, cold depths to start your journey back to the equator along the sea bottom. You thought it would be dark and desolate here, but a shower of tiny bioluminescent animals is putting on an exquisite light show. On the bottom, you're lucky enough to drift through beautiful gardens of white and red tube worms that stand three feet tall and surround 20 foot high pipes of dark, sparkling minerals. The pipes spew scalding water heated by rising magma within the Earth.

You continue your slow drift southward over a submerged mountain range that runs down the middle of the Atlantic Ocean. You are hot from the lava spewing from undersea volcanoes that may someday become new islands like Iceland, Hawaii, and Montserrat. Without warning, the water shudders from a series of undersea earthquakes that help relieve the stresses caused by magma rising into the Earth's crust. Sometimes these quakes occur under land where the Earth's great plates collide and shake the ground hard enough to destroy buildings and bridges.

Suddenly the volcano over which you drift erupts into a boiling cauldron of seawater. You are caught in a mammoth bubble that carries you 2,500 meters up to the surface of the ocean. Superheated steam from the bursting bubble wafts you another 4,500 meters up into the troposphere where you are immediately swept eastward by the 320 kilometers per hour winds of the jet stream.

A week later and half a world away, you precipitate in a blizzard of snow over Mount Redoubt in Alaska. The heat from this awakening volcano melts the ice and snow under you, and the whole white veneer starts sliding down the side of the mountain. Within minutes you're caught in a blinding white wall of powder moving at 160 kilometers per hour, ripping up trees by their roots, knocking down chalets, and covering everything in your path. Finally, the avalanche deposits you in a warm valley, where you melt and flow through a braided stream back into the Pacific Ocean. You've arrived here about 500 years sooner than if you had completed the same journey through the deep waters of the world's oceans.

But "Pacific Ocean" is a misnomer; it is not always pacific and peaceful. Besides the huge typhoons that seasonally stir its waters into a tempest, the surrounding "Ring of Fire" is the most seismically active region in the world; it is the birthplace of more volcanoes, earthquakes, and tsunamis than anywhere else on Earth.

Floating placidly now in Blying Sound along the western shore of the Gulf of Alaska, you hear a growing roar in the distance that sounds like a bursting dam. A huge wave traveling up the inlet sucks the water out of the bay and pulls you out in the strongest current you've ever felt. Fish are left flapping helplessly on the dry seafloor as you rush past. You are lifted towards the sky by a tsunami 12 meters tall and growing as it approaches the shore at more than 95 kilometers per hour. It starts to curl over the town of Seward, then crashes down on the streets and buildings 20 meters below. You smash through the town driven by the great weight of water behind you, battering everything in your path. In a few minutes that seem to last forever, you toss and tumble over the landscape and turn the town into a trash heap. As you surge inland over the highways, buildings, and neighborhoods, the water around you fills up with big chunks of trees, homes, and entire vehicles.

The energy packed into this great wave (and the ones to follow) is unbelievable. It rips up or knocks down everything in its path. When the valley in which the town lies finally fills to its brim, the water recedes slowly at first, then in a gathering rush. Everything that was ripped up by the incoming surge is now carried out to sea by the ebbing maelstrom.

This tsunami, spawned 10 hours ago by an earthquake 8,000 kilometers away, moved through the water at 800 kilometers per hour. It started out only a couple of feet high in a deep open ocean trench and moved unnoticed past ships. But as it scraped the ocean floor closer to shore, energy-packed water piled up on itself. Fortunately, an alert issued by the Pacific Tsunami Warning System allowed most people to reach the safety of high ground.

Ultimately, you are sucked back into the cold waters of the Gulf of Alaska, and you meander into a great current of water circulating slowly across hundreds of miles of the North Pacific Ocean. Overhead, a low-pressure trough off the Canadian coast churns up the wind and sea to produce a thick, dank haze of microscopic water droplets draping the ocean; air and water become indistinguishable, and the horizon indiscernible. You are one of the droplets that evaporate and are carried southeastward by the gathering storm to warmer climes. As you approach the rugged coast of the western United States, you rise with the wind to scale the high mountains. You cool down, condense, and fall on the slopes of the Cascades as rain.

You filter down through the normally arid soils until you reach rock, and you flow ever downward along its surface. The dirt above the rock slowly absorbs you and turns into mud. The earth begins to slip, slip, slip down the hill with the added weight and lubrication. As it gains speed, it grows into a catastrophic landslide that sweeps houses off their foundations and dumps them into the valley below.

One good thing about landslides is that they deliver new topsoil to the valley floor, creating an environment where life can bloom. You are content now in your new surroundings and with your new role—encouraging new plant life to poke through the fresh topsoil. It's satisfying to be helpful at last after wreaking so much havoc in your journey around the world.

After you have introduced all the relevant background material, it is time for students to start writing. The assignment is for them to imagine that they are droplets of water caught up in a natural disaster of their choice. For example, students might imagine they are caught up in a spiral arm of a hurricane. They should first conduct basic research on hurricanes to gain knowledge on the science behind the disaster. Then they should write a creative, fictional story that explains how they—that is, the arm of the hurricane—formed, where they traveled, what damage they caused to towns, and when and under what conditions they were downgraded to tropical storm status. The possibilities for story ideas are limitless, as are the powers of the imagination.

The goal of this exercise is to simultaneously get students to express their understanding of a scientific concept such as natural disasters, while exercising their imaginations and having fun writing a creative story. This type of exercise can be adapted for use in conjunction with almost any science topic.

You might want to limit the length of the stories and request that each story include a specific number of concepts, depending on the length of time you want to devote to the project and the ability level of your students. At a minimum, students should have a weekend to work on their narratives, but I recommend that they have at least a week to develop them. During the week, give students time to research their topics. A starting point could be the basic sidebar information included in the online version of "The Life of A Drop of Water" located at *waves.marine.usf.edu/disaster_menu/disaster_menu_article.htm*. Clicking on the names of past natural disasters will bring you to additional information about each event.

Integration and Assessment

This activity is a great opportunity to involve teachers in other subject areas. Such interdisciplinary activities stress the interconnectedness of the disciplines and encourage students to integrate skills developed in other classes. Students are also eager to work on projects that they can receive credit for in more than one class.

Each teacher that participates should develop a rubric based on his or her own subject area. For example, the language arts rubric should assess students' grammar, spelling, and composition. You, of course, will focus on the scientific accuracy of the story. Assessment by the social studies teacher would make sure that the correct parts of the world have been identified during the water droplet's travels over land formations and bodies of water. The social studies staff could also insist that students refer to specific real-life events, such as Hurricane Andrew or the eruption of Mount Pinatubo in the Philippines. Art teachers could judge the creativity and presentation of any graphics produced to accompany the stories. The math department could check the accuracy of any statistics, measurements, and graphs that are included.

Internet Resource
Making Waves
waves.marine.usf.edu

Chapter 38

Volcano Résumés

By Sandra Rutherford and Cindy Corlett

T
ired of building a papier-mâché volcano to teach about plate tectonics? Do you want to connect science and writing? Then the volcano résumé project is perfect for you. This one-week project requires students to research a specific volcano and create a résumé for it that describes its location, physical characteristics, eruption history, and additional information of interest. Students must also include references for the information on their own résumés. Figure 1 outlines the résumé requirements. It also compares a human résumé to a volcano résumé. Figure 2 (p. 216) is a sample resume for the Sakurajima volcano near Kagoshima, Japan.

Figure 1. Volcano résumé requirements	
Human résumé	**Volcano résumé**
Identifying information Name, address, phone number, cell phone number, fax number, e-mail address Other personal data or details	Identifying information Volcano name Volcano location, including latitude and longitude and closest city or country Optional picture of the volcano
Description of yourself Qualifications Education Additional training Licenses, certifications, or accreditations	Volcano description Type of volcano (shield, cinder cone, or composite) Eruption style Magma composition Current status (dormant, extinct, or active)
Employment history or work experience Work history Background	Eruption history Local history Past eruptions
Additional information Accomplishments Scholarships and awards Portfolio	Additional information Formations or other features created are reported. Economic loss and loss of life are reported. An interesting story is given; for example, when Mt. Pelée erupted, one survivor was found in the local jail. Safety precautions, sirens, and escape routes are discussed. Benefits for the area are discussed. For example, after the Japanese volcano Sakurajima erupted, the island produced a good crop of kumquats because the soil was enriched by volcanic ash.
References People who know you and will vouch for your credibility	References Bibliography of sources used to gather the information

Figure 2. Sample volcano résumé

Sakura-jima

I am located near Kagoshima, Japan. The latitude and longitude are 31.6 N, 130.7E and the elevation is 3,663 feet (1,117 meters).

Volcano Description
I am a an andesitic stratovolcano on an small island in an inlet on the island of Kyushu, Japan. My eruptions are explosive with many bombs and ashfall. The eruptions are classified as Strombolian. I also produce pyroclastic and debris flows that can be very dangerous.

Eruption History
I am a highly active volcano. I first erupted in A.D. 708 and since then I have been erupting constantly which makes it difficult to provide a list of my history.

I had many large eruptions between 1471-1476, 1779, and 1781. My most current eruptive phase began in 1955 and I have erupted between 100– 200 times each year since. For example I erupted 126 times in 1994.

Additional Information
I am monitored by the Sakurajima Volcano Research Center which was founded in 1960. I have not caused too many people to die except in 1914. I am mostly an inconvenience due to showering nearby people with ash.

References
Earthquake Research Institute, University of Tokyo, 1996, Welcome to Decade Volcano: Sakurajima, http://hakone.eri.u-tokyo.ac.jp/unzen/sakura/sakura.html, accessed on September 14, 2007

Kyoto University Disaster Prevention Research Institute, 2007, Sakurajima Volcano Research Center, http://www.dpri.kyoto-u.ac.jp/~kazan/default_e.html, accessed on September 14, 2007

Volcanoworld, 2007, Sakura-jima, Japan, http://volcano.und.edu/vwdocs/volc_images/north_asia/sakura.html, accessed on September 14, 2007

The grading rubric (Figure 3) should be handed out when the project is assigned so students know what is expected of them. Sample résumés from past years can also be posted in the classroom to serve as inspiration. In those school districts that have implemented standards-based grading (Guskey 2001; Colby 1999), the first five elements of the rubric can be used to assess the content knowledge and the last two elements can be used to assess the work habits of effective learners.

Figure 3. Volcano résumé grading rubric			
Element	**Exemplary (5 points each)**	**Proficient (3 points each)**	**Developing (1 point each)**
Identifying information volcano name and location	The volcano's identifying information is thoroughly listed. A picture of the volcano is also included.	The volcano's identifying information is adequately listed. Very little information is missing.	The volcano's identifying information is poorly listed. Much information is missing.
Volcano description	The description of the volcano is thorough. Eruption types, magma composition, and the status of the volcano are all listed.	The description of the volcano is adequate. Eruption types, magma composition, and the status of the volcano are partially listed.	The description of the volcano is poor. Eruption types, magma composition, and/or the status of the volcano are not listed.
Eruption history	A thorough summary of the eruption history is listed.	An adequate summary of the eruption history is listed.	A poor summary of the eruption history is listed.
Additional information	Additional information is thoroughly reported.	Additional information is adequately reported.	Additional information is poorly reported.
References	There is a minimum of three sources listed in proper bibliographic manner. If an internet source is used, the author of the page, date when it was found, and the complete web address taking the reader directly to the web page used are listed.	There are fewer than three sources listed in proper bibliographic manner.	The sources are not listed in proper bibliographic manner.
Design and format	There is good use of color, borders, and pictures. The résumé is only one page in length and the paper is filled. Name and class period are on the back of the page.	There is adequate use of color, borders, and pictures. The résumé is close to the required length. Name or class period is missing from the back of the page. This information is written on the front of the page.	There is poor use of color, borders, and pictures. The résumé is not the required length. Name and/or class period are missing.
Conventions	There are no spelling or capitalization errors. Paragraphs, stanza divisions, and other textual markers are used correctly to enhance meaning.	There are very few spelling or capitalization errors. Student eliminates or manipulates sentence fragments for emphasis and stylistic effect.	There are some spelling and capitalization errors. Student begins to manipulate punctuation for emphasis and stylistic effect.
Total: _____ /35			

Many volcanoes can be used for this project, such as Kilauea, Paricutin, Vesuvius, Krakatau, Fuji, Surtsey, and Mount St. Helens. I recommend that you choose volcanoes that you will be using during your plate-tectonics unit, but you can also have students select their own. To get them started, you can point students toward helpful websites. I recommend the following:

Earth's Active Volcanoes: *www.geo.mtu.edu/volcanoes/world.html*
USGS, Cascade Volcano Obervatory: *http://vulcan.wr.usgs.gov*
Hawaiian Volcano Observatory: *http://hvo.wr.usgs.gov*

Conclusion

Project-based learning is a good way to augment lessons. This project gives students the opportunity to show the teacher their creative sides. The finished résumés can be posted on the classroom walls for all to see. For the teacher, projects can be a way to integrate writing into their science classes and also determine if students really understand the concepts they are being taught. In other words, this is another form of assessment, but one that is fun, interesting, and motivating for students.

References

Colby, S. A. 1999. Grading in a standards-based system. *Educational Leadership* 56 (6): 52–55.
Guskey, T. R. 2001. Helping standards make the grade. *Educational Leadership* 59 (1): 20–27.

Chapter 39

Reading and Writing Nonfiction With Children

Using Biographies to Learn About Science and Scientists

By Rebecca Monhardt

Biographies are sometimes considered to be a bridge between fact and fiction (Hillman 2003). As students read real-life accounts of scientists, they can expand their views of what kinds of things scientists do; realize that all kinds of people do science; find out how the scientific community influences the acceptance of scientific knowledge; learn that science is a collaborative effort; and learn about barriers certain groups encountered in their efforts to become part of the scientific community. Children as well as adults are often fascinated with real people and their life stories. Biographies of scientists—the living, the dead, the famous, and the not so famous—all have a place in the science classroom. Reading about the lives of people who engage in science emphasizes that science is indeed a human endeavor—it is something that people do rather than just an accumulation of facts. Scientific knowledge is a result of the efforts of people engaged in science.

In selecting biographies for use in a science classroom, the factual accuracy of the text is very important to consider (Hillman 2003). The degree to which this is achieved can vary and biographies fall into several different categories based on the amount of fiction that they include (Huck et al. 1997). Authentic biographies are carefully researched histories in which almost everything included about the person's life can be substantiated as fact. Fictionalized biographies are not quite so factual, and the author includes aspects of invention, supposition, and inference. In some cases, authors create these kinds of biographies to tell a more engaging story, but in other cases, the dramatization is a necessity due to lack of documentation. This is often true of historical figures about whom all the life details are simply not known. Biographical fiction has little accuracy, and the purpose of books that fall into this category is to tell an engaging story, not to create an accurate account of a person's life.

In reading biographies, students can identify examples that reflect aspects of the nature of science and scientists. The activities using different kinds of science biographies that follow are ones that I have found successful in getting students to expand their understanding of science and to consider jobs that perhaps they had not thought of as within the realm of science.

Activity One: The Nature of Science

Background

Before doing the following activity using children's picture book biographies, talk about what science is. The following descriptors can provide a framework for students as they look at biographies of scientists to develop a better understanding of the nature of science and scientists. Discuss each item on the list with the class before distributing it to students. Teachers may want to rephrase ideas somewhat, depending on the age of students.

- **Science is empirical.** It is based on observations both direct and indirect, and it seeks to find out about the natural world. Science deals with things that can be measured and/or counted, things that can be perceived with the five senses, with or without the use of various instruments.

- **Scientific claims are testable/falsifiable.** Data can be obtained that support or refute each claim.

- **Scientific tests or observations are repeatable.** Experiments or observations can be repeated by other investigators. Conclusions can be confirmed by repeated investigations by other researchers.

- **Science is tentative/fallible.** Science is not a rigid unchanging body of "right" answers. Scientific knowledge evolves over time.

- **Science is self-correcting.** The recognition that science is fallible and that replication of crucial studies is important leads to the elimination of error.

- **Science places a high value on theories that have the largest explanatory power.** The greater the number of diverse observations that can be explained by a theory, the more likely it is to be accepted by the scientific community.

- **Science values new ideas.** Scientists value theories that raise new questions that have not been asked before or that facilitate new ways of looking at the world.

- **Science values open-mindedness.** Good science seeks to be unbiased and objective.

- **Scientists value simple explanations.** Accurate explanations may, of course, be quite complex, but scientists prefer theories that are relatively simple.

- **Scientists demand logical coherence in explanations.** Scientific explanations must be able to withstand careful scrutiny of their logic and employ sound argumentation.

■ **Scientists value skepticism.** No conclusions are accepted on face value without careful analysis of the evidence supporting and refuting the claim.

■ **Curiosity, creativity, and chance play important roles in science.**

■ **Science is a way of knowing and should not be considered the only way of knowing.** (Smith and Scharmann 1999)

This activity uses picture book biographies to help students develop an understanding of the nature of science and scientists (see Figure 1). Picture books work well because they can be read aloud rather quickly, and many excellent examples are currently on the market. Some suggested titles include the following:

■ Anholt, L. 1998. *Stone girl, bone girl*. New York: Orchard Books.

■ Hong, L. T. 1995. *The empress and the silkworm*. Morton Grove, IL: Albert Whitman & Company.

■ Lasky, K. 1994. *The librarian who measured the Earth*. Boston: Little, Brown and Company.

■ Martin, J. B. 1998. *Snowflake Bentley*. Boston: Houghton Mifflin Company.

■ Sis, P. 1996. *Starry messenger*. Ontario, Canada: HarperCollins Canada.

■ Sis, P. 2003. *Tree of life*. New York: Frances Foster Books.

Figure 1. The nature of science

For this activity, your group has been assigned a book that deals with a specific scientific discipline. As a group, your task is to identify unique aspects of this discipline and the people who practice it. Begin by having one member of your group read the book aloud. As the other members listen, they should take notes about how the science and scientists are described in the book. The objective isn't to describe the science content, but rather to describe the processes and people involved in science. Then write a short paragraph that the publisher could use on the book jacket to tell the reader what this book says about science. You will share these with the whole class and also give us a short summary of the book.

For this activity, divide students into small cooperative groups, and determine roles within the group so every group member has a task. For example, roles may include a team leader who makes sure everyone stays focused on the task at hand, a recorder who writes down the group's ideas, and a reporter who shares the group's work with the whole class. Reading the picture book aloud is a task that can be assumed by one student or shared among the group members. Ideal group size for this activity is four to five students. Extent of previous experience working in cooperative groups dictates how much teacher instruction is necessary in establishing groups. Students who have experience with cooperative learning need less teacher direction than those who have little experience with this. Approximately two class periods should be allowed to complete this activity.

Activity Two: Pop-Up Biography

Background

In this activity, students create a simple pop-up book on a scientist of their choice. Rather than comprehensive biographies, these pop-ups are an introduction to a scientist and should highlight a particular scientific attitude that is illustrated by that particular person's life. Creating pop-up biographies, even simple ones, is a rather large project that may take several weeks to complete and requires a great deal of teacher direction. In middle schools, this would be a great integrated project that can include the language arts, reading, art, and science teachers—each of whom could provide classroom instruction related to their area of expertise.

Before beginning the pop-up books, ask students to think about some characteristics or scientific attitudes that previously have been identified. I use the following list compiled by Simpson et. al (1994). As I share the list with the whole class, I ask students if they can think of specific examples from their own lives that would illustrate any of these attitudes.

- **Longing to know and understand**—A belief in the idea that knowledge is important and seeking knowledge is a worthy investment of time and energy.

- **Questioning of all things**—All statements and "truths" are open to questioning.

- **Search for data and their meaning**—Seeking and making sense of data is prized because it is from data that evidence is provided to support ideas.

- **Demand for verification**—Scientific data are subjected to public scrutiny so that others can test the validity or accuracy of a claim before it is generally accepted.

- **Respect for logic**—Drawing of conclusions from data is based on some kind of logical scheme.

- **Consideration of consequences**—The short- and long-term effects that a certain kind of inquiry may have should be considered.

After talking about these particular attitudes, give students the opportunity to look at various biographies that are provided by the teacher. I like to set these up as a reading center and give students the opportunity to look at these books for about a week. Then we revisit our list of scientific attitudes, and students share examples of how a person they read about exhibited one of these attitudes. Here are some examples that I have included in a reading center:

- Batten, M. 2001. *Anthropologist: Scientist of the people.* New York: Houghton Mifflin.

- Bradby, M. 1995. *More than anything else.* New York: Orchard Books.

- Burleigh, R. 2003. *Into the woods: John James Audubon lives his dream.* New York: Atheneum Books for Young Readers.

- Ehrlich, A. 2003. *Rachel: The story of Rachel Carson*. New York: Harcourt.

- Fabiny, S., C. Kees, and C. Shields. 2003. *Rainforest animal adventure*. New York: Sterling.

- Fisher, L. 1999. *Alexander Graham Bell*. New York: Atheneum Books for Young Readers.

- Holmes, T. 1998. *Fossil feud: The rivalry of the first American dinosaur hunters*. Parsippany, NJ: Julian Messner.

- Jackson, D. 2002. *The bug scientist*. New York: Houghton Mifflin.

- Jackson, D. 2002. *The wildlife detectives*. New York: Houghton Mifflin.

- Jackson, E. 2002. *Looking for life in the universe*. New York: Houghton Mifflin.

- Montgomery, S. 1999. *The snake scientist*. New York: Houghton Mifflin.

- Osborn, E. 2002. *Project ultra swan*. New York: Houghton Mifflin.

- Sayre, A. 2002. *Secrets of sound: Studying the calls and songs of whales, elephants, and birds*. New York: Houghton Mifflin Company.

- St. George, J., and D. Small. 2002. *So you want to be an inventor?* New York: Philomel Books.

- Thimmesh, C. 2002. *The sky's the limit*. New York: Houghton Mifflin.

- Towle, W. 1993. *The real McCoy: The life of an African-American inventor*. New York: Scholastic.

- Walker, S. 2002. *Fossil fish found alive*. Minneapolis, MN: Carolrhoda Books.

After having the opportunity to look at the books provided and to think about the lives of the scientists portrayed in terms of the list of scientific attitudes, students select one scientist whose life they will use to create a pop-up biography and complete a short information form (Figure 2). Provide students with information on paper engineering that gives them ideas on how to actually construct their books. While I sometimes show students examples of professionally created pop-up books, the examples I use with them are very simple ones, often aimed at younger children. *The Wide-Mouthed Frog* by Keith Faulkner uses simple pop-up techniques, and *Dear Zoo* by Rod Campbell, which is even simpler, uses easily constructed flaps that can be opened to reveal a picture. These examples give students the general idea without overwhelming them.

Figure 2. Pop-up biography

Name of scientist I have chosen:

Why I personally thought this person was of interest:

Three sources I consulted to find information about this person:
1.
2.
3.

The scientific attitude that we talked and that I will use as a theme in creating my pop-up biography:

Information I found out that I might use:

Students begin by writing the text, making revisions until they have attended to all language arts conventions that are necessary in a book that will be shared with others. The construction process engages students in a problem-solving process not unlike what many scientists do in their particular fields of study. After giving students adequate time both in class for initial instruction and outside of class to work on their pop-up books, have students share the final projects with the class and read them to younger students. From start to finish, the process usually takes about two weeks. It is also useful to create a scoring rubric that can be used to grade finished pop-up books. The teacher and students, working together, can decide what is important to include in the rubric. A rubric clearly defines expectations for students as they create their books. My students opted to create an evaluation form that the listeners use to provide feedback (Figure 3).

Figure 3. Evaluation form

Evaluation form
Title of book_____   My name_____
Author_____   Grade level _____

	Yes	No	Somewhat	Comments
I enjoyed reading this book.				
The information I learned interested me.				

One thing I learned from the book was:

Some characteristics of the scientist in this book are:

While the pop-up books of Robert Sabuda are marvels of paper engineering, they tend to intimidate students in their first attempts at creating their own pop-ups. Save these to show later. Becoming proficient in creating pop-ups using paper engineering is definitely a problem-solving activity and requires some quality "messing-around time." A center with paper, glue, and reference books for students on how to create different pop-up features provides a nice learning environment in which students can experiment with paper engineering in preparation for creating their own books. There are also websites that provide excellent detailed directions for creating pop-ups (see Internet Resources).

References

Campbell, R. 1999. *Dear zoo: A lift-the-flap book.* New York: Little Simon.

Faulkner, K. 1996. *The wide-mouthed frog: A pop-up book.* New York: Dial Books for Young Readers.

Hillman, J. 2003. *Discovering children's literature.* 3rd ed. Upper Saddle River, NJ: Pearson Education.

Huck, C. C., S. Hepler, J. Hickman, and B. Kiefer. 1997. *Children's literature in the elementary school.* New York: Harcourt.

Simpson, R. D., T. R. Koballa, S. Oliver, and F. E. Crawley. 1994. Research on the affective dimension of science learning. In *Handbook of research on science teaching and learning*, ed. D. Gabel, 212. New York: Macmillan.

Smith, M. U., and L. S. Scharmann. 1999. Defining versus describing the nature of science: A pragmatic analysis for classroom teachers and science educators. *Science Education* 83: 493–509.

Resources

Grinstein, L., C. Biermann, and R. Rose, eds. 1997. *Women in the biological sciences*. Westport, CT: Greenwood Press.

Hiner, M. 2002. *Paper engineering for pop-up books and cards*. Norfolk, England: Tarquin Publications.

Jackson, P. 1993. *The pop-up book*. New York: Henry Holt.

Matyas, M., and A. Haley-Oliphant, eds. 1997. *Women life scientists: Past, present, and future*. Bethesda, MD: The American Physiological Society.

National Academy of Sciences. 1995. *On being a scientist*. Washington, DC: National Academies Press.

National Research Council (NRC). 1996. *National science education standards*. Washington, DC: National Academies Press.

Watt, F. 1997. *The Usborne book of paper engineering*. Tulsa, OK: EDC.

Internet Resources

Robert Sabuda
   http://robertsabuda.com/popmakesimple.asp

Pop-Up Lady: Joan Irvine
   http://joanirvine.com/default.aspx

Enchanted Learning
   www.enchantedlearning.com/crafts/cards/flowerspopup

Chapter 40

Journals of Discovery

Incorporating Art and Creative Writing Into Science Journals Leads to Meaningful Reflections on Learning for Both Students and Teachers

By Cathy Livingston

Madison was intently coloring in her science journal. On one page, she had written facts about the Earth, neatly listing distances, sizes, name origins, and signs. On the opposite page, she was busy illustrating the Earth, coloring the continents and oceans using markers. Later I looked at her picture. Around the edges of the planet she had meticulously written "not actual size" and "not actual continents." I had to laugh, but in her way, she was demonstrating that she understood the concept of scale and map accuracy.

Ryan, in a short story he had written about what life would be like on Mercury, said, "The only way to get water is to put a cup on the dark side, then let it freeze, then take it to the fire side and melt it. So, you don't get a bath too often. P.S. Save me." After reading his journal entry, I knew that he understood that the lack of an atmosphere in combination with Mercury's nearness to the Sun provides for dramatic and sudden changes in temperature.

Since I began incorporating art and creative writing, along with the traditional vocabulary and textbook facts, into my fifth-grade students' science journal assignments two years ago, I've been treated to numerous insightful messages about students' progress. These integrated science journals have also provided me with valuable insights into my teaching—reflecting how engaged students were in learning about a particular topic and providing information about how successful (or not) I was in conveying the intended science concepts to students.

One of the most helpful projects of my teaching career has been studying my students' journal entries and *really reflect* upon their contents. The more I reflected on their journals, the more I learned myself. Soon I began passing my understandings on to the students themselves, so they too could learn to analyze their own work to generate deeper understandings. I share some of our insights here.

Journal Makeover

Our science journal makeover started when, as a way of integrating art and helping students remember the meaning of vocabulary words more easily, I began requiring students to illustrate their vocabulary words in their journals. Because this was a new concept for the children, I modeled everything on the board, giving them suggestions on ways they could illustrate the different concepts and words. The students, many of whom had resisted writing out definitions, were more interested in creating what they considered an "art project" in their science journals. This activity was also more collaborative, as students compared their drawings and discussed them with one another.

This art element seemed successful, and before long, I also began requiring students to also write a "piece" before and after each unit of study. These were "quick writes," usually taking only 5 to 10 minutes. The prewriting pieces were very short, as students had not studied the topic yet. These usually ended up being only a few sentences or a single paragraph. The postwritings took more time to complete and ran anywhere from a half a page to almost two pages in the journal.

Writing provided students with opportunities to reflect on what they thought about a topic before we studied it as well as what they had learned during the study. It was also a way to bring creative writing into the science process. Creative stories enabled students to incorporate facts and vocabulary in a unique manner, which assisted them in recalling that information at a later time. And, their journal writings helped me assess what students had learned individually.

Analyzing Journals

My assessment of students' journal use was based on my review of the science journals themselves and on my in-class observations. I used checklists to chart behaviors I observed as the children used their journals during class. Using codes, such as "C" for content and "Cr" for creativity, I was able to quickly evaluate the journals.

One of the most interesting things I discovered as I reviewed students' journals was a connection between student interest and the quality of work the children produced. Consider the following experience from a unit on seeds: We began a seed-growing project using beans and corn seeds. Students were given precise instructions and, for the next several days, were asked to check their seeds as part of their morning work and draw and write about their observations in their journals.

Kelly, a bright and conscientious student, was very enthusiastic about the project. His initial entries were filled with detailed drawings colored with map pencils. The descriptions were detailed and informative: "We put the cup in the plastic bag but didn't close the bag. The reason is because it needs air. Every day we have to blow on it so it can get carbon dioxide. I am hoping my plant will grow."

After a few days, several seeds in the classroom began to sprout, but Kelly's did not. At this point, I noticed that the quality of Kelly's drawings began to fall off and the writings had fewer details. Midweek, his entries were neat but not as long or as detailed as they had been initially. By the end of the week, despite the fact that his bean had finally beguan to sprout, it was too late to reclaim Kelly's interest. He had to be reminded to make a journal entry, and he wrote and drew quickly, immediately closing the journal and returning it to his desk.

The failure of the seed to sprout should have been a clue that for Kelly and his classmates in a similar situation, the study was over. When his seeds were slow to germinate, he became less interested in the project, lowering the quality of his work in the science journal and his ability to attend mentally to the project and learn. This was true for the journals of other students whose beans did not sprout either.

Reflecting on this experience, I was reminded of the importance of paying attention to the level of student interest and recognizing when it's time to move on to something else. I should have been more aware of what was happening with Kelly and paired him with another student who had a more successful outcome. By creating a partnership, I could have kept Kelly's attention centered on this project until the unit was completed.

Before and After Reflections

After that realization, I continued to collect data on students' use of journals, deciding to tally the checklists I used to record my class observations of students onto one master list. I noticed students who had more checks in the "student interest" category also had more checks in other areas on the chart. They used more science vocabulary, were more creative in their writing and art, used their grammatical skills, added more content, and had higher quality work in their journals. This reinforced my conclusion of what I had observed while watching Kelly work in the seed unit.

Our next unit was on rocks and minerals, and as always, journals were an integral part of the experience. This time, students were required to start the study by writing a short piece that answered the question, "What is a mineral?"

To begin the study, Kelly wrote a few sentences, stating, "I think it is something that comes from rocks. I'm not really sure what it is, so I just guessed."

After the study, which included textbook readings, journaling, videos, and a hands-on project in which the students attempted to identify individual minerals by their characteristics, I repeated the prewriting question. This time, Kelly wrote an entire page, discussing different minerals, what they are used for, how they are identified, and which he liked. He incorporated vocabulary and descriptions from the projects. I had noticed that he was interested in the topic and enjoyed the group identification project, and this interest was reflected in the quality of his journal work.

Every student in the class, including a special-needs learner with significant difficulties in written and verbal expression, showed progress on this pre- and postwrite. Kevin wrote, "I think a mineral is something of a rock that has minerals in it and helps whole rocks to form into bigger rocks." After the study, his journal contained this entry: "Now I know about minerals. Minerals will have color and streak and will have metallic-luster and will fool you too. And when you think the rock is a crystal rock, it turns out to be a gypsum rock."

Cassie stated in her prewrite that she believed all minerals taste salty, then continued, "I also think it's formed together by salt that's why I think if it's salty it's a mineral." In her postwrite, Cassie focused on how to identify minerals and wrote, "Well, I'll tell you how to identify one. First you can streak it and see what color it is on the outside, then you can get a magnet and see if it's magnetic. If you get a magnifying glass and you look really closely at it you might see something that you probably won't see just looking at it."

Several students believed during the prewrite that a mineral was "pieces of sand made into a rock." In the postwrite, they used many of the science vocabulary words, stating, "You can tell a mineral by if it has color, chemical composition, metallic, cleavage, hardness …" Students' journal entries supported my belief that when students experience science with all their senses, as they did in the rocks and minerals unit, their creative writings and art contain more science vocabulary, factual information, and detail.

If there was little activity over the space of days, such as the seed experiment where many seeds failed to sprout, journaling became poorer with careless drawings, shorter definitions, and sloppier and less creative work.

Figure 1. Student journaling rubric scale

Name:_____

Please tell me what you think about your science journals. I would like you to consider these things:

A.   Does writing in your journal help you remember the things we study in science?   1 2 3 4 5 Why or why not?_____

_____

_____

B.   How much does it help you remember vocabulary words when you draw pictures about the words and color them? 1 2 3 4 5 Tell me what you like or don't like about making the drawings. _____

_____

_____

C.   We have written some stories in our journals this year using science facts in the stories. How well do you think it helps you remember facts when you use them in a story? 1 2 3 4 5 It does /doesn't help because _____

_____

_____

D.   If you were the teacher, what would you do with your students' journals to make them better? What would help your students learn more about science and remember what they learned? _____

_____

_____

Student Analysts

Next I wanted the students to examine their own journals to self-reflect on their work, asking them to comment on the strengths and "weaknesses," or areas of improvement, for their journals. After reading students' reflections, it was evident they were able to analyze their work and make similar observations to my own. Student comments under strengths included the following: "I liked my 'It Would be Cool to Live on a Planet' story"; "I really liked what I wrote on what I learned at the end of the chapter"; and "I liked how I organized my facts."

Improvements to make in their journaling included such ideas as "Make sure I spell things right" and "Be neater, try harder, and be more creative."

I also gave the children a rubric scale (Figure 1) and asked them to rate how they liked aspects of journaling and explain why they selected the rating they picked. The majority of students gave the journals a high rating, stating that writing and drawing their vocabulary assisted them in remembering the words. Students' comments included the following statements: "I like making the drawings because it's a lot easier to remember things later on, especially if you draw funny pictures." "You can look and see how stuff is actually happening that you read about." "I can visualize what it looks like through the picture."

When I asked if using science facts in a story was helpful, one boy wrote, "It does help me remember things because every word I write down pretty much gets stuck in my head." Another student shared, "I love writing, and I think I'm pretty good at it. When I look back at the story, I enjoy reading it, but also remember the facts about it."

The students' evaluations showed that some children liked different parts of the journal but that everyone liked some aspect.

These classroom successes have strengthened my resolve to continue incorporating scientific writing, creative writing, and art into the science curriculum. Used in conjunction with traditional textbooks, art and writing enhances student learning and the amount of knowledge that is retained over time is increased. Students who are competent writers in all areas of study will be much better prepared for their future education and careers.

Resource

National Research Council (NRC). 1996. *National science education standards.* Washington, DC: National Academies Press.

Chapter 41

Science Interactive Notebooks in the Classroom

By Jocelyn Young

Writing is one of the ways in which children learn in science. When students explain—in writing—what they have seen and why they think this occurs, they are forced to clarify their thoughts and organize these ideas in a way that others can understand (Azimioara, Bletterman, and Romero n.d.). Science interactive notebooks are a tool used to strengthen student learning of curriculum (the input) through increased student participation (the output). They can be used in class daily to promote student learning and prove to be successful because they use both the right- and left-brain hemispheres to help sort, categorize, and implement new knowledge creatively. The right side of the spiral notebook is for writing down information given by the teacher (notes, vocabulary, video notes, labs, etc.). The left side of the spiral shows the processing of the information from the right side (brainstorming, reflections, drawings/figures, worksheets, etc.).

Science interactive notebooks are important for many reasons. By using notebooks, students model one of the most vital and enduring functions of scientists in all disciplines—recording information, figures, and data. A second reason for maintaining a science interactive notebook is that it provides a ready reference for each unit, as well as a resource to consult for review. The notebook is also a means of communicating with the teacher and parents/guardians. Keeping a notebook also enhances students' writing skills, therefore connecting science with other areas of the curriculum. Extensions in the notebook can include poems, cartoon drawings, figure drawings, stories, songs, and notes from research on any given topic.

Finally, the science notebook offers the teacher a unique means of assessing student progress in the classroom. The notebook, beginning with the first lesson of the unit and continuing to its conclusion, can be used to assess the growth in students' understanding as well as their abilities to summarize and express their thoughts and feelings. Think as a scientist … record as a scientist … and reflect as a scientist!

Getting Set Up

A 200-page spiral-bound notebook or a large-size composition book should be used. These notebooks with hard or plastic covers seem to be the most durable and can last for at least one semester. The key is to not have the students rip out or add any pages. However, papers are periodically glued into the notebook.

Require all students in the class to organize their notebooks in the same manner, using the right side for input (e.g., lectures, labs) and the left side for output (e.g., drawings, reflections, worksheets). Each student should have the same thing on each page of the notebook (see Figure 1). A rubric glued into the front of the notebook will inform students and parents on how the notebook will be scored. Information as to what goes where (left side versus right side) can also be glued in the front of the notebook. A table of contents can be glued in at the beginning of each unit or after a few units, or the teacher may choose to have the students construct the table of contents. Students should always date their entries and number the pages consecutively throughout the entire notebook.

Figure 1. Science interactive notebooks

Left side	Right side
The left-side page demonstrates your understanding of the information from the right-side page. You work with the input, and INTERACT with the information in creative, unique, and individual ways. The left side helps focus your attention and guides your learning of the science content and concepts.	Science interactive notebooks are used to help you learn and remember important scientific concepts. Why do they work? This notebook style uses both the right- and left-brain hemispheres to help you sort, categorize, remember, and creatively interact with the new knowledge you are gaining.
What goes on the left side? Output goes on the left side!	**What goes on the right side?** Input goes on the right side!
Every left side page gets used! Always use color and organize information. It helps the brain learn.	Always write the date on each page and label each assignment!
What could go on the left side? • Brainstorming • Mind maps • Concept maps • Venn diagrams • Pictures • Drawings • Diagrams • Writing prompts • Flow charts • Lab and self reflections • Poems • Songs • Worksheets	**Guidelines:** • The right side has only odd numbered pages. • The right-side page is for writing down information you are given in class (input). • When the teacher lectures, you take notes on the right side. • When you take book notes or video notes, they ALWAYS go on the right side. • You may use Cornell Style Notes on the right page. • Laboratory activities go on the right side. • Any other type of INPUT you get in class.

The Writing Habit

Students who have not used science interactive notebooks previously may need initial guidance on how to use them most effectively. A good way to begin is by facilitating a brainstorming session designed to increase students' awareness of the importance of maintaining a notebook. We brainstorm on "how notebooks will help us learn the course material and organize ourselves," then review the guidelines on the reference pages glued into the front of the notebooks.

It is helpful to encourage the students' understanding of their notebooks in two major ways. First, they should "take notes" on information they have been given. As they move through the daily lessons, students should also "make notes"—that is, ask questions, sketch, and record comments. Emphasize the importance of always writing clearly and of expressing thoughts in an organized way. Encourage students to incorporate tables, graphs, figures, and diagrams as much as possible. The left third of each page is used for study questions to be completed when appropriate; the right two thirds is used for note taking during class.

Providing daily notebook writing time can be challenging. With proper planning, however, writing becomes a natural part of the rhythm of the science class. It does not require a complete overhaul of previous lesson plans. Everything the teacher has been doing in the classroom previously stays the same—simply adjust the curriculum to fit into a notebook and add some writing pieces. Integrating the notebook does not take large amounts of extra time and, after the initial year, planning for subsequent years becomes easier.

Incorporating writing time depends on the nature of the classroom activity on any given day. What is most important is that students have sufficient time and opportunity to write each day. Worksheets, demonstrations, lectures, lab activities, and figure analyses are all examples of possible daily entries in the science interactive notebook. During some labs or activities, things may go more smoothly if students suspend their hands-on investigations at certain points, reflect on the activity, write in the notebook, and then resume their activity. In other cases, the best time to write is after the activity or lab ends. Even though students have used their notebooks repeatedly during a lesson, a few minutes should always be left at the end of a lesson for students to reflect and write on what they have learned and to address questions that have arisen. Guided reflection can take a number of forms to focus the students learning. Lab reflections can be done after each laboratory experience, and self-reflections are done at the end of each unit so students can think about the chapters covered.

Assessing the Notebooks

Explain to the students early on that when the notebooks are reviewed, many things will be considered. These should include how complete the entries are and how much effort has been put into the writing. Students should think of the information in their notebooks as a work in progress; however, that does not excuse messiness, a lack of readability, or grammar and spelling errors. Teachers should emphasize writing across the curriculum. What the student learns in English and math also goes for science. The teacher should sit down with a language arts teacher and review what is expected of each grade level in their writing classes, so the science teacher can incorporate the same basic requirements. If each teacher requires something different, students will get confused.

It is essential to check the students' notebooks often. A glance at the notebooks during class, and collection of them on the day of a unit test for a more detailed review, should provide sufficient evaluation. Feedback may be given to students in many ways. Some teachers prefer to use sticky notes, while others write on the notebook page itself. Some may prefer to enter their comments in the back of the book or on the table of contents. Also, at the end of each unit, the students are required to have their parents/guardians review their work and sign their notebooks. Incorporating the parents/guardians into the curriculum to evaluate the students' learning progress allows critical communication to occur and for the parent to review the work before a grade is assigned.

Feedback should be positive and constructive. Grade students on completeness and effort. When scoring, include any homework assignments in the notebook. Using a clear scoring rubric enables the students to understand how he or she can improve. Rubrics can be created

	Figure 2. Science interactive notebook rubric
6	Notebook contents are complete, dated, and labeled. Pages are numbered (odd: right side; even: left side). Right-side/left-side topics are correct and contents are organized. Lecture notes go beyond basic requirements. Student uses color and effective diagrams. Student shows impressive, in-depth self-reflections.
5	Notebook contents are complete, dated, and labeled. Pages are numbered (odd: right side; even: left side). Right-side/left-side topics are correct and contents are organized. Entries include most of the traits of a "6," but lack excellence in all areas. Most areas meet requirements but don't go beyond. Student shows in-depth self-reflection.
4	Notebook contents are complete (at least 90%), dated, and labeled. Pages are numbered (odd: right side; even: left side). Right-side/left-side topics are correct and contents are organized. Student uses color and some diagrams. Information shows basic understanding of content topics. Some areas meet requirements, but don't go beyond. Student shows limited but real self-reflection.
3	Notebook contents are complete (at least 80%), dated, and labeled. Pages are numbered (odd: right side; even: left side). Right-side/left-side topics are somewhat organized. Student uses minimal color and few diagrams. Information shows a limited understanding of content topics. Few areas meet all requirements. Student shows some real self-reflection.
2	Notebook contents are incomplete. Some attempt at dating and labeling of entries is made. Right-side/left-side is inconsistent and contents are unorganized. Information and concepts show only a superficial understanding of the subject matter and/or show serious inaccuracies. Notebook is not neatly written. Student shows little real self-reflection.
1	Notebook turned in but is too incomplete to score.

on a general basis or may be specific for a particular assignment or entry. (See Figure 2 for an example.) Make the assessment simple to facilitate grading all the notebooks in a timely manner and enable the students to better understand what is expected of them.

Conclusion

Science interactive notebooks fill many roles. They facilitate students' science learning and give students an opportunity to enhance their writing skills. They help students better appreciate the process of scientific inquiry. They help students organize their learning and, by the end of the unit, realize how much they have learned. For teachers, the interactive notebook is a unique means of assessing student learning and organization.

These guidelines emphasize the many benefits that science interactive notebooks bring to the classroom. The notebooks can transform classrooms into dynamic learning environments. In the process, students connect their prior experiences with new material and learn to acquire knowledge in ways that will make them lifelong learners.

Reference

Azimioara, M., C. Bletterman, and P. Romero. n.d. *Another approach to the scientific notebook. A collection of articles and rubrics.* Tustin School District: Tustin, CA.

Chapter 42

Using Science Journals to Encourage All Students to Write

By Joan C. Fingon and Shallon D. Fingon

I t seems that everyone is using science journals or notebooks lately. As a middle school science teacher, I use science journals as a tool to enhance students' knowledge and understanding of content and to reinforce students' writing skills. However, although research shows, and many teachers agree, that there are several benefits to using science journals, most teachers want more support in helping students who are reluctant or lack motivation to write. Here we share how we use science journals to motivate students to write about science in middle school classes.

What Is a Science Journal?

Ruiz-Primo, Li, and Shavelson describe science journals or notebooks as a "compilation of entries that provide a partial record of the instructional experiences a student had in her or his classroom for a certain period of time" (2002, p. 2). The writing is usually descriptive or narrative and centered around authentic tasks such as collaborating, researching, analyzing, and interpreting information. Journals can be more than places to record data and facts—they also assist students in exploring, predicting, and engaging in scientific thinking that may be oral, written, or symbolic.

Why Use Journals?

Journals can be used as a warm-up activity or discussion generator, or for closure, self-reflection, or assessment. Journals can also be used to

- build a personal connection or rapport between the student and teacher;
- provide evidence at parent-teacher conferences of what children are learning;
- provide documentation at parent/staff team meetings for students with special needs;

- allow expression of ideas through written and visual or graphic representations;

- allow written response to investigating, observing, and hypothesizing from lab experiments and class discussions;

- provide opportunity for students to explore questions and answers related to science topics not studied in class; and

- help students learn time-management skills.

Journal Logistics

All students are given a black-and-white, 9¾- × 7½-inch composition journal, which is stored in a page protector inside a larger science subject-area binder. Using glue sticks, students glue a listing of the journal requirements and the rubric for assessment inside the front and back covers of their journals. (See Figures 1 and 2, p. 243, for more details on journal requirements and the rubric.) In addition, the journal requirements and rubric are also written on large posters and placed in a corner of the classroom where students hand in their journals in different wired baskets identified by their class section. Students must print their names and class sections on the front covers and can choose to decorate their journal covers. It is also recommended that parents be informed of what is expected of their children—a newsletter or notice can be sent home at the beginning of the year explaining journal requirements and assessment.

Figure 1. Journal requirements

- Three legible handwritten pages (single-sided) per week. Entries may also be typed if the student prefers.
- A date and a title for each entry.
- Two entries for prompt # 1: *In science class, discussion, or lab this week I learned ...* Specific science words or vocabulary presented in class must be used in prompt #1.
- One entry for prompt #2: *What I am curious about in science is ...*
- A written response to the teacher's question or comment.

Guiding Journal Entries

At the beginning of the year, before students start journal writing, the class brainstorms a list of what they think should be in the science journal. This list is displayed on colorful posters in the journal section of the classroom and serves as a reminder to students to self-check whether they answered the prompts and fulfilled other requirements before handing in their journal. Some examples of students' brainstorming follow:

- Write in your own words what you are learning.

- Use science terms and vocabulary.

- Record observations and make predictions from lab work.

- Write your own questions and explore ways to find answers.

- Use different ways to express yourself, such as drawing or writing poetry.

- Use your curiosity to think of questions and explore the world around you.

- Connect science to your everyday life!

- Stay focused on science. Journals are not appropriate for writing personal thoughts about your classmates, creative drawings, or other information not related to science.

Next I introduce two creative-writing prompts that best promote student writing. They are

- In science class, discussion, or lab this week I learned...

- What I am curious about in science is...

Using the first prompt, students include specific descriptions, examples, ideas, key vocabulary, facts, and questions from science lessons and labs written in their own words. These entries also contain drawings, charts, or graphs to support their writing. Overall, this prompt helps the teacher determine how well students grasped concepts of the week's lessons and whether additional instruction is needed.

In response to the second prompt, student writing is designed to be more open-ended. It provides an opportunity to increase students' motivation to write about their own connections and experiences about science that they are making outside of science class. For example, students can write about a science program they watched on TV, or animals or plants they observed around their communities, and so on. Essentially, the intent is to allow students an opportunity to describe their interests in science that might not be currently included in the curriculum. Students are also encouraged to provide references or sources that they used to problem solve or answer their questions.

Motivating Students to Write to Learn Science

After journal use is underway, the teacher's most important task is motivating students to write. During the first week of school, students complete a survey about their reading and writing interests and attitudes toward science. Some survey questions include the following: How do you feel when you come to science class? What kind of grades do you usually get in science? What do you hope to learn in science this year? This survey gives the teacher a much better understanding of students' interest in science topics and how they perceive their strengths and needs. In addition, students are instructed about what data are and how to find statistics, record data, make observations, and write scientific questions. In conjunction, the teacher uses visuals and models by writing questions to help students begin to think like scientists.

However, students need to do more than just write in their journals; they must learn how to engage in writing to learn science (Owens 2001). To achieve this, different students require different levels of support. Some students are less motivated or lack prior knowledge of science and need more encouragement, while others write off topic or struggle with getting started in their writing. Regardless of the situation, it is best to give students options to support their writing. For example, sharing samples of journals from previous years is one way to help students get ideas. Teachers new to journal writing may want to model and use a strategy called a think-aloud whereby the teacher writes down ideas and questions on an overhead to share with students to encourage them to record what they are thinking.

Another way to initiate and help students begin their writing is by reviewing key concepts and ideas taught in lessons throughout the week and recording this information on a smaller whiteboard placed in the journal section of the room. For those students who require additional support with their writing, sentence starters can also be used as something to refer to as they begin their writing. These prompts can be glued on the first page of students' journals. Examples include the following:

- Today I learned that …

- In lab or class this week, I thought _____ was interesting because _____.

- What we did today in science reminds me of …

- I am confused about …

- I previously thought _____, but now I think _____.

- I was wondering about …

- I would like to explore _____ because _____.

- I really understood … [give details].

- I am trying to find the answer to …

- When I visited _____, I observed _____.

- While watching _____, I noticed that _____.

- In another subject [social studies, reading, math] we talked about _____, which related to science because …

Teacher Feedback

Providing timely feedback is key to keeping students writing, and praise can boost student confidence in writing and in their understanding of science. Encouraging, gently nudging, and reminding students to reread their entries before handing in their journals tends to help students write more and be more confident about what they are writing. Teacher comments or questions written in the margins of the journals asking for more clarification (e.g., "How much?" "Why do you think that?") can also encourage more critical thinking.

Besides providing encouragement, feedback may be used to differentiate instruction for students who need it. In addition to journal entries assessed based on a rubric, comments and questions are also included. Figure 2 offers a sampling of teacher feedback that I have found to be very helpful. The comments are divided into three basic categories: (I) praise and confirmation, (II) teacher questions, and (III) comments for students who need more support overall.

Figure 2. Sampling of teacher feedback and comments

I. Praise/confirmation: This feedback is used more at the beginning of the year to encourage student writing and isnonjudgmental in nature.
1. Great idea, ok, awesome point, etc.
2. Keep telling me more!
3. Good question!
4. I enjoyed reading this!
5. Good connections and good thinking!

II. Teacher questions: This feedback, written in the form of a question, suggestion, or directive, requires a response from the student. A student is asked to respond to at least one question per week.
1. What would it look like? Draw it for me.
2. What if you did … , then what might have happened?
3. Give me an example of what you mean.
4. Please check your answers again, something doesn't seem right. [Or, "Tell me more about your results."]

III. Needs more support: This feedback is used for students who do not follow directions, are not writing enough, or are writing off topic.
1. You have only listed the facts or information from the lesson. Where are your ideas? Come and see me and let's talk more about this, OK?
2. OK, I think I understand, but you haven't written enough. Let's look at the sentence starters together and see how I can help you.
3. This writing is off topic. How do your ideas connect to what we are doing in science class? Let's chat, OK?
4. What happened? I think you may need some help with your question, writing, etc.
5. Please do not try this on your own—it is not safe. Come and ask me more about this.

Students With Special Needs

Students with special needs can also write in journals but may need modified requirements. A child's Individual Education Plan will be the best starting point to meet individual needs. Common modifications include the following:

- Shorter page requirements

- Students who cannot write on their own dictating to a scribe

- Multiple avenues for written expression, e.g., poetry, graphs, sketches

- Providing books and resources that match students' reading abilities and interests

Assessing Journals

Teachers are always in need of more ideas and support for assessing science journals. In my classes, journals count for 15% of students' final grade each quarter and are assessed based on a rubric (see Figure 3). In addition to students completing periodic quizzes, tests, and lab reports, hand-in dates for journals are staggered among my five classes—two classes are assessed on Monday and three classes are assessed on Wednesday each week. If students have time after completing their lab reports or other classwork, they are allowed to write journal entries in class or as homework. Grades and feedback can be handwritten in red or green ink in the margins of the journals and are given back to students the next day. Using this approach, Monday's journals are returned with comments on Tuesday, and Wednesday's journals are given back on Thursday. That way, no journals are read over the weekend. Students who are absent or do not complete their journals on time have until Friday morning to hand in their work. I do not grade journals during holiday weeks, standardized testing times, or any other time that is considered extremely stressful for students or me.

Figure 3. Science-journal rubric

√ ++ = 100% (Exceptional!)
- Three dated entries, at least one page each, with titles, and neatly written
- Several ideas *all related to science,* classroom discussions, or labs
- Wide variety of science terms or vocabulary spelled and used correctly, detailed description in student's own words (outside sources or visuals labeled and fully explained)
- Highly detailed response to the teacher's question or comment, shows additional curiosity, thought, or ideas and more in-depth research

√ + = 85% (Very good!)
- Three dated entries, one page each, and neatly written
- Few/some ideas, all related to science, classroom discussions, or labs
- Many science terms spelled and used correctly, some description in student's own words (outside sources or visuals labeled and mostly explained)
- Detailed response to teacher's question or comment, shows some curiosity, thought, and research

√ = 75% (Passing)
- Three dated entries, one page each, and neatly written
- At least one idea related to science, classroom discussions, or labs
- Some science terms or vocabulary spelled and used correctly, mostly described in student's own words (either an example or visual or outside source used and explained somewhat in student's own words)
- Response to teacher's question or comment shows limited curiosity, thought, ideas, or research

√ – = 50% (Needs improvement)
If a student receives this grade, a consultation or one-on-one conference is scheduled between the student and the teacher.
- Less than three entries, or entries that are less than one page each, or writing doesn't make sense
- Ideas not related to science or off topic
- No science terms used, or spelled or used incorrectly, or not written in student's own words (no outside sources or visuals)
- No response to teacher's question or comment

Although reading journals can be time consuming, I am able to assess one class, or 25 journals, during one preparation period (40 minutes) or less. By the end of the year, students have usually completed 95 dated entries in two composition notebooks. Students who forget or misplace their journals are allowed to write their responses on separate pieces of paper to be assessed and stapled into their journals at a later date. Occasionally, there are students who do not write enough or misunderstand the assignment, and a one-on-one conference is necessary. Typically, students are asked to reread their entry and to revisit the requirements found on posters located in the journal section of the classroom before the teacher-student visit begins. After students have reread their work and journal requirements and conferred with the teacher, they usually understand their mistakes and make corrections. Students who do not turn in their journals that week receive no credit and must have their journals signed by a parent.

Another way for teachers to assess journals is to collect them from all classes on the same day and return journals by the end of the week. For those who need more time, assess journals every other week, or allow students to respond to fewer prompts. Regardless of the approach the teacher uses, the feedback must be timely to keep students engaged in the writing process.

Conclusion

When students are given a variety of opportunities to express themselves, they may be more willing and motivated to write. Providing support to students and encouraging them to explore their own interests and their curiosity about the world around them may increase achievement, knowledge, and understanding of science. Regardless of the teacher's time and approach to assessing journals, journal writing presents a viable option that can help students learn science. Specifically, science journals are one effective tool that teachers can use to help build students' interest and motivation to learn to write and write to learn about science. Journals can also provide evidence and timely feedback to teachers to improve their own teaching during this current time of heightened teacher accountability.

References

Owens, C. V. 2001. Teachers' responses to science writing. *Teaching and learning: The Journal of Natural Inquiry.* Summer: 22–35.

Ruiz-Primo, M. A., M. Li, and R. J. Shavelson. 2002. Looking into students' science notebooks: What do teachers do with them? *CSE Technical Report* 562. National Center for Research on Evaluation, Standards and Student Testing.

Chapter 43

Learning Logs
Writing to Learn, Reading to Assess

By Daniel Heuser

Just what do children get out of inquiry? Good inquiry activities help students hone their inquiry abilities and teach them about the nature of science. But inquiry is also a way to teach science content, and teachers need to know if this instruction is helping children gain these important ideas. So, how do we know what students are learning? Try a "Learning Log," a tool to help build knowledge from inquiry activities. This article describes a color and light activity I did with my first and second graders, and how a rubric for learning logs helped me make accurate judgments of what my students learned. However, learning logs can be used effectively in any grade level and on many topics.

What Is the Hottest Color?

"What is the hottest color?" asked a student one day as we brainstormed questions during a lesson on color and light. This seemed like an excellent question to help consolidate our unit. As we discussed the question, it became clear that to many students, the answer was simple: Red is the hottest color. Why? "Because it's the color of fire." When I held up a piece of aluminum foil, however, many of their initial thoughts changed. Silver became the hottest color of choice, because "It's metal, and metal is hot" and "Once I touched some aluminum foil at a picnic, and it felt hot."

This question focused so well on the unit objectives—light produces heat and can be reflected and absorbed, and materials of different color react differently to light—that I wanted the whole class to investigate. So, as a group, we designed a plan to answer this question and help students refine their natural inquiry abilities. Several issues arose as we discussed possible investigation plans.

First, it became obvious that most students thought they could tell small differences in temperature with their hands. I challenged several students to close their eyes and tell me which of two pieces of paper (one red and the other a lighter color) was the "hottest" just by touch. After a few trials in which students inconsistently picked the "warmest" paper, the group started to entertain the idea that the hand was not the best device for this task.

Soon, a child suggested using thermometers, which gave me a chance to point out that scientists use instruments such as thermometers because they increase accuracy.

A second opportunity for children to refine their inquiry abilities came when we had to decide where the papers would be placed in relationship to the afternoon Sun. To several students, it was a given that the paper closest to the Sun would be the hottest—even though the few feet involved was nothing in comparison to the Sun's five million miles distance from Earth. This seemed like a natural point for me to bring up the idea of multiple trials.

"Scientists have a way of dealing with that problem," I said. "We could put out two pieces of each paper color, one closer to the Sun and one farther away. That way it will make our test fair for all of the colors. We can also see if it's the color that makes a difference or the distance from the Sun."

Soon we had our investigative plan: We would put pieces of paper in several colors—plus a sheet of aluminum foil—out in the Sun during their music class. A thermometer would be placed on top of each. After music class, we would read the thermometers and see what happened. The results are shown in Figure 1. Thanks to our fairly high-quality thermometers, there was only one degree difference in our two sets of blue paper. Because of this, we later had a discussion about how instruments can lead to varying measurements.

Figure 1. Experiment results

Color	Temperature
Black	103°F (39°C)
Blue	98 and 99°F (36°C and 37°C)
Red	91°F (33°C)
White	90°F (32°C)
Silver (aluminum foil)	89°F (31°C)

Explanation: Darker paper absorbs more of the Sun's rays, and visible light energy is converted to heat energy. Aluminum *reflects* more of the Sun's rays.

Time for Reflection

Each science investigation I conduct ends with reflection in which we talk and write about the activity. In this instance, I guided the conversation by providing several discussion prompts:

- What is the hottest color?
- Why do you think that is?
- What else did you notice about the data?
- Have you ever noticed how some colors seem hotter than others when you are outside?

Students shared their thoughts, debating several interpretations and explanations of the data. Their ideas reflected their varying abilities. While trying to explain why the black paper was the hottest, one child said, "The Sun is trying really hard to warm the black paper up." Another shared a more sophisticated explanation by suggesting the idea of materials reacting with light: "Black holds light in it, but white doesn't." A third child expanded on this comment by asserting, "You're not supposed to wear a black shirt on a sunny day because you'll get too hot because black absorbs the light." Note that this child used the term *absorbs* and brought up a practical application of absorption.

We also discussed that though our investigation question asked, "What is the hottest color?" it's not actually colors themselves that were hot but that colors absorb or reflect heat in differing amounts. This post-activity discussion is vital preparation for constructing new knowledge during the learning log writing that follows (Rivard and Straw 2000).

Is this the time to teach children what happens at the molecular level as light and colored materials meet? No. It is more important that inquiry for children of this age focus on observable phenomena. According to the *National Science Education Standards*, "The changes that occur when materials interact provide the necessary precursors to the later introduction of more abstract ideas in the upper grade levels" (NRC 1996, p. 121).

Learning Logs

Following our discussion, I usually put two writing prompts on the board for my students to respond to in their learning logs. The first is simply to answer the inquiry question—in this case, "What color is hottest?" The second prompt is to help children extend their knowledge beyond the initial question. This second prompt is usually quite general so that children can take aspects of the activity and discussion and build knowledge in directions that best fit their abilities and interests. For this lesson, the second prompt was "What does sunlight do to papers of different colors?"

Writing about science experiences can be difficult for children. I've found it best to start using learning logs early in the year with my first graders so they become accustomed to the task. In fact, I now start so early in the year that sometimes I cannot even read their writing, and I have students dictate their responses to me. I'm not able to do this with every student every time, however, and that's fine. The power of reflective writing is more in the thought that the writer puts into it, rather than the final product.

Here are several other tips for using learning logs:

- Generally, spelling and punctuation can be ignored. I want students to put thought into the content rather than the conventions.

- Have students write to a time limit. "Everyone writes for 10 minutes," usually leads to more detailed and thoughtful writing than simply asking children to respond to the prompt. I do not accept an "I'm done" before the time limit is over. Instead I encourage students to expand their thoughts. Challenging them to fill out a whole sheet (or two) is another motivator.

- Circulate and read children's logs as they write. For adults it is considered rude to look over another's shoulder. With learning logs, however, it is a crucial habit to get into. As I read what students are writing, I often ask for clarification, ask questions, and offer encouragement. These probes push children to build new understanding.

- Finally, read and learn from the finished entries. Using a rubric makes the assessment of learning logs easier and more accurate.

Learning Log Rubric

Once students have responded in their learning logs, I assess what they've written. I evaluate each child's response to the first prompt using the rubric shown in Figure 2 (p. 250). At the very least, I want children to reach a reasonable conclusion from the activity. While reflection can and should focus on inquiry processes and other aspects of science, this rubric is for assessing content knowledge.

Basic conclusions are just the beginning, however. Writing that goes beyond reporting results has been called "knowledge-transforming writing" (Bereiter and Scardamalia 1987). For example, research suggests that when students write to explain the results of hands-on activities, they are building new understanding as they connect past knowledge to the inquiry (Palincsar, Anderson, and David 1993). These extensions of thinking often take the form of explanations, justifications, applications, and generalizations.

Figure 2. Learning log rubric

Level	Student	Examples
4	Correctly interpreted results to answer the question, and included *two* other pertinent comments (explanation, application, generalization, or justification).	**Explanation** • The sun is attracted to dark colors. • The sun was trying very hard to make black a light color. • Black absorbs heat. Light colors like silver will reflect light. • Black made the light stay in it. • The sun pays attention to the darkest colors like black. **Application** • If it is a hot day you should wear light colors to stay cooler. • That's why blacktop is so hot on your bare feet. **Generalization** • No matter where the color is if there are two of the same colors they will always be the same temperature. • Different colors are different temperatures. • Dark colors are hot, light colors are not. **Justification** • Black is the hottest. The black thermometer was the highest.
3	Correctly interpreted results to answer the question, and included *one* other pertinent comment.	(shown in level 4 examples)
2	Correctly interpreted results to answer the question.	• Black is the hottest, white is the lowest, yellow is in the middle. • The hottest color is black.
1	Incorrectly interpreted results.	• Yellow is the hottest color because it's the color of the Sun (ignored, was not swayed by, or did not understand data). • Tinfoil is 89, black is 103, blue is 98 … (listed data without interpreting it).
0	Log provided little or no information in which to make a judgment.	Includes logs that are illegible or off topic.

Explanations

One of the main aims of inquiry is to help children "use their observations to construct reasonable explanations" (NRC 1996, p. 121). The Standards acknowledge, however, that this is a difficult task for many K–4 students. For this reason, the rubric makes no distinctions between explanations that are fairly accurate and complex and those that are naïve and basic. From a constructivist viewpoint, children's explanations reflect their individual experiences and intellects. These early explanations are necessary to the later development of more accurate concepts. As they wrote, I asked several children, "Why do you think the darker colors had the highest temperatures?" Probes like this lead children to think about explanations.

Justifications

Children should be encouraged to justify their conclusions with evidence, which most often are observations from the investigations. Probes such as "How do you know that black is the hottest color?" prompt children to back up their assertions with facts, such as that the thermometer on the black paper had the highest reading.

Applications

Children need to see how science is applicable beyond the walls of the classroom. Students who connect conclusions to experiences outside of school or to previous science lessons are applying knowledge. When teachers ask, "Have you ever touched something black that was in the Sun? Write about that!" children think of how these concepts apply in the world at large. An example that may come to mind is, "That's why blacktop is so hot on your bare feet."

Generalizations

Children develop generalizations by identifying patterns across the investigation data. Being able to see beyond the phenomena to an overview of the data is a step toward generating powerful explanations (Tytler and Peterson 2004). "What kind of colors had the highest temperatures?" is an example of a probe that may lead children to generalizations: "Dark colors are hot. Light colors are not."

An Authentic, Valuable Tool

With learning logs, no learning time is lost since the assessment—students written log entries—is not separated from instruction but embedded in it. Learning log responses offer an authentic view into students' learning. As students respond to the prompts, they essentially are "answering the question and presenting the results to others"—part of what inquiry is all about (NRC 1996, p. 122). They are developing inquiry skills in a meaningful way, yet another reason learning logs are such valuable tools for students and teachers.

Resources

Bereiter, C., and M. Scardamalia. 1987. *The Psychology of Written Communication.* Hillsdale, NJ: Lawrence Erlbaum Associates.

National Research Council (NRC). 1996. *National science education standards.* Washington, DC: National Academies Press.

Palincsar, A. S., C. Anderson, and Y. M. David. 1993. Pursuing scientific literacy in the middle

grades through collaborative problem solving. *The Elementary School Journal* 93 (5): 643–658.

Rivard, L. P., and S. B. Straw. 2000. The effect of talk and writing on learning science: An exploratory study. *Science Education* 84 (5): 566–593.

Tytler, R., and S. Peterson. 2004. From "try and see" to strategic exploration: Characterizing young children's scientific reasoning. *Journal of Research in Science Teaching* 41 (1): 94–118.

Chapter 44

Using Web Logs in the Science Classroom

By Staycle C. Duplichan

As educators we must continually ask ourselves if we are meeting the needs of today's students. The science world is adapting to our ever-changing society; are the methodology and philosophy of our educational system keeping up? China is revising textbooks to include resources that teach technology skills, South Korea is developing an educational technology infrastructure, and the United Kingdom is producing major educational technology programs (Richardson 2006). How are we preparing our students to work in this new world?

The good news is that our children are social beings; they naturally want to personalize and discover new information (Huffaker 2005). They are learning new skills when they use their Xboxes, iPhones, iPods, Flip camcorders, and digital cameras. Students also read, edit, and create multimedia projects using MySpace, YouTube, Facebook, and Xanga. Educators can tap into these technology skills by using web logs as a resource for the science curriculum.

Web 2.0

Technology has evolved from the time when the internet was used only as a reference library to today's social, interactive online world. When the internet was born, users had to know the exact URL address to retrieve any information. We now refer to this time as the Web 1.0 era. Internet users saw the need to organize information in the form of websites and to create search engines. Organizing internet data heralded the Web 1.5 era. Today the internet has evolved into the Web 2.0 era that allows participants to invite others to view and possibly edit documents, pictures, websites, and spreadsheets. This era is marked by a system of inviting collaborators to actively join and share information. Web 2.0 offers many educational resources, such as web logs, social bookmarking sources, wikis, Google resources, and podcasts. Web 2.0 is not a perfect system. All of these tools require registration and most require an e-mail address. Not all of the information is accurate and controlled. However, technology is arguably on the cusp of a Web 2.5 era in which internet sites are being created so that information can be monitored and controlled (Solomon and Schrum 2007). One important tool that persists in the Web 2.5 era and can be used in the science classroom is web logs.

Web Logs

Web logs were given the name *blogs* by the American blogger Jorn Barger in 1997 (Lanclos 2008). Web logs have an important place in the science curriculum. Students need to know how to write, problem solve, and form educated opinions to be science literate. Blogging can be the answer by engaging learners to reflect on real-world problems by learning how to express themselves and communicate through writing. Teachers might be surprised at how well even quiet, shy students express themselves when blogging (Kajder and Bull 2003).

Figure 1. A screen shot of student postings

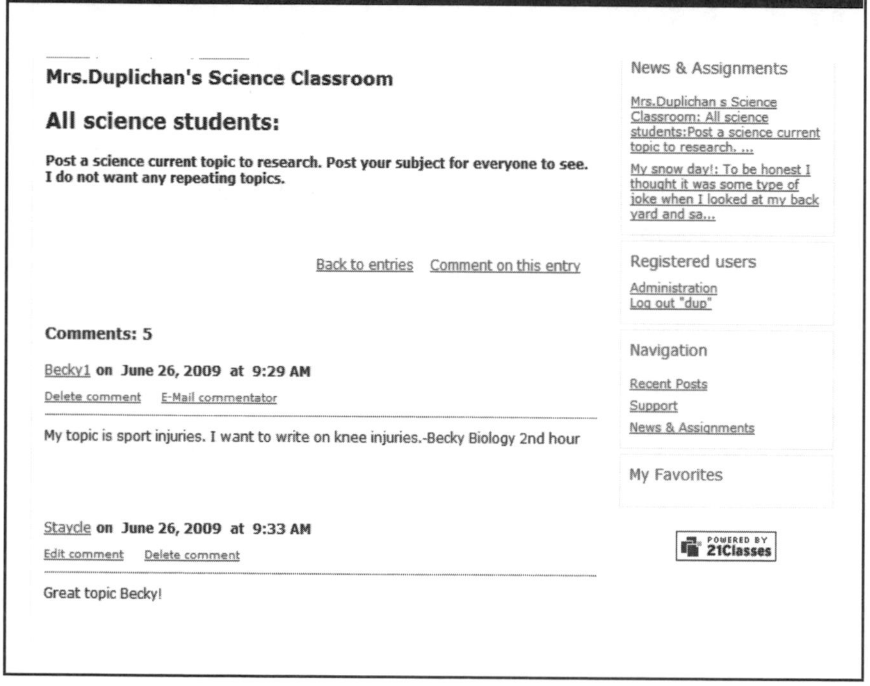

Mrs.Duplichan's Science Classroom

All science students:

Post a science current topic to research. Post your subject for everyone to see. I do not want any repeating topics.

Back to entries   Comment on this entry

Comments: 5

Becky1 on June 26, 2009 at 9:29 AM
Delete comment   E-Mail commentator

My topic is sport injuries. I want to write on knee injuries.-Becky Biology 2nd hour

Staycle on June 26, 2009 at 9:33 AM
Edit comment   Delete comment

Great topic Becky!

News & Assignments
Mrs.Duplichan s Science Classroom: All science students:Post a science current topic to research. ...
My snow day!: To be honest I thought it was some type of joke when I looked at my back yard and sa...

Registered users
Administration
Log out "dup"

Navigation
Recent Posts
Support
News & Assignments

My Favorites

POWERED BY
21Classes

Blogs are a multi-genre, multimedia, visually minded medium that can be used to promote student engagement. For example, the teacher could post a question or writing prompt, which students answer by posting a blog entry. The example given in Figure 1 demonstrates how teachers can assign a writing prompt to their science students. All students can read postings by their classmates and write a response to their classmates' postings. Students benefit from collaborating with one another. Blogs can also act as an online filing cabinet by allowing students to post and keep their assignments online. Students can store their writing assignments in a folder on the web log. Essentially, web logs can become an online portfolio (Kajder and Bull 2003).

Let's Get Blogging

The first step in creating a web log is to obtain permission from your school district or principal to use blogging websites in your classroom. Permission must also be obtained from students' parents. All students must be given a permission slip that they sign and have signed by a parent before they can participate in this project (Figure 2). Alternative assignments can be created if a student is not allowed to blog. For example, the student could be given paper and pencil to do the web log assignment.

Figure 2. Student permission slip

Dear parent/guardian,

Our _____class will be using a web log (blog) this year to encourage your child to write more and to improve on your child's writing skills. All students must follow these class rules:

- Think of all consequences before making a post to the blog.
- Keep all personal identification secure. Do not use your last name on any post.
- Do not post any inappropriate images or language to the blog.
- Follow all school and Internet-use policies.
- Remember all copyright rules discussed in class!
- I understand that it is my choice to blog. I can answer my assignments using paper and pencil.

I understand that if I do not abide by these terms and conditions, I will lose all computer privileges.

_____
Student signature

_____ _____
Parent signature   Date

Once permission has been given, the teacher should look at examples of web log classroom sites. Figure 3 lists examples for teachers to view. The internet offers many different, and free, education web log sites for students (Figure 4). Most web log sites do not require an e-mail address from your students. Students are given a username and password by the teacher. When they log in, they can view and post their assignments. The students' postings are not directly posted on the web log site. The teacher has the option to view each assignment and post the students' entry to the web log.

Figure 3. Examples of excellent educational web logs for teachers

Darren Kuropatwa—A Difference
  http://adifference.blogspot.com
Educational Weblogs—Zimbio
  www.zimbio.com/Educational+Weblogs
Tim Lauer—Education/Technology
  http://timlauer.org
Sarah, Plain and Tall by Patricia MacLachlan
  http://sarahplainandtall.blogspot.com
Leader Talk—Education Week
  www.leadertalk.org
Kathy Schrock's KaffeeKlatsch
  www.kathyschrock.net/blog
Anne Davis—EduBlog Insights
  http://anne.teachesme.com

Figure 4. Examples of web log servers

Blogger
  www.blogger.com/start
Bravenet
  www.bravenet.com/webtools/journal/index.php
21Classes Cooperative Learning
  www.21classes.com
Edublogs
  http://edublogs.org
Class Blogmeister
  http://classblogmeister.com

Create your home page by writing a message for your students. *Sarah, Plain and Tall by Patricia MacLachlan* (see Figure 3, p. 255) is an excellent example of a classroom web log. Figure 5 contains a screen shot of my classroom's home page. The picture is important to my students. For the first time in their lifetime, it snowed! The students wanted to share their experience. The web log gave them a place to share their experiences and feelings about the snow. I took the snowy home page photo with my digital camera. Be careful with students' pictures—most school districts do not allow photographs of students in any publications.

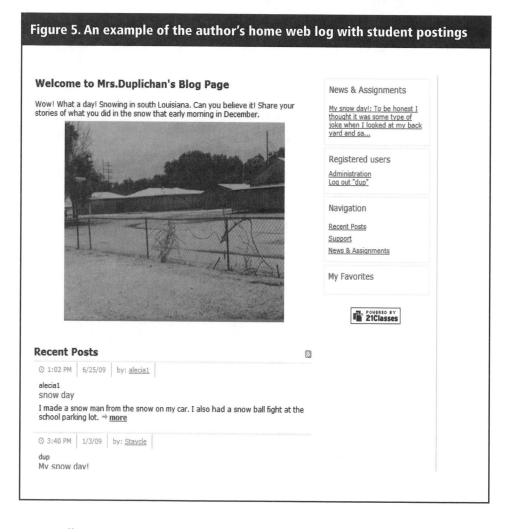

Figure 5. An example of the author's home web log with student postings

Welcome to Mrs.Duplichan's Blog Page

Wow! What a day! Snowing in south Louisiana. Can you believe it! Share your stories of what you did in the snow that early morning in December.

News & Assignments

My snow day!: To be honest I thought it was some type of joke when I looked at my back yard and sa...

Registered users

Administration
Log out "dup"

Navigation

Recent Posts
Support
News & Assignments

My Favorites

POWERED BY
21Classes

Recent Posts

⏱ 1:02 PM | 6/25/09 | by: alecia1

alecia1
snow day
I made a snow man from the snow on my car. I also had a snow ball fight at the school parking lot. → more

⏱ 3:40 PM | 1/3/09 | by: Staycle

dup
My snow day!

Finally, create an account for each student. Most web logs require only typing in a user-name, password, and students' names. I only use each student's first name or first name and last initial when forming my students' accounts.

The next step in creating a web log is to decide what you want to accomplish with your blog and brainstorm ways of using this writing resource in your classroom (Figure 6). A blog can be a resource that will teach students to explain scientific concepts in the form of writing. Let's say you want students to think critically on a science topic, such as the legal ramifications of DNA testing. Start with one assignment and then gradually add to your blog.

Figure 6. Examples of how web logs can be used in the science classroom

Current event	Ask a classmate	Book club	Report
• Students are required to post a summary of a current event, such as global warming, for each grading period.	• Students post a question for other classmates to answer. An example of a possible post is, "How can I remember the difference between interphase and prophase?"	• Students reflect on their favorite science book.	• Students are assigned a subject to research. Each student or group could be assigned a scientist, theory, organ, kingdom, or disease to report on.

Creative writing	What if	Debate	Online reading
• Students write how a cell is like a factory. Each student posts one example. • Students write a complaint letter from the heart to the cholesterol molecule. • Students write a love letter from the lungs to an oxygen molecule.	• Students are asked if their life would be different if their knee joint became a ball and socket joint. Each person posts one example and responds to others. • Students are asked, "What if pollution killed all of the earthworms?" • Students are asked to reflect on how the Earth would be different if the temperature rose 20 degrees.	• Students are asked, "What are the legal ramifications of DNA testing?" • Students are asked, "What is your opinion on using animals for testing products?" • Students are asked, "Should stem cell research be allowed?"	• Students are assigned to read an article from Google Scholar.

Visual aids	Lab report	Study habits
• Students post digital pictures of lab setups. • Students post digital pictures of pictures of lab procedures. • Students draw steps for any lab procedure. • Students draw and label a key scientific concept.	• Students post their lab results. • Students post their data for comparision.	• Students post how they remember vocabulary or facts. • Students give examples of how they study for tests.

Before students post to your blog, remind them of proper posting etiquette. Review their permission slip. Post the blogging rules in the computer lab, so students will be reminded of them often (summarized as part of Figure 2, p. 255). Finally, consider how students' posting will be assessed. A rubric similar to Figure 7 (p. 258) can be used.

Figure 7. Web log assessment

Multimedia project: Writing a blog

Teacher name: _____   Student name: _____

CATEGORY	4	3	2	1
Rough draft	Brought in on due date. Student shares with peer and extensively edits based on peer feedback.	Brought in on due date. Student shares with peer and peer makes edits.	Provides feedback and/or edits for peer, but own rough draft was not ready for editing.	Rough draft not ready for editing and did not participate in reviewing draft of peer.
Mechanics	No misspellings or grammatical errors.	Three or fewer misspellings and/or mechanical errors.	Four misspellings and/or grammatical errors.	More than four errors in spelling or grammar.
Content	Covers topic in depth with details and examples. Subject knowledge is excellent.	Includes essential knowledge about the topic. Subject knowledge appears to be good.	Includes essential information about the topic but there are one to two factual errors.	Content is minimal OR there are several factual errors.
Originality	Shows a large amount of original thought; creative and inventive ideas.	Shows some original thought; new ideas and insights.	Uses other people's ideas (giving them credit), but little evidence of original thinking.	Uses other people's ideas, without giving them credit.

If your students do not have access to a home computer, all of the assignments can be posted in a school computer lab. Time can be given at the beginning or the end of the class period for students to post on the web log site. If students are working in groups or pairs, the teacher decides whether one person in the group posts the assignment or if each student in the group posts to the web log.

Enjoy using the blogging world. You will be amazed by your students' excitement and participation. Happy blogging!

References

Huffaker, D. 2005. The educated blogger: Using web logs to promote literacy in the classroom. *AACE Journal* 13 (2): 91–98.

Kajder S., and G. Bull. 2003. Scaffolding for struggling students. *Learning & Leading with Technology* 31 (2): 32–35

Lanclos, P. 2008. *Weaving Web 2.0 tools into the classroom.* Portland, OR: Visions Technology.

Richardson, W. 2006. *Blogs, wikis, podcasts and powerful web tools for classrooms.* Thousand Oaks, CA: Corwin.

Solomon, G., and L. Schrum. 2007. *Web 2.0 new tools, new schools.* Washington DC: Iste.

Chapter 45

Interactive Reflective Logs
Opening Science Notebooks to Peer and Teacher Feedback

By Cynthia Minchew Deaton, Benjamin E. Deaton, and Katina Leland

Although some students flourish during classroom discussions, other students become more reserved and withdrawn. How do we as educators ensure that all students are given the opportunity to respond? How do we engage students who are embarrassed to speak in front of others? How can students participate in a science learning community? One way to encourage students' communication with their peers and teachers is through the use of a reflective journal, which engages students in expressing their understanding of and questions about science concepts.

We created an interactive reflective log (IRL) to provide teachers with an opportunity to use a journal approach to record, evaluate, and communicate student understanding of science concepts. Through a two-part design, the IRL allows (1) students to demonstrate their understanding of science concepts and (2) teachers and other students to question or guide students' understanding. Unlike a traditional journal, the IRL incorporates prompts to encourage students to discuss their understanding of science content and science processes and to reflect on their science activities. The IRL provides a structured approach to journaling and encourages teachers and students to participate in a community of learners by sharing their IRL entries with one another. This is unlike traditional journal entries that are usually kept to oneself or only shared with the teacher. Traditional journal entries also usually result in open-ended responses that do not always show students' understanding of science content, science processes, and evidence.

Creating an IRL

Each log is broken into five sections: science content, science process, explain, questions/interests, and refine activity (see Figure 1, p. 260, for a blank IRL). These sections guide students in (1) writing about their understanding of content and procedures for investigations or inquiries, (2) developing explanations based on their evidence, (3) extending their knowledge by posing new questions, (4) listing insights they gained from their inquiry, and (5) examining and evaluating their investigation.

Figure 1. Interactive reflective log for science investigations

Student	Reflective Partner
1. Science content a. What did you know about _____? b. What questions do you have about _____? c. What did you learn about _____?	P: _____ _____ _____ T: _____ _____ _____
2. Science process a. What happened? b. What did you do? c. What did you find? d. What safety procedures did you follow?	P: _____ _____ _____ T: _____ _____ _____
3. Explain a. What caused _____? b. Why?	P: _____ _____ _____ T: _____ _____ _____
4. Questions/interests a. What other questions do you have? b. What was interesting to you?	P: _____ _____ _____ T: _____ _____ _____
5. Refine activity a. What would you do differently? b. What do you wish you could have done?	P: _____ _____ _____ T: _____ _____ _____

To aid students in completing successful writing about their science experiences, the IRL provides students with basic prompts to guide their writing about their science investigations. Although the science content prompts on the IRL were selected to support students in developing communications skills and explanations for a specific activity, they can be revised easily. Teachers can easily fill in the following questions to develop prompts for that section:

What did you know about _____?
What questions do you have about _____?
What did you learn about _____?

The science process section encourages students to think about what they did during an activity and uses broad prompts. These prompts can remain the same for any activity. The explain section uses prompts that encourage students to compare and contrast findings and use evidence to develop explanations. This section can also be easily revised as teachers complete the following questions:

What caused _____?
Why did it cause _____?
How do you know it caused _____?

The questions/interests section of the IRL, like the science process section, uses broad prompts and can easily remain the same from activity to activity.

Making It Reflective

Our third-grade students used an IRL to record their investigation of Earth's layers. As they participated in the Layer-Cake Earth activity (Tedford and Warny 2006), students responded to the IRL questions using both words and drawings. The Layer-Cake Earth activity provides a hands-on approach to learning geology concepts and investigating Earth's layers. In this activity, teachers use a layered cake to represent the sediment layers that students can take core samples from and investigate. As they responded to our prompts (Figure 2, p. 262), the students listed the procedures they used to collect samples and what they found in each layer, and they developed explanations for the location of each fossil. Most students chose to list, draw, and label their sample and fossils. By using the IRL, students were able to record and reflect on the procedures they used and their findings. They used the IRL in lieu of more traditional methods of recording their science activities. The prompts in the IRL supported students in discussing the processes they used to collect their evidence and the evidence they collected. It also encouraged them to use evidence to explain their findings.

Figure 2. Sample interactive reflective log

Student	Reflective Partner

1. Science content
a. What did you know about Earth's layers?
   There are four layers.
   They can be solid or liquid.
 	
b. What questions do you have about
   Earth's layers?
   How bright is the Earth's inner core?
   How hot is the Earth's core? Has anyone taken the
   temperature of the inner core? If there was not a
   crust, would the mantle spill out into space?
 	
c. What did you learn about Earth's layers?
   How to find sample. The different layers. How big
   they are. I didn't know there was an inner and outer
   core. What a trilobite was.
	P:_____
	_____
	_____
	T: I like your questions. It would be nice if you could research them and share what you find with the class. What could you do to find the answers to your questions?
	
	I am also glad you learned some new things. You learned how to collect samples and that there is an inner and outer core. What did you learn about the Earth's crust?

2. Science process
a. What happened?
   We found 3 shark teeth and Dinosaur bones. The 3
   shark teeth in the first layers and dinosaur bones in
   the second layers. Dinosaur bones in the pink layer.
 	
b. What did you do?
   We dug into different layers of the earth. We got
   the sample from the field scientist in our group. We
   found 3 shark teeth and dinosaur bones. They were
   cool.
 	
c. What did you find?
   We found 3 shark teeth and dinosaur bones. We
   didn't find a trilobite.
 	
d. What safety procedures did you follow?
   We did not run in the room. We took turns getting
   materials. We were careful when digging. We
   cleaned up the floor and desk. We did not eat
   anything or throw anything.
	P:_____
	_____
	_____
	T: I'm glad you know what your group did to investigate the Earth's layers. What was your role in your group? How did you help during the investigation?
	
	I am glad that you followed the class rules and were safe during the investigation. Did you use any science tools during your investigation? How did you safely handle those tools?

3. Explain
a. What caused another sample to look different?
   Shape, size, color, and layer you found them in.
 	
b. What caused another sample to look the same?
   Where you took your sample. Where you cored at.
   Layers you cored.
 	
c. Why do you think the sample looked different?
   Dug into different spots. Each spot was different.
   Some were thick. Some were thin. Each layer was a
   different color. Different things in each color layer.
 	
d. Why do you think the sample looked the same?
   Dug in same spot. Dug right next to the spot we dug
   the first time.
	P:_____
	_____
	_____
	T: Do you think the location of the other group's core sample made their sample look different than your group's sample? Why?

Continued on the next page

Figure 2. Sample interactive reflective log (cont.)

4. Questions/interests a. What other questions do you have? *What was my partners' favorite thing?* *Can we do this for real?* *Can we make 2 cakes and have more things?* b. What was interesting to you? *Finding things. To get the sample out. Core.*	P:_____ _____ _____ T: What other fossils do you think we could add if we had another cake? What could we use to represent the fossils? Why did you enjoy finding things?

Making It Interactive

Once students complete their IRL, the teacher selects a reflective partner for each one. Teachers may select reflective partners based on who works in the same science group, reading and writing abilities, and previous interactions in class. If students are asked to write about their investigations, another member of their learning community should read their comments. Our thinking was that when students know teachers or other students will take the time to read their responses and elaborate on them, their motivation to write may increase.

When students are allowed to review their peers' work, they act as reflective peers. This role allows them to add questions and comments on their peers' IRLs. For example, they may question their peers' use of (1) scientific terminology, (2) investigation procedures, (3) data collection, and (4) explanations developed from data. It also allows group members to communicate with one another and help refine other members' ideas and explanations. Students can use their science group's or science partner's questions and comments to elaborate on or revise descriptions and explanations they developed while participating in the science investigation and completing the IRL. Their group's or partner's feedback may also enhance future use of the IRL to organize their thoughts and record their science investigation.

Many students need support in developing as a reflective partner. For students to understand how to provide feedback to their peers, they first need to understand what appropriate feedback looks like. Teachers need to model appropriate feedback and talk about their expectations for reflective partners. Teachers may also develop prompts to support students in examining their peers' IRL entries. For example, they can ask reflective peers to provide feedback on investigation procedures (e.g., Do you understand the procedures they used during their investigation?), use of science terminology, or use of evidence when explaining the findings.

Our IRL allows both students and teachers to comment on or question students' responses to the prompts. Teachers may wish to be the only person commenting on students' IRLs, or they may like their comments to support questions or comments asked by other students. This choice provides teachers with a flexible approach for involving members of the learning community. In our case, teachers took on the role of the reflective partner. Through this role, we were able to provide students with questions and comments that valued their participation, their knowledge about Earth's layers, and the data they collected. Comments encouraged students to clarify and extend their responses to their IRLs. Other comments were used to provide students with positive reinforcement as they reflected on their findings and responses. Although the questions and comments may have varied from student to student, they all helped students reflect on the investigation.

By participating as reflective partners, teachers can seamlessly act as participants in the community of learners. Like reflective peers, teachers use comments and questions to guide students to further examine the content, processes, and data from their investigations. Their questions can be used as enrichment or remediation questions for certain students. Reading and responding to students' IRLs affords teachers the opportunity to assess student understanding, identify concepts they need to revisit, and challenge students to extend their understanding of a concept.

Amplified Assessment

Although the IRL itself provides teachers with a way to assess students' science understanding, the IRL rubric supports teachers in assessing students' science understanding and participation as reflective partners. The IRL rubric assesses both students' use of the IRLs for recording their investigations and their participation as reflective partners. By having peers and teachers respond to their IRLs, students can use comments and questions posed by their peers or teachers to refine their writing or future investigations. Feedback from a teacher on the IRL through questions and comments and by using the rubric can also help students reflect on how they connect science terms and concepts, develop clear explanations, and reflect on the procedures and outcomes of their investigation. Depending on the students, teachers may need to revise the descriptors in the IRL rubric so that they are easily understood.

Reflective Thinkers

Not only does the IRL provide students with a guide for writing their investigations, it can encourage students to reflect on their investigations and communicate with their peers. Questions and prompts from the IRL can be used to encourage future investigations and provide teachers with an understanding of students' interests and knowledge about science concepts. In addition, IRLs can enhance the classroom community as students trust one another to provide feedback on their responses about and understanding of scientific investigations.

Reference

Tedford, R., and S. Warny. 2006. Layer-cake Earth. *Science and Children* 44 (4): 40–44.

Chapter 46

A Laboratory of Words
Using Science Notebook Entries as Preassessment Creates Opportunities to Adapt Teaching

By Jeanne Clidas

"Living things move and make sounds. For example, a cat moves its feet to make it go from place to place and it says meow. A tree is a living thing too. So are people, dogs, plants, and bugs."

This is an entry from a student's science notebook in response to my question "How do you know if something is alive?" Like his fourth-grade classmates, this student brings a wealth of knowledge to each new science inquiry. The background knowledge of my students varies depending on their past experiences, but each one usually has something to contribute to a new science inquiry. Not all of the ideas presented in their science notebooks are accurate, however, so I wondered how the children acquired them and what role they would play in learning.

Although I have always used science notebooks as a place to record observations, data, and conclusions, I decided to add a step to bring students' existing ideas out for examination. Before each lesson, I started asking the children to write what they knew about the topic in a "quick write." A quick write entails me asking an open-ended question and having the students write all they know in three minutes. When the quick writes are finished, the students discuss their thoughts with partners or in small groups.

As students record what they already know before each science inquiry and then document the inquiry process (i.e., data, observations, and questions), there is opportunity to revisit and reflect on how the old and the new relate. Science notebooks in my classroom are a laboratory of words that support conversations and continued inquiry.

Assessing Prior Knowledge

To assess what students already know, before each inquiry experience I ask them to do a quick write consisting of a simple question or directive (Figure 1, p. 266). When we study the seasons, I ask them to write what they believe causes the different seasons. When we explore the ecology of the Norwalk River, I ask them to write what they know about how water moves.

I want to know what the students believe and understand, but I also want to know where the class's knowledge supports new learning and where it might need clarification or challenging.

For example, at the beginning of our inquiry into plants, Tara writes, "A plant is a living thing that does not move. A plant reproduces itself. A plant is a flower with leaves. Some plants look ugly, some look nice. There are all kinds of plants." In assessing Tara's ideas, I can build on her understanding that a plant reproduces itself when we investigate seeds and experiment with other ways plants propagate, but I need to challenge her idea that plants have flowers because not all do (Figure 2).

Figure 1. A student example

> What is a rock?
>
> A rock is anything that comes out of a volcano and cools. It gets old and grows so that is how it changes colors and the ones that are smooth get smooth by getting hit on a lot and getting run over. Rocks are made out of minerals. —Kelly

Figure 2. A student example

> What is a plant?
>
> A plant is a (living) thing that does not move. A plant (reproduces) itself. A plant is a flower with leaves. Some plants look ugly, some look nice. there are all (kinds) of plants
>
> How do plants get food?
>
> Plants get food from there roots. When it rains the water seeps into the ground and the roots of the plant suck it up. some other plants catch food by when the fly lands on its tong the mouth closes up.

Unfortunately, many of the ideas students bring to science inquiry are incomplete or incorrect because they have never been shared, discussed, or challenged. These preconceptions are tenacious and resistant to change. Because the quick writes bring the preconceptions out to be examined, they are less likely to interfere with new learning.

All inquiry starts with a question, but to generate a question a student must have some prior knowledge about the subject. Writing one's own ideas offers the learner time to think, organize, and choose the ideas with the most personal meaning and connection. The individual quick writes allow me to assess where the similarities and differences in student knowledge are. I can also see which students have a deeper understanding of the topic and which have a more surface or limited understanding.

Composing a Quick Write

Students first need to know how to successfully compose a quick write. At the beginning of the year, I model this process by asking an open-ended question about our topic and have the students orally contribute some ideas. I show them how I would write their ideas in sentences and name the process a *quick write*. We read the quick write together and discuss how it states what we currently know. I point out the keywords and circle them so it is obvious my sentences are specific and not general. It is important for students to know that quick writes are personal and unique to each individual, so I give them another open-ended question about the same topic and have them share their responses with partners. This gives every student a chance to contribute. It also encourages discussion and negotiation of key ideas. An example of a student discussion follows:

- "Tell me what you know about photosynthesis." (Teacher)
- "It is something plants do. It is also green and needs light." (Student 1)
- "I think it's when plants make food. The food is green and we can eat it." (Student 2)
- "It needs sunlight. It needs water. Only plants with flowers do photo-synthesis." (Student 3)
- "Plants do it. They use Sun and water. Flowers can do it too." (Student 4)
- "It's what makes plants green." (Student 5)

Not all of the responses are completely accurate or comprehensive, but the students tell me what they know. This provides the starting point. I use the students' ideas to write a sentence that all the students can see and read: "I think photosynthesis is something green plants do when they use sunlight to make food." This sentence is a model for what they will do. The class discusses these ideas and there is often a debate as to whether the sentence is correct. Because there is agreement that photosynthesis has something to do with plants, I ask the students to respond in writing to a new question: "What is the relationship between plants and photosynthesis?" The students are given three minutes to write down their answers. This maximizes the time on task and time to uncover the most commonly held ideas. Examples of student quick write responses follow:

- "I think photosynthesis is what plants do when they mix sunshine and water to make food."
- "I think plants do photosynthesis to make food."
- "I think only green plants use photosynthesis."
- "Photosynthesis is when green plants make food."

When the quick writes are complete, it is time to share, analyze, and consider the value/accuracy of what is believed. Figure 3 (p. 268) presents the steps for writing and analyzing the quick write entries. As I walk around and listen, I am able to discern what the class knows or believes about the topic. I use the information from the quick writes and discussions as the foundation for future instruction. As our investigation, research, and inquiry proceed, I direct the students' attention back to this entry so new knowledge and ideas can be compared to what was originally thought or believed. I have found this to be an important step. Reminding the students where their ideas started from helps them decide which new ideas to add to their existing knowledge and which ideas from the quick write to abandon or modify.

Figure 3. Steps for using science notebooks for assessing background knowledge	
1.	Present an open-ended question or directive statement related to the science topic.
2.	Tell the students to write their responses in their science notebooks. Allow 3–5 minutes.
3.	Have students read their quick writes to partners and compare their ideas.
4.	Ask students to choose an idea from their quick writes that they think other children also have written.

Composing Writing Prompts

I discovered I needed open-ended, higher-level questions to use as prompts for the quick writes. The best questions require more than simple "yes" or "no" answers. Explanations often occur as a result of good questions. Open-ended questions also allow the students to focus on the personal connections they can make rather than on the "correct" answer. The students know there are many possible ideas related to the question and so feel encouraged to record their ideas rather than what they think the teacher wants. Example student responses to the question "How does the water in our river move?" follow:

■ "The water is strong and so it pushes over the rocks and moves down the river." (Josh)

■ "The water in the river comes from a pond up in the mountains. It falls out of the pond and flows down the mountain. Where we see it, the water is going fast because a lot of water has come together and runs fast." (Mariah)

■ "Water moves from high places to low places. At the river site, we had to walk up a hill to see part of the river. The end of the trail was lower so I know it was going downhill. It goes fast because of all the rocks that are in the way." (Dante)

■ "Sometimes the water doesn't move. I think it moves most when it rains and the river gets full. The water pushes around the rocks in the water." (Katie)

I know many of their ideas are based on our experience at the river site, which gives me a context into which to put our inquiry. I also know which ideas need to be explored or examined. For example, I ask Josh to explain *strong* to understand more about his idea. One of my favorite questions is "Help me understand where your idea comes from?" It is important to know what is behind the students' ideas before judging them as incorrect. The assessment of the students' ideas drives my instruction and allows me to differentiate based on the range of correct, incorrect, and incomplete notions.

Using the Quick Writes

After listening to students discuss their ideas about how water moves, I decided to have them revisit the observation notes they wrote during our first two visits to the river and look for any notes related to the movement of the water. They find some interesting ideas:

■ The river is fastest and has more bubbles where it gets narrow.

- The wider parts of the river don't look like the water is moving very much.

- The water moves faster at the bottom of the hill.

- There are foam and bubbles around the rocks.

- In the winter, the water moves under the ice.

Using the information from the quick writes and the observation notes, the students generate the question "What variables affect the flow of water?" An inquiry activity in which students test their ideas about the questions allows them the opportunity to explore their quick write ideas and their observation notes. Using simple materials, the students create channels through which water can flow. The students test variables such as the width or incline of the channel. At this point, it is my role to observe. The students' ideas guide their inquiries. In this way, they confirm, challenge, clarify, and extend their own ideas about the movement of water. During the inquiry, they record their thoughts, questions, observations, and processes.

Because the notebooks contain quick writes that indicate a starting point, observation notes, drawings, diagrams of what was seen or discovered, questions that arise during inquiry, and summaries, the students have many opportunities to revisit and compare their ideas. The new information collected through inquiry is added to their laboratory of words.

Notebooks Become Record

Students use the tools of scientists when keeping a science notebook. They also keep track of their thinking and the changes to their original ideas. Because the original ideas are always available for revisiting, the students can refer to the quick write when they encounter new or different ideas. The students use their writing skills to play with and learn the science vocabulary and concepts. Their inquiry is supported by the writing process as the notebooks become a record of how they developed deeper understanding of new science concepts.

Resources

Ausubel, D. 1968. *Educational psychology: A cognitive view.* New York: Rinehart and Winston.

Banchi, H., and R. Bell. 2008. The many levels of inquiry. *Science and Children* 46 (2): 26–29.

Clidas, J. 1993. The Emerging Scientist: A Case Study of Fourth-Grade Students' Science Journals. Unpublished diss., Fordham University.

Doris, E. 1991. *Doing what scientists do: Children learn to investigate their world.* Portsmouth, NH: Heinemann Books.

Lindsfors, J. W. 1999. Children's inquiry: *Using language to make sense of the world.* New York: Teachers College Press.

Marek, E. 1986. They'll misunderstand, but they'll pass. *The Science Teacher* 53 (9): 32–35.

Shaw, E., P. Baggett, and B. Salyer. 2004. Kidspiration for inquiry-centered activities. *Science Activities* 41 (1): 3–8.

Chapter 47

The Art of Reviewing Science Journals

Questions to Consider When Planning and Assessing Students' Journal Entries

By Daniel P. Shepardson and Susan Jane Britsch

Science journals are wonderful tools. They offer a glimpse into children's science understandings, and they are both diagnostic and pedagogically informative to teachers. Examining and reflecting on children's journal work lets teachers embed assessment in curriculum and instruction. However, effectively analyzing children's journal writing and drawing takes practice.

Over the past few years, as teacher-educators involved in the Children's Literacy and Science Project (CLASP), a research and professional development program funded by Toyota USA Foundation, we've taught teachers how to improve their understanding of children's journal responses, what to look for in children's responses and what these responses reveal about students' levels of understandings, and how these responses can guide subsequent instruction.

Through our experience, we've identified several questions and components important in helping teachers better analyze student journal responses:

- Do I comfortably understand the science being taught? (Conceptualizing the Science)

- What are common misconceptions about the study topic? (Identifying Possible Misconceptions)

- Are the instructional goals conducive to inquiry? (Structuring the Instruction)

- Is the response developmentally in line with what children of this age are capable of? (Age-Appropriate Responses)

- What do I analyze and what shows understanding? (Deciding What to Look For and At)

■ What does the response tell me about this child's understanding? (Interpreting the Work)

■ How do I change my instruction to adjust to these findings? (Making Decisions)

With these seven considerations in mind, each of which is discussed in more detail below, teachers will be able to learn more about the children they are teaching and their own instruction.

Conceptualizing the Science

This one is quite simple—we must understand the concepts we are teaching to adequately analyze and appreciate our students' work. For example, in a unit on sound, if teachers understand that pitch means how high or low a sound is (not its loudness) and that a higher pitch has a greater frequency of vibration, they might analyze children's work for ideas about the cause of high-pitched sounds. Without that understanding, however, a teacher is more limited in helping children develop science knowledge of that concept and may miss opportunities to further advance student understanding.

As unexpected questions emerge during the investigation, teachers can seek out topic-oriented resources to fill in their background knowledge. For example, if children are not understanding that sound is a form of energy, teachers might augment their understanding by consulting resources like Friedl (1997) or Wenham (1995), which provide activities accompanied by scientific explanations.

Identifying Possible Misconceptions

We have also found it useful for teachers to familiarize themselves with possible misconceptions children might have before beginning a topic of study.

For example, the research on children's ideas and understandings about sound indicates that older children may understand that sound production involves vibration (context-specific; Driver et al. 1994). However, younger children may conceptualize sound as an attribute of the object itself, not as something that is caused by vibration. Teachers might then examine children's journal responses with an eye for these identified understandings.

Misconceptions abound, and many common ones are identified and described in research literature, a valuable resource. Rosalind Driver and her colleagues (1994) contributed some of the foundational work on children's conceptions; this remains a central resource for teachers. Other resources provide information about misconceptions that relate to a variety of science topics (e.g., Black and Lucas 1993; Glynn and Duit 1995; Glynn, Yeany, and Britton 1991).

Structuring the Instruction

The level of inquiry experienced in the classroom can influence the ways in which some children use their journals. In general, responses in structured inquiry activities are characterized by a reliance on listing procedures and labeling diagrams. Teachers in CLASP have observed that open-inquiry activities tend to elicit more detailed observation, student-generated questions based on evidence, and references to science concepts than do more structured inquiry activities.

CLASP teachers have also noticed that highly teacher-structured journal pages tend to limit the ways in which children use their science journal to learn. Journal pages that are overly circumscribed by teacher-created headings or designated spaces for either writing or drawing affect the depth, detail, extensiveness, and range of purposes for which the children use visual and written elements on the journal page. For example, a child may respond only to the teacher's questions without enlisting his or her own experience or knowledge base. The teacher-structured journal page can also limit the child conceptually by confining the response to certain teacher-indicated boundaries on the page (e.g., lines or boxes).

In an open-inquiry investigation about pendulums using an unstructured journal page, children are able to relate their own experiences and ideas to the science topic. This space allows students to illustrate and link pendulums of different kinds with other ideas from past and current experiences.

To ensure the best responses, when teachers plan instruction they should consider how they structure journal pages and the ways in which this could impact children's ways of using the journal. Ask yourself, Does the structure of the page permit children to represent their ideas verbally but not visually? Does the page setup signal the importance of certain ideas to the exclusion of others?

Age-Appropriate Responses

Like other forms of assessment, children's journals must also be evaluated in developmentally appropriate ways. It would be unrealistic, for example, to expect very young children to understand the relationship between a sound's volume (loudness) and the air movement caused by each sound wave. On the other hand, young children can understand that a guitar string plucked softly has a narrow width of movement or vibration (producing a soft sound), whereas the same string plucked harder has a greater width of vibration and thus a louder sound. These concepts may be seen (e.g., string vibration) and heard (e.g., soft/loud sound).

Figure 1. A student's illustration about sound

Deciding What to Look For and At

After the first four components have been considered, teachers should decide what to focus on in analyzing children's journals. When deciding what to look for, teachers determine if students express understanding of a specific concept. For example, in the unit on sound, does the teacher examine the children's journal entries for the understanding that the thickness and length of an object influence pitch? Or look for the understanding that a higher pitch means more vibration?

What the teacher decides to look at—e.g., illustrations that show movement—becomes the evidence for children's science understandings and abilities. For example, in Figure 1 (p. 273) the child has extended lines outward from the girl's mouth. This tells a teacher that the child understands that sound travels outward from its source.

Interpreting the Work

Evidence found on the journal page can be interpreted in light of the scientific understanding, possible misconceptions, developmental level, and instructional context. Teachers can then draw conclusions about the child's scientific understandings and abilities and plan for instruction.

The journal entry shown in Figure 1 reflects a child's ideas prior to instruction. We can make the following interpretations: For this child, objects or people make sounds, different objects make different sounds, and people hear sounds.

Her ideas are similar to her classmates' ideas and are not much different from those of other children as reported in the research literature: (1) Sound is produced as a result of the physical attributes of the object, and (2) a force is needed to produce a sound (Driver et al. 1994).

Based on the teacher's conceptual understanding, we see that the child understands sound in the following ways:

- Sound travels outward from the source, but not necessarily as a wave.
- Sound can move through air, but there is no indication that sound can move through liquids or solids.

We can also see what the child does not understand:

- The vibration of the object produces the sound. Objects cannot produce sound unless they are vibrating.
- Pitch is caused by the frequency of vibration; the higher the pitch the greater the frequency of vibration.
- An object's thickness, length, and tightness influences its pitch by affecting its vibration.

Making Decisions

Finally, based on the interpretation of the child's work, teachers make decisions about the child's performance, teaching, and learning. The analysis of the illustration in Figure 1 gives the teacher an idea of which concepts to address in instruction and how to teach them.

For example, the teacher might use a tuning fork to demonstrate that sound is produced when the tuning fork vibrates. The teacher could place the vibrating tuning fork in water or place it next to a suspended Ping-Pong ball (Friedl 1997) to show how sound is produced by vibration (e.g., water splashes, Ping-Pong ball moves).

The teacher might also ask children to investigate different rubber bands to see how pitch changes with length and thickness.

Effective Analysis

With the continuing popularity of science journals, it is in the teacher's best interest to learn and practice how to best interpret these vital reflections of children's understandings. By keeping these components of effective journal analysis in mind and having an organized approach, teachers can use journals to their best advantage as informative tools for teachers and students.

References

Black, P. J., and A. M. Lucas, eds. 1993. *Children's informal ideas in science*. London: Routledge.

Driver R., A. Squires, P. Rushworth, and V. Wood-Robinson. 1994. *Making sense of secondary science: Research into children's ideas*. London: Routledge.

Friedl, A. E. 1997. *Teaching science to children: An inquiry approach*. New York: McGraw-Hill.

Glynn, S. M., and R. Duit, eds. 1995. *Learning science in the schools: Research reforming practice*. Mahwah, NJ: Lawrence Erlbaum Associates.

Glynn, S. M., R. H. Yeany, and B. K. Britton, eds. 1991. *The psychology of learning science*. Mahwah, NJ: Lawrence Erlbaum Associates.

National Research Council (NRC). 1996. *National science education standards*. Washington, DC: National Academies Press.

Wenham, M. 1995. *Understanding primary science ideas, concepts, and explanations*. London: Paul Chapman Publishing.

Chapter 48

The P.O.E.T.R.Y. of Science
A Flexible Tool for Assessing Elementary Student Science Journals

By Jennifer C. Mesa, Michelle L. Klosterman, and Linda L. Cronin-Jones

Inquiry-based science offers rich hands-on and mind-on experiences that encourage students to ask and search for answers to their own questions. Writing about inquiry-based science experiences can provide students with opportunities to communicate their questions, observations, and reflections while expanding our instructional and assessment options as teachers. But how can teachers encourage and assess student writing in science? In this article, we describe P.O.E.T.R.Y., an authentic assessment tool that can be used to analyze elementary student science journal entries and track the development of skills and concepts in both language arts and science.

What Is a Science Journal?

The terms *science journal* and *science notebook* are often used interchangeably. Although both provide students with opportunities to write about their individual science learning experiences, journals and notebooks differ significantly in both format and purpose. Consider these two examples:

Example 1

In Mr. Mendez's classroom, students record their observations and measurements from an investigation of the physical properties of water (cohesion and adhesion) in their science notebooks. They may also paste their instruction sheet and copy notes from the board into their notebooks.

Example 2

In Mrs. Nelson's classroom, students record their predictions, observations, and measurements during an investigation of seed germination in their science journals. After completing the investigation, they reflect on their predictions and use their own observations and measurements to explain what factors are essential for seed germination. Students are also encouraged to write about their own prior experiences growing plants from seeds and share information they remember from a previous week's video about the life cycle of plants.

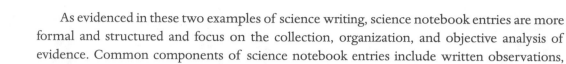

As evidenced in these two examples of science writing, science notebook entries are more formal and structured and focus on the collection, organization, and objective analysis of evidence. Common components of science notebook entries include written observations, scale drawings, diagrams, and numerical data such as charts, data tables, and graphs. Journal entries are more flexible in their format and may contain written and drawn observations and interpretations of observations, as well as personal reactions or perceptions (Dirnberger, McCullagh, and Howick 2005). Simply put, science notebooks focus on recording what students have done while journals focus on what students have learned.

What Is P.O.E.T.R.Y.?

The acronym P.O.E.T.R.Y. stands for Predict, Observe, Explain, Think, Reflect, and Yearn to learn more (Figure 1). P.O.E.T.R.Y. was adapted from White and Gunstone's POE (Predict-Observe-Explain) strategy (1992), which is typically used to guide student learning during an inquiry-based science investigation or demonstration. While the POE strategy focuses on three science-process skills, P.O.E.T.R.Y. emphasizes these three science-process skills as well as higher-order processes (thinking and reflecting) and scientific habits of mind (yearning to learn more). In addition, whereas POE is primarily designed for use in inquiry-oriented science lessons, P.O.E.T.R.Y. focuses on process skills, thinking skills, and habits of mind that represent essential elements of inquiry in both science and language arts contexts.

Uniting Science and Language Arts

Time is a limited commodity in elementary classrooms, and therefore P.O.E.T.R.Y. was designed to incorporate key elements of both national language arts and national science standards. Combining science and language arts skills in one assessment tool was both logical and desirable because so many of the skills standards for the two subjects clearly complement

Figure 1. Explanation of the P.O.E.T.R.Y. acronym	
	Description
Predict	The student makes a prediction about what is to occur and explains her reasoning. Example: I think the bean plant will grow toward the light because it needs light to grow.
Observe	The students makes accurate observations or measurements. Example: The length of the feather is 5.5 cm. The feather is gray and soft.
Explain	The student uses evidence to evaluate his or her prediction and to develop an explanation for his or her observations. Example: I predicted the temperature of the bag would not change, but I felt the bag get hotter after I added the water. I think a chemical reaction happened because a temperature change is a sign of one.
Think	The student devises alternative explanations for the observations. Example: I think paper airplane B flew farther not because it was lighter but because there was a little bit of wind that helped it go farther.
Reflect	The student evaluates the approach used to collect data. Example: I think we should have measured the amount of water we gave each of the plants during our experiment. Some of the plants may have gotten more water than others, making them grow more.
Yearn to learn more	The student generates new questions and approaches to investigate her questions. Example: I want to find out if earthworms can see. I will put a bunch of earthworms near a light and see if they move away.

Figure 2. P.O.E.T.R.Y scoring rubric						
	Predict	**Observe**	**Explain**	**Think**	**Reflect**	**Yearn**
Advanced	The student provides a reasonable prediction that is related to the topic at hand and uses many details from prior knowledge to support it.	The student provides a detailed description of many characteristics of an object or person.	The student evaluates the prediction and poses a reasonable explanation, using many details from prior knowledge and observations.	The student poses a reasonable alternative explanation, using many details from prior knowledge and observations.	The student evaluates how information was gathered and suggests many reasonable ideas for improvement.	The student poses many new questions to investigate that are related to the topic at hand and suggests reasonable methods for investigating them.
Proficient	The student provides a reasonable prediction that is related to the topic at hand and uses a few details from prior knowledge to support it.	The student provides a detailed description of a few of the characteristics of an object or person.	The student evaluates the prediction and poses a reasonable explanation, using many details from observations.	The student poses a reasonable alternative explanation, using many details from observations.	The student evaluates how information was gathered and suggests a few reasonable ideas for improvement.	The student poses a few new questions to investigate that are related to the topic at hand and suggests reasonable methods for investigating them.
Basic	The student provides a reasonable prediction that is related to the topic at hand and uses at least one detail from prior knowledge to support It.	The student attempts to describe more than one characteristic of an object or person.	The student evaluates the prediction and poses a reasonable explanation, using at least one observation.	The student poses a reasonable alternative explanation, using a few details from observations.	The student attempts to evaluate how information was gathered and provides at least one reasonable suggestion for improvement.	The student poses at least one new question to investigate that is related to the topic at hand and suggests a reasonable method for investigating it.
Developing	The student provides a reasonable prediction that is related to the topic.	The student attempts to describe at least one characteristic of an object or person.	The student evaluates the prediction or poses a reasonable explanation, using at least one observation.	The student poses a reasonable alternative explanation, using at least one observation.	The student attempts to evaluate how information was gathered or provides at least one reasonable suggestion for improvement.	The student poses at least one new question to investigate that is related to the topic at hand.
Circle One:		Advanced	Proficient		Basic	Developing

and reinforce one another. For example, the National Science Education Standards require that students "use data to construct a reasonable explanation," while the National Language Arts Standards require students to "gather, evaluate, and synthesize data from a variety of sources" (IRA/NCTE 1996; NRC 1996).

Scoring Through P.O.E.T.R.Y.

To determine if the P.O.E.T.R.Y. assessment tool was understandable and easy to use when analyzing student journals, we worked with a local third-grade teacher who had her students keep science journals for an entire school year. To get a more authentic picture of how science journals are actually used in elementary classrooms, we did not prompt her with specific instructions regarding the content or format of the journals; nor did we provide any specific writing prompts. To determine whether the P.O.E.T.R.Y. assessment tool could be used to identify differences in the quality and content of student science writing over time, three journal entry samples were selected from the beginning, middle, and end of one third grader's science journal (Figures 3, 4, and 5, p. 282). Each entry was then "scored" using the traditional version of the P.O.E.T.R.Y. tool (Figure 2, p. 279).

Entry #1: Developing

The first entry (Figure 3) received an overall rating of *developing* for two reasons: (1) The entry indicated a limited understanding of how to make good predictions, observations, and explanations; and (2) the entry did not include significant examples of thinking, reflecting, or yearning to learn more. In this early entry, the student wrote about an activity investigating a mysterious substance called "goo yuck." She was challenged to conduct several different tests to determine whether goo yuck was a solid or a liquid. The student provided a *prediction* and a list of *observations*, but she did not provide any reasoning for her predictions. Nor did she provide much detail in her observations. The beginning of an *explanation* can be seen at the end of the entry where she attempted to draw a conclusion about the physical state of the substance. Although she came to different conclusions (solid versus liquid) for different tests, there was little evidence of *thinking* because she did not attempt to summarize and compare the relative number of tests that indicated solid versus liquid but instead formed separate conclusions for each test. Furthermore, in this entry, she did not *reflect* on her experience or indicate a *yearning* to know more.

Although the predictions and observations in the first entry were more characteristic of a science notebook, the student used several language arts skills to develop her ideas. Accessing prior knowledge of the terms *liquid* and *solid* was necessary to form an appropriate prediction, organizational strategies were used to communicate the observations in a list appropriate for science, and the use of symbols in her explanation showed knowledge of alternative forms of written language.

Figure 3. Sample entry #1

What Is Goo?

Prediction: Goo is a liquid.

Observations
- Liquid on top
- Solid on the bottom
- Sinks
- Light green
- Cold
- Stinks
- Smooth
- Gooey

Experiment #1=solid
Experiment #2=liquid

Figure 4. Sample entry #2

Heat Energy Lab

Yesterday in lab we started talking about ENERGY. This is what I know about energy. I know that it is run by the Sun.

When we went outside to measure temperatures, or heat energy, on different surfaces around my school yard, I noticed that you had to count to 50 to make a difference in the temperatures. My highest temperature was a rock. It was 84°F and 28°C.

My noticings:

- The road was the second hottest because it was dark colored.
- I thought the grass was going to be the coldest, and it was because grass is actually cool.
- We observed metal, wood, asphalt, concrete, brick, and rock.
- The range wasn't that great because it was a cool day.

The kids in my class always want to get a drink of water at the wing because the water is colder. It is colder because it is in the shade and the other one isn't.

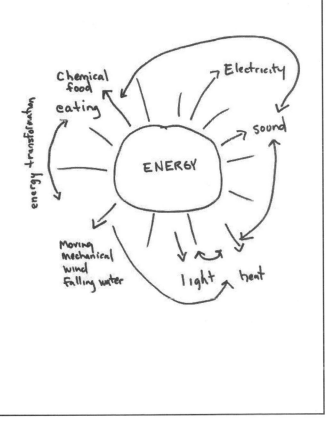

Entry #2: Basic

This second entry (Figure 4) received an overall rating of *basic*. More P.O.E.T.R.Y. skills were included and the entry contained more detail, but the student still did not demonstrate an understanding of alternative explanations or a desire to know more about the topic being explored. In this entry, the student was asked to reflect on an energy lab conducted the previous day. Her *prediction* was advanced because she used several past experiences with heat and energy (such as her classmates' water fountain choices and the coolness of grass) to make the prediction "I thought the grass was going to be the coldest." Her *observations* were *basic* because several of them (such as temperature ranks of the rock and road) did not include detailed descriptions. As in the first entry, her *explanation* was not supported with evidence, no alternative explanations were included, and no evidence of higher-order *thinking* was included. The second entry did contain some evidence of *reflection* when she described the process of reading her thermometer. However, nothing in her writing indicated a *yearning* to know more.

Regarding language arts skills, her basic language skills did improve in the second entry. Her predictions, observations, and explanations were more detailed and employed a greater use of symbols to convey meaning (e.g., emphasizing "energy" by surrounding it with rays

like the sun). She also used alternative forms of technology (e.g., reading a thermometer) to support her ideas.

Entry #3: Developing

The third entry (Figure 5) received an overall rating of *developing* because it contained fewer P.O.E.T.R.Y. elements and lacked supporting details for each element. This third entry was much stronger in terms of language arts skills than science inquiry skills. In terms of science skills, she did not offer a *prediction*. She proposed that lichens can live only in specific types of locations (*explanation*) but did not provide any of her own *observations* to support her claim. The entry consisted of things she was told about lichens but did not include evidence of any of her own *thinking, reflection,* or *yearning to learn more* about lichens.

Interestingly, with no prompting, the student drew on her own knowledge of phonics to examine and comment on the sounds in the word *lichen,* which is characteristic of making *predictions* in language arts. Another language skill demonstrated in this entry was the use of a word web to communicate the meaning of the term *lichen.* This is characteristic of making *observations* and *explanations* in language arts.

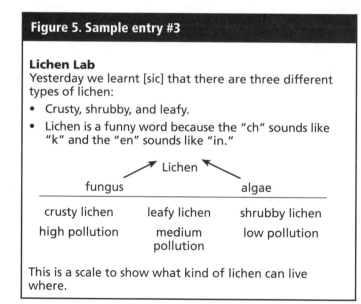

Figure 5. Sample entry #3

Lichen Lab
Yesterday we learnt [sic] that there are three different types of lichen:

- Crusty, shrubby, and leafy.
- Lichen is a funny word because the "ch" sounds like "k" and the "en" sounds like "in."

Lichen
fungus   algae

crusty lichen   leafy lichen   shrubby lichen

high pollution   medium pollution   low pollution

This is a scale to show what kind of lichen can live where.

Informing Through P.O.E.T.R.Y.

Analyzing these three journal entries provides valuable insights into this student's mastery of three science-process skills, two higher-order thinking skills, and an essential scientific habit of mind. Without the aid of a tool such as P.O.E.T.R.Y., a teacher might conclude that since the second and third entries were longer and more detailed than the first, this student's scientific thinking and understanding significantly improved over the course of the school year. However, when examined more closely, results of the P.O.E.T.R.Y. assessment indicate that while this student's language arts skills improved, a corresponding growth in her ability to think scientifically did not occur. In this case, the teacher we worked with assumed that her students' abilities to think scientifically naturally improved as a result of required journaling time. She now realizes that her students need more specific prompts for journal entries, especially if her goals include helping students improve their abilitieis to think and reflect and promoting a desire or yearning to learn more about the world around them.

Other classroom teachers can use P.O.E.T.R.Y. as both a formative and summative assessment tool. In its simplest application, it can be used to assess individual journal entries regarding one specific science inquiry activity, and future instruction could be adjusted to address identified areas of weakness. As a more holistic assessment, multiple student writing samples could be scored and compared throughout the year to document student growth and progress over an extended period of time.

P.O.E.T.R.Y. can also be used to inform your own instruction. After scoring student journal entries, you may find that you need to provide more or less structure in a science inquiry activity, provide more explicit instruction regarding how to make good predictions and observations, provide more examples or prompts to promote thinking, provide more links with previous learning to promote reflection, or even include more creative/unusual experiences to stimulate a greater yearning to learn more.

Regardless of how the scoring guides are used, P.O.E.T.R.Y. offers a more complete picture of your students' mastery of the skills and habits of mind used in true scientific inquiry while also assessing development of key language arts skills. This easy-to-use tool can help you make the most of your classroom journaling time and promote the development of both language arts and scientific thinking skills in the process.

References

Dirnberger, J. M., S. McCullagh, and T. Howick. 2005. Writing and drawing in the naturalist's journal. *The Science Teacher* 72 (1): 38–42.

International Reading Association and National Council of Teachers of English (IRA/NCTE). 1996. *Standards for the English language arts.* Newark, DE: International Reading Association.

National Research Council (NRC). 1996. *National science education standards.* Washington, DC: National Academies Press.

White, R. T., and R. F. Gunstone. 1992. *Probing understanding.* New York: Routledge.

Index

Aeronautical engineering, 131
Age appropriateness, 273
Amplified assessment, 264
Analytical rubrics, 49–55
Analyzing science journals, 228–229
Anonymous peer-editing lab, 112
Ant investigation worksheet, 185
Assessment rubrics, 179
Assessment tools, books as, 162–164
Assessments
    amplified, 264
    journals, 142–143, 244–245
    notebooks, 235–236
    P.O.E.T.R.Y. tool, 278
    prior knowledge, 265–266
    science journals, 244–245
    science notebooks, 235–236
Attitudes, scientific, 222

Background knowledge, assessing, science
        notebooks for, 268
Biography, 219–225
Biological engineering, 131
Blogs, 253–258
    assessment, 258
    student permission slip, 255
    with student postings, 256
    for teachers, 255
Books
    as assessment tools, 162–164
    brainstorming, 173
Brainstorming, 92, 173

Chain of evidence, 20
Chapter from student-authored book,
        sample, 6
Chart, data, sample, 155
Chemical engineering, 131
Children's Literacy and Science Project, 271
Civil engineering, 131

CLASP. *See* Children's Literacy and Science
        Project
Class discussion, 61
Class inquiry questions, 92
Class question, constructing, 92
Collaborative writing, 19–20
Communication
    concepts regarding, 82–83
    as science inquiry skill, 14
Community involvement, forensic science,
        190–191
Concepts, communication of, 202
Conducting experiments, 95–96
Connecting knowledge, 32
Consequences, consideration of, 222
Content accuracy, 53
CORE Model of Instruction, 31–35
Creative writing, 211–214
Critical attributes, identifying, 19
Critical thinking, 47–48
Current events science journal, 124
Current science, 123–125
Curricula connections, 183–187
Custom ABC books, 7

Data charting, 47, 155–156
    sample, 155
Directions, 57–61
    student, 57–61
        sample, 60
Discussion webs, 47–48
    sample, 48
Draft, 53
    final, 53
Dramatic writing, lesson, 57–58
Drawing, 75–80

e-mails to scientists, 7–8
Ecosystem journalism, 177–181
    student newspaper, 177–181

Index

Editing, peer, 111–113
Educational web logs for teachers, 255
Electrical engineering, 131
Elementary grades, 31–39
Engineering careers, 131
English immersion, 69–74
English language learners, 75–80
    drawing, 75–80
Entry in journal, sample, 157
Environmental engineering, 131
Essays, 139–141, 175
Evaluation form, 224
Experiment procedures, 95
Explaining, as science inquiry skill, 14
Exploration, 205–209
Extensions, 98

Feedback, 2, 242–243
Field guides, 145–151, 153–160
    page, 148, 158
        sample, 148, 158
    rubrics, 150
        sample, 150
Final draft, 53
First grade, 153–160
Flipbook, 101
    construction, 102
    text example, 103
Focus statements, 34
Forensic science, 189–192
    community involvement, 190–191
    mock case, 191–192

Generalizations, 251
Genetic engineering, 131
Graphic organizers, 33
Graphs, 96
    evaluation of, 97
GRASP strategy, 46–47
Guiding journal entries, 240–241
Guiding science journal entries, 240–241

Haiku writing, 115–121
    assignments, 119

benefits of, 116
children writing, 117–119
extensions, 120
student perspectives, 119–120
Home web logs, with student postings, 256
Hypothesizing, 95
Hypothetical letters, 19

Identifying critical attributes, 19
Illustrated information books, 161–166
Imaginative writing, 29–30
Immersion in English, 69–74
Inference charts, observations, contrasted, 6
Inquiry assignments, 130
Inquiry skills, 14
Insights, 38
Interactive notebooks, 233–237
    rubrics, 236
    strategy, 208
Interactive reflective logs, 259–264
    amplified assessment, 264
    creating, 259–261
    interactive nature of, 263–264
    reflective thinkers, 264
    sample, 262–263
Interactive science notebooks, 208, 233–237
Interpreting data, as science inquiry skill, 14
Inverted-pyramid writing, 131
Investigation, 85–89, 91–99
IRLs. *See* Interactive reflective logs

Journal entries, 157
    sample, 157
Journal prompts, student responses, 5
Journal rubrics, 230, 244
Journal scale rubrics, 230
Journal writing, 70
Journaling rubric scale, 230
Journalism, student newspaper, 177–181
Journals, 5–6, 139–143, 227–231, 239–245
    analyzing, 228–229
    assessment, 142–143, 244–245
    before/after reflections, 229–230
    defining, 239

essays, 139–141
feedback, 242–243
guiding journal entries, 240–241
letters, 141–142
logistics, 240
makeover, 228
motivation, 241–242
notebooks, contrasted, 277
notebooks contrasted, 277
poetry, 142
reviewing, 271–275
    age-appropriate responses, 273
    Children's Literacy and Science Project, 271
    conceptualizing science, 272
    decision making, 274
    instructional structuring, 272–273
    interpretation, 274
    misconceptions, identifying, 272
    view selection, 273–274
student analysts, 230–231
students with special needs, 243
value of, 239–240
Justifications, 251

K-W-L chart, 159
Key-word process, 203
Kinesthetic writing, 101–103

Lab report rubrics, 107, 113
Lab reports, 105–109
    assessing success, 108–109
    demonstrating learning, 107–108
    hands-on activity, 105–106
Label analysis, 20–21
Learning logs, 247–252
    applications, 251
    explanation, 251
    generalizations, 251
    justifications, 251
    reflection, 248–249
    rubrics, 249–251
Letters, 141–142
Letters to authors, 28

Linear strings, 33
Listing variables for experiment, 93
Logic, respect for, 222
Logistics, journals, 240
Logs, reflective, interactive, 259–264
    amplified assessment, 264
    creating, 259–261
    interactive nature of, 263–264
    reflective thinkers, 264
Longer projects, strategy for, 202

Maps, 154
Measures of success, 37
Mechanical engineering, 131
Misconceptions, identifying, 272
Mock case, forensic science, 191–192
Mode continuum phases, 70
    experimenting, 70
    journal writing, 70–71
    learning key vocabulary, 70–71
    teacher-guided reporting, and, 70–71
Motivation, 241–242
Multigenre lab reports, 105–109
    assessing success, 108–109
    demonstrating learning, 107–108
    hands-on activity, 105–106
    rubrics, 107
Mystery box writing, 167–172
Mystery plant identification worksheet, 147

National Science Education standards, 116
Nature detectives, assignments for, 155
Nature of science, 221
News clips, 22
Newsletters, 135–137
    student, sample, 136
Newspaper task sheet, 129
Newspapers, 127–133, 177–181
    content ideas, 131
Nonfiction, 5–9, 219–225
Notebook entries, 76
Notebook rubrics, 236
Notebooks, 76, 233–237, 265–269, 277
    assessing, 235–236

assessing background knowledge, 268
becoming records, 269
interactive, 233–237
journal, contrasted, 277
journals, contrasted, 277
prior knowledge assessment, 265–266
quick writes, 266–269
as records, 269
science journals, contrasted, 277
writing prompts, 268

Observational skills, 14, 115–121
Observations, inference charts, contrasted, 6
Organizing information, 32–33
Outlines, 53

Peer editing, 111–113
Persuasive writing, 26
Plagiarizing, 45–48
Planning, as science inquiry skill, 14
Pluto project, 27
Poetry, 142
P.O.E.T.R.Y. assessment tool, 277–283
  acronym explanation, 278
  scoring rubric, 279
Pop-up biography, 222–224
Prairie resources, 179
Prediction, as science inquiry skill, 14
Prelab investigation, 92
Prior knowledge assessment, 265–266
Process steps analysis, 19
Prompts
  sample, 36
  writing, 5, 34, 36, 51–52, 268
Proposal writing, 21–22
Publishing student newspaper, 179

Questioning, as science inquiry skill, 14
Quick writes, 266–269

Rationale for science writing, 1, 193–196
Reading comprehension, 11–16
Records, science notebooks as, 269
Reflection, 33–35, 248–249

student, sample, 159
Reflective logs, 259–264
  amplified assessment, 264
  creating, 259–261
  interactive, sample, 262–263
  interactive nature of, 263–264
  reflective thinkers, 264
Reflective thinkers, 264
Refutational-text grading rubric, 53
Refutational texts, 50
Refutational writing prompt, 51
Related variables sets, 94
Reporting on accidents, 20
Reports, 8
Research, 63–65
  via web, 22
Reviewing, as science inquiry skill, 14
Reviewing journals, 271–275
  age-appropriate responses, 273
  Children's Literacy and Science Project, 271
  conceptualizing science, 272
  decision making, 274
  instructional structuring, 272–273
  interpretation, 274
  misconceptions, identifying, 272
  view selection, 273–274
Role playing, 26–28
Rough drafts, 53
Rubrics, 37, 98, 159
  analytical, 49–55
    science writing, 49–55
  assessment, 179
  field guide, sample, 150
  interactive notebook, 236
  journals, 230, 244
  lab reports, 98, 113
  learning log, 249–251
  multigenre lab report, 107
  P.O.E.T.R.Y. scoring, 279
  refutational-text grading, 53
  sample field guide, 150
  science interactive notebook, 236

Safety procedures, 96

Sample chapter, student-authored book, 6

Sample data chart, 155

Sample discussion web, 48

Sample field guide page, 148, 158

Sample field guide rubrics, 150

Sample interactive reflective log, 262–263

Sample journal entry, 157

Sample prompt, corresponding writing, graphic organizer, 36

Sample science journal entry, 157

Sample student directions, 60

Sample student newsletter, 136

Sample student reflection, 159

Sample writing technique, 197–203

Scavenger hunts, 154

Science careers, 131

Science-cognition-literacy framework, 11–16

Science interactive notebooks, 234, 236
    rubric, 236

Science journals, 5–6, 139–143, 227–231, 239–245
    defining, 239, 277–278
    entry, sample, 157
    logistics, 240
    makeover, 228
    prompts, student responses, 5
    reviewing, 271–275
        age-appropriate responses, 273
        Children's Literacy and Science Project, 271
        conceptualizing science, 272
        decision making, 274
        instructional structuring, 272–273
        interpretation, 274
        misconceptions, identifying, 272
        view selection, 273–274
    rubric, 244
    rubric scale, 230
    science notebook, contrasted, 277
    writing, 70

Science newspaper task sheet, 129

Science notebooks, 76, 233–237, 265–269, 277
    assessing, 235–236
    becoming records, 269
    interactive, 233–237
    journal, contrasted, 277
    journals, contrasted, 277
    prior knowledge assessment, 265–266
    quick writes, 266–269
    as records, 269
    science journal, contrasted, 277
    science journals, contrasted, 277
    writing prompts, 268

Science wheel, writing in, 41, 43

Science writing
    analytical rubrics, 49–55
    as assessment tool, 25–30
    biographies, 219–225
    blogs, 253–258
    creative writing, 211–214
    current science, 123–125
    curricula connection, 183–187
    dramatic writing, 57–58
    drawing, 75–80
    ecosystem journalism, 177–181
    editing by peers, 111–113
    English language learners, 75–80
    field guides, 145–151, 153–160
    first grade, 153–160
    forensic science, 189–192
    haiku, 115–121
    illustrated information books, 161–166
    interactive reflective logs, 259–264
    interactive science notebooks, 233–237
    investigation, 85–89, 91–99
    journals, 139–143, 227–231, 239–245
    kinesthetic writing, 101–103
    lab reports, 105–109
    learning logs, 247–252
    learning tool, 41–44
    multigenre lab reports, 105–109
    mystery box writing, 167–172
    newsletters, 135–137
    newspapers, 127–133, 177–181
    nonfiction, 5–9, 219–225
    peer editing, 111–113

plagiarizing, 45–48
P.O.E.T.R.Y. assessment tool, 277–283
reading comprehension, 11–16
reasons to write, 193–196
refutational texts, 49–55
reviewing journals, 271–275
sample writing technique, 197–203
science inquiry skills, 11–16
science notebook, 265–269
scientist's view, 81–83
strategies for, 17–23
structured English immersion science,
    69–74
student-authored books, 6
student directions, 57–61
student writing, 63–67
third grade, 173–175
trade books, 183–187
upper elementary grades, 31–39
web logs, 253–258
Scientific attitudes, 222
Scientific directions, 21
Scientific reporting, 21
Scientist's view, 81–83
SCL framework. *See* Science-cognition-
    literacy
SEI. *See* Structured English immersion
Servers, web logs, 255
Solar cooker lab, 92–97
Sources, integrating, 47
Special needs, students with, 243
Story writing, 22
Strategies for writing, 17–23
Streamlining, 66–67
Structured English immersion, 69–74
Student-authored books, 6–7
Student-centered labs, 91–92
Student directions, 57–61
    sample, 60
Student journals, 139–143
    assessment, 142–143
    essays, 139–141
    letters, 141–142
    poetry, 142

Student maps, 154
Student newsletters, 135–137
    sample, 136
Student newspapers, 127–133, 177–181
Student permission slip, web log use, 255
Student reflection, 159
Student research paper, key-word process, 203
Student surveys, 64–65
Students with special needs, 243
Success, measures of, 37
Supporting details, 34
Supports in science writing, 1–2

Task organization, 42
Task sheet, genetics assignment, 43
Teachers' insights, 38
Technical directions, 21
Techniques, 197–203
Testable problems, 94
Thinkers, reflective, 264
Third grade, 173–175
Trade books, 183–187

Upper elementary grades, 31–39

Value of science journals, 239–240
Variables sets, relation of, 94
Verification, 222

Water cycle, 211–214
Web discussion, 47–48
    sample, 48
Web logs, 253–258
    assessment, 258
    servers, 255
    student permission slip, 255
    for teachers, 255
Web quest research, 22
Web research, 22
Wheel, science, writing in, 41, 43
Writing
    analytical rubrics, 49–55
    as assessment tool, 25–30
    biographies, 219–225

blogs, 253–258

creative writing, 211–214

current science, 123–125

curricula connection, 183–187

dramatic writing, 57–58

drawing, 75–80

ecosystem journalism, 177–181

editing by peers, 111–113

English language learners, 75–80

field guides, 145–151, 153–160

first grade, 153–160

forensic science, 189–192

haiku, 115–121

illustrated information books, 161–166

interactive reflective logs, 259–264

interactive science notebooks, 233–237

investigation, 85–89, 91–99

journals, 139–143, 227–231, 239–245

kinesthetic writing, 101–103

lab reports, 105–109

learning logs, 247–252

learning tool, 41–44

multigenre lab reports, 105–109

mystery box writing, 167–172

newsletters, 135–137

newspapers, 127–133, 177–181

nonfiction, 5–9, 219–225

peer editing, 111–113

plagiarizing, 45–48

P.O.E.T.R.Y. assessment tool, 277–283

reading comprehension, 11–16

reasons to write, 193–196

refutational texts, 49–55

reviewing journals, 271–275

sample writing technique, 197–203

science inquiry skills, 11–16

science notebook, 265–269

scientist's view, 81–83

strategies for, 17–23

structured English immersion science, 69–74

student-authored books, 6

student directions, 57–61

student writing, 63–67

third grade, 173–175

trade books, 183–187

upper elementary grades, 31–39

web logs, 253–258

Writing center activities, 170

Writing prompts, 5, 34, 36, 51–52, 268

Writing technique, sample, 197–203

Xanga, use of, 253

Xboxes, 253

Zoology, 131

Zoom-ins, 146, 149

blogs, 253–258
creative writing, 211–214
current science, 123–125
curricula connection, 183–187
dramatic writing, 57–58
drawing, 75–80
ecosystem journalism, 177–181
editing by peers, 111–113
English language learners, 75–80
field guides, 145–151, 153–160
first grade, 153–160
forensic science, 189–192
haiku, 115–121
illustrated information books, 161–166
interactive reflective logs, 259–264
interactive science notebooks, 233–237
investigation, 85–89, 91–99
journals, 139–143, 227–231, 239–245
kinesthetic writing, 101–103
lab reports, 105–109
learning logs, 247–252
learning tool, 41–44
multigenre lab reports, 105–109
mystery box writing, 167–172
newsletters, 135–137
newspapers, 127–133, 177–181
nonfiction, 5–9, 219–225
peer editing, 111–113
plagiarizing, 45–48

P.O.E.T.R.Y. assessment tool, 277–283
reading comprehension, 11–16
reasons to write, 193–196
refutational texts, 49–55
reviewing journals, 271–275
sample writing technique, 197–203
science inquiry skills, 11–16
science notebook, 265–269
scientist's view, 81–83
strategies for, 17–23
structured English immersion science, 69–74
student-authored books, 6
student directions, 57–61
student writing, 63–67
third grade, 173–175
trade books, 183–187
upper elementary grades, 31–39
web logs, 253–258
Writing center activities, 170
Writing prompts, 5, 34, 36, 51–52, 268
Writing technique, sample, 197–203

Xanga, use of, 253
Xboxes, 253

Zoology, 131
Zoom-ins, 146, 149

DATE DUE

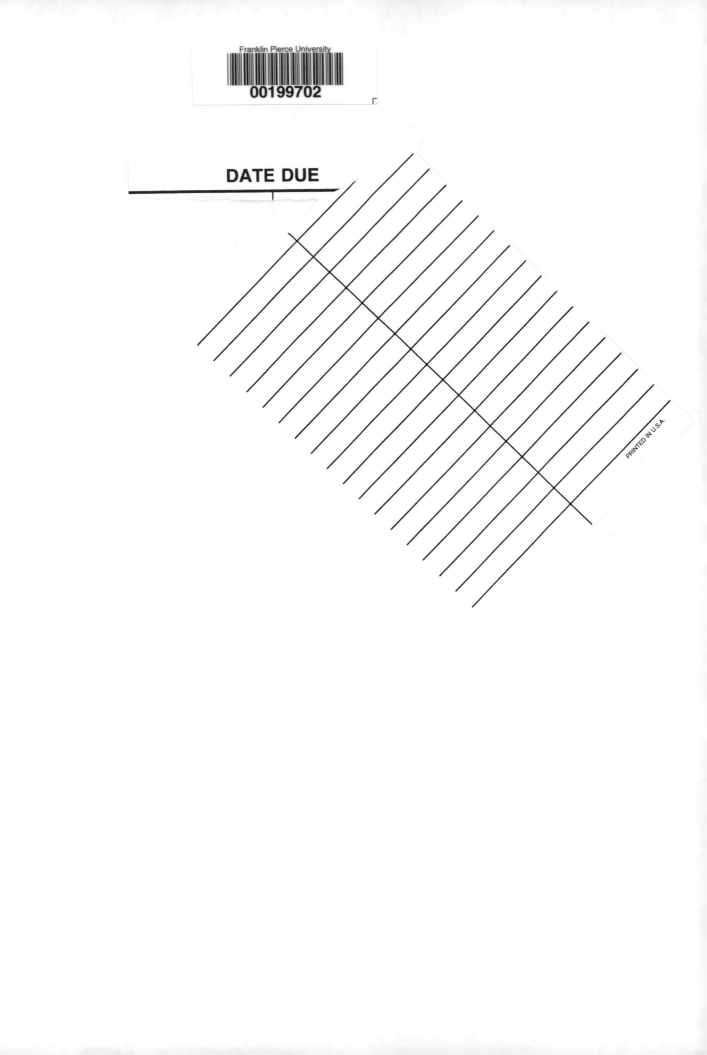

PRINTED IN U.S.A.